AF734915

Practical Strategies for Developing Large Software Systems

Practical Strategies for Developing Large Software Systems

ELLIS HOROWITZ, Editor
University of Southern California

with contributions by Barry Boehm,
Jules Schwartz, Winston Royce, Ray Wolverton, John Brown,
Ellis Horowitz, Leon Stucki, and Harvey Bratman

ADDISON-WESLEY PUBLISHING COMPANY
Reading, Massachusetts · Menlo Park, California
London · Amsterdam · Don Mills, Ontario · Sydney

 Printed in the United States of America. Published simultaneously in Canada. Library of Congress Catalog Card No. 74-28818.

ISBN 0-201-02977-4
ABCDEFGHIJ-MA-798765

Contents

Preface

How Did This Book Start?

In July 1974 a one-week seminar was held at USC entitled "Modern Techniques for the Design and Construction of Reliable Software." There was a great interest in the topic as evidenced by the large number of attendees. This interest was clearly a manifestation of what has become a major crisis in the computer field today, the software bottleneck. Our inability to effectively construct complex software systems has impeded our ability to make good use of our computer resources. But on the positive side there have been many recent developments which aim to solve this problem. Strategies such as structured programming, chief programmer teams, and model-driven software design are just a few of these new and promising techniques.

My idea as an organizer of this seminar was to collect experts from industry who were intimately involved with the software productivity issue. By emphasizing this industrial point of view my hope was that the attendees would get a truer assessment of the extent to which all of these new strategies are really practical. This is precisely what happened.

The following selection of papers represents a written and edited version of that seminar plus some additional material to round out the coverage. The papers have been organized so that they cover the four basic phases of the software development process: requirements, design, coding and testing, plus a section on management. The first section contains two overview articles by authors who have had vast experience in this area, Barry Boehm and Jules Schwartz. Dr. Boehm sets the stage by synthesizing the results of several studies and comes up with a quantitative assessment of how time and money are consumed in each phase of the software cycle. This factual data backs up the growing concern in our industry for improved productivity. Jules Schwartz draws upon his 20 years of experience in the computer field to describe the unique challenges and pitfalls which can arise when managing a large computer software project. Each remaining article presents and evaluates the latest thinking on means for improving the quality of software. Many of the authors have reached their conclusions only after extensive data was gathered through experiments run within their companies. Our major goal has been to present tested techniques backed up by a careful analysis of their merits and demerits.

Whom is This Book For?

This book is intended for people who are involved in virtually any phase of the software development process, programmer to manager. The section on requirements analysis contains two articles. Winston Royce makes the case for carefully doing requirements analysis and discusses how it should be done. Ray Wolverton draws upon the data of two large command and control systems to describe sizing and costing methodology. His detailed revelation of the costing algorithm makes this article one of the very few which significantly discuss this usually confidential topic. Barry Boehm presents his concept of model-driven software design and compares its advantages to existing design methodologies. The coding and testing section contains three articles, each espousing its own favored technique. Brown describes his "co-ordinated commentary programming," Horowitz presents an analysis of structured FORTRAN backed up by experience at six installations, while Stucki describes a performance measurement tool for producing source program profiles. Bratman then describes how management control functions can be automated so that project monitoring can be improved.

Though an effort has been made to make these articles applicable to as wide an audience as possible, there remains at least two biases which I will make clear so that the reader may keep them in mind. The first is the fact that most of the authors are connected with firms that primarily do software contracting with the military. Thus their orientation is on the single-release, large aerospace application. Such applications do contain many similarities with other types of software systems, but they have some unique characteristics as well. The second bias or viewpoint taken here is that the software is being developed within a large organization. This allows the luxury of tool development which so often cannot be afforded by smaller commercial shops. Nevertheless, these people are among the first to have experimented with these new ideas, and their conclusions, I believe, have broad significance.

Finally, the book has been augmented so that it can be appropriately used as a textbook for a course. Several curricula descriptions have included courses which are supposed to have this subject matter within their scope. These are Software Design (C4) and Systems Design (D2) as described in the report Curriculum Recommendations for Graduate Professional Programs in Information Systems (C. ACM, 5/72), also Large Scale Information Processing Systems (A8) as described in Curriculum '68 (C. ACM, 3/68), and Software Design (UC4) and System Design and Implementation (UD9) as described in the report Curriculum Recommendations for Undergraduate Programs in Information Systems (C. ACM, 12/73). Nevertheless one present deficiency of many computer science programs is their lack of presentation of material concerned with large software construction. Perhaps not enough is yet known to give such a course and, if so, my hope is that this book will stimulate some efforts toward this end. In any case an annotated bibliography of recent and available literature has been included to facilitate further study.

It is impossible to summarize here all of the key ideas which have emerged over the course of editing this book. But certainly the most exciting development for me has been my new awareness of these problems coupled with the many creative and promising solutions contained within these articles.

Acknowledgments first go to the authors who contributed their time, ideas, and experience. Special thanks go to Barry Boehm for his suggestions on needed articles to round out the balance of the book. Also to Martin Cohen who helped with the bibliography and to Robert Kashef for his initial stimulus to run the course.

Author Biographies

DR. BARRY BOEHM received his B.A. from Harvard and his M.S. and Ph.D. from UCLA. From that time until 1973 he was employed at the RAND Corporation ultimately as head of its information sciences and mathematics department. There he was director of a substantial Air Force study on software assessment, (CCIP-85). He serves on a variety of technical committees for the National Bureau of Standards, NASA, and the National Academy of Sciences in Brazil. He is the author of a book on trajectory computation, editor of a book on community information utilities and the author of numerous book chapters and research papers on topics in software design automation, data structures, numerical analysis, simulation, computer-communications systems, and future implications of computer technology. He has recently been appointed Director of Software Research and Technology at TRW.

MR. HARVEY BRATMAN has been a project head in SDC's software Engineering Branch since December 1972. The Software Engineering Branch has been concerned with developing techniques to increase programmer productivity and software reliability. For most of his fifteen years at SDC, Mr. Bratman has been involved in the design and development of compilers and programming support systems. Before his sojourn at SDC, Mr. Bratman was employed at Lockheed Aircraft Corporation in the Mathematical Analysis Department with responsibility for mathematical and utility programs. Mr. Bratman has written several papers on supervisory control, compiler design, interactive programming support. He received his B.A. in Mathematics at UCLA in 1950.

MR. JOHN BROWN is currently on staff to the Site Defense Program Manager at TRW. There he is required to evaluate the state of the art of software production methodology and to assess the feasibility of new technology in the existing program. He has been staff engineer in the Product Assurance Office of TRW since October 1969 specializing in procedures and tools for software product assurance. He recently managed a study into the fundamental properties of software reliability and formulated a technique for quantitatively assessing software reliability through continuous measurement of software testing thoroughness. He is the author is six technical papers dealing with quality assurance, automated tools, software costs, and programming methodology. He has a B.S. and M.S. from the University of Washington.

DR. ELLIS HOROWITZ received his Ph.D. in computer science from the University of Wisconsin. He was on the faculty at Wisconsin and Cornell before assuming his present post at the University of Southern California. Dr. Horowitz has published in JACM, CACM, JCSS, SIAM Journal of Computing, Acta Informatica and Mathematics of Computation on topics concerned with the design and analysis of efficient algorithms. He has been an ACM National Lecturer and is currently vice-chairman of SIGSAM. He serves on a variety of professional committees and is a member of AAAS, ACM, IEEE, SIAM and Sigma Xi. He recently organized the short course at USC entitled "Modern Techniques for the Design and Construction of Reliable Software" of which this book is a direct result.

DR. WINSTON W. ROYCE is a graduate of the California Institute of Technology where he received a B.S., M.S., and Ph.D. He served there as an Assistant Professor until 1961 when he joined TRW. There he had project responsibility for designing an optimal mission planning and orbit selection system for spacecraft. Responsibility for this large software system was followed by his involvement in a series of ground systems which gave him varied experience with providing large, complex deliverable software. Since that time he has designed several new techniques for improving the management of software projects.

MR. JULES I. SCHWARTZ is currently Director of Senior Staff, Commercial Division, Computer Sciences Corporation. The staff serves as consultant, management, or as members of teams working on a variety of commercial, and other systems. Mr. Schwartz has over 20 years experience with compilers, languages, operating systems, time-sharing, data management, real-time and batch systems for commercial and government applications. He is one of the original designers of the JOVIAL language which is still actively used by the Air Force.

MR. LEON STUCKI received his B.A. in mathematics from the University of Utah in 1968, an M.B.A. from the University of Southern California in 1970, and is currently a candidate for a Ph.D. in computer science from the University of California, Los Angeles. He is an information scientist in Advanced Computer Systems Department at McDonnell Douglas Astronautics Company in Huntington Beach, California. Recently he was the principal investigator for the design, prototype implementation and production verification and validation of the Program Evaluator and Tester system. In the areas of software validation and reliability, he serves on a software quality assurance committee examining the problems involved in large-scale, complex systems. His software validation efforts have included numerous presentations and critiques on the subject to the Army, Air Force, and Navy. He has newly been appointed editor of the L.A.-chapter SIGME newsletter.

MR. RAY WOLVERTON received his B.S.E.E. from Stanford University in 1950 and he has done graduate work at USC and UCLA. Since 1955 he has been with the TRW Systems Group working in the fields of real-time command and control operations, computer software development and test management and project management. His present interests include large-scale computer program management, cost modeling and forecasting, and reliability. He is a member of various honorary and professional societies and currently is a member of the American National Standards Institute.

1

Introduction and Overview

An introduction to the Introduction may seem needless, but let me set the stage for what follows. In this year it is hard to believe that anyone in the computer field has not yet been alerted to the high rise in software costs. Nevertheless, the hard facts have not been well publicized for a variety of reasons. The first paper by Barry Boehm draws upon many of the available studies and puts together a clearer picture of where the money is going. His own experience includes an extensive study done for the Air Force called Information Processing/Data Automation Implications of Air Force Command and Control Requirements in the 1980s, CCIP-85 for short. This study has provided a host of statistics on how time and funds are consumed in the software development cycle. And 33 percent of Air Force software is of the MIS type, so many of the conclusions are relevant to data processing in general. But Dr. Boehm also draws upon many other reports to piece together a comprehensive picture of the state of such matters. And in addition to all the useful facts and figures, he highlights the high leverage areas. These are the specific phases of the software development process where some effort at improvement will go a long way.

The building of large software systems is like no other large-scale industrial effort. Therefore the management of such projects has its own unique characteristics which need to be understood and mastered. Successful management has remained almost a "black art" and the application of discipline strongly resisted by the technical personnel. For any manager of a software group the article by Jules Schwartz will be indispensible. From SAGE to MULTICS and beyond Mr. Schwartz talks about the problems of project management. His mood is one of caution and his emphasis is on getting the right answers to the questions: what should be produced, should it be produced, and can it be produced. He gives a scathing portrait of today's programmer community and discusses exactly where discipline must be applied. In the end it is careful attention to detail and the ability to see beyond the myths which will lead to an on-time, on-budget, functioning and relevant software package.

THE HIGH COST OF SOFTWARE

Barry W. Boehm

INTRODUCTION

The high cost of software should be considered more of an opportunity than a problem. Nobody can say for sure to what extent software "costs too much." However, the high cost implies that additional improvements will lead to significant savings, which should justify additional investment to streamline some of the institutions, techniques, and procedures which often hinder software productivity.

This chapter will address three main questions:

- How high is the cost of software?
- Where do the costs go?
- What factors influence the costs? (or, what can we do about them?)

For reference, "software production" here includes all the effort involved in producing and maintaining the necessary executive, support, and applications programs and their documentation, starting from a reasonably well-defined functional specification. Most of the software data come from the Air Force, primarily from the CCIP-85 study(1) and the recent Air Force-Industry Software Cost Workshop, but they are probably fairly representative of other software activities elsewhere.

HOW HIGH IS THE COST OF SOFTWARE?

In 1961, Gilchrist and Weber(2) estimated the number of software personnel in the U.S. at 360,000. They also estimated that this number was growing at the rate of 30,000 per year, implying a total of about 450,000 in 1974. Multiplying by a fairly typical software manpower cost of $35,000 per burdened man-year yields a total U.S. expenditure on software of about $16 billion, or over one percent of the 1974 Gross National Product.

In the Air Force, in fiscal year 1972, the annual expenditure on software was somewhere between $1 and 1.5 billion per year,or about 4 to 5 percent of the total Air Force budget. In comparison, the cost on hardware was something between $300 and $400 million. For the Worldwide Military Command and Control System, the relative costs were even more dramatic; an estimated $722 million for software, compared to $50 - 100 million for hardware. The comparison is even more dramatic if you look at what you are really paying for when you pay for this thing called hardware. A relatively small fraction of a typical large manufacturer's cost goes into boxes, the chips, and the wires that you receive; generally about twice as much currently goes into software. Currently, though, both hardware and software costs are typicall dominated by the remaining costs incurred for R & D, sales, service, profits, lawyers, etc.

Figure 1 shows the likely trends in the relative costs of hardware and software, even considering the cost of hardware as the rental cost paid by the user. In the late 1950s the hardware was only 20 to 30 percent of the cost. Right now, software is about 70 percent of the cost, and by the 1970s it appears it's going to be about 90 percent of the cost, as hardware costs continue to go down and people costs continue to go up.

The discussion above covers only the direct cost of software. It turns out that the indirect costs of software are even greater. The effects of software delays and errors on audit trails, equipment resupply and repair, cash flows, and other operations-oriented concerns lead to many other significant dollar losses in the national economy.

WHERE DO THE COSTS GO?

Nationwide, it is difficult to determine the breakdown of software expenditures by type of software. Figure 2 represents the second iteration of an effort to find out within the Air Force how much of the cost goes for various types of software. [3] As seen in Figure 2, the expenditures for critical real-time software such as command and control and intelligence (21 percent), and for on-board space and avionics type software (10 percent) are dominated by the expenditures on management information

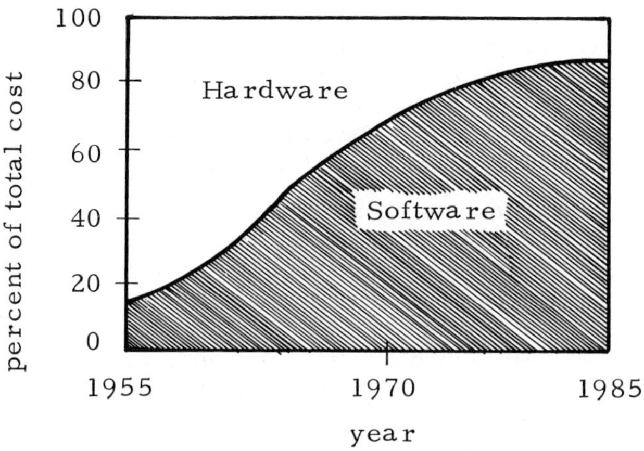

Figure 1. Hardware/Software Cost Trends

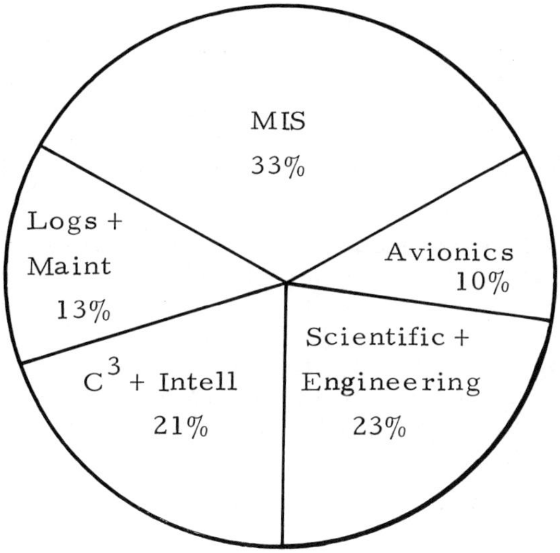

Figure 2. Estimated Distribution of USAF Software Costs

system (MIS) software (33 percent), logistics and maintenance (13 percent), and scientific and engineering software (23 percent). The percentages are not exact; they could be off by a factor of one-third either way (e.g., MIS could be 44 or 22 percent and I wouldn't be too surprised). However, even rough estimates are fairly important because of the distrbutions of software cost vary between application areas.

Figure 3 shows some of the differences between real-time software and batch scientific or business-type software. For example, for business-type software, relatively little time goes into testing. The programs are simpler; most of the errors are in formatting and the like which are fairly easy to get out, rather than errors in timing which are extremely difficult to get out. Another difference is that documentation costs tend to be much higher for the business type of program. The 100 percent estimate of additional time required for documentation was a business-type application; the 9 percent estimate was for batch scientific programs.

One pitfall to avoid in looking at these software development cost statistics, and in worrying about the fact that software is on the critical path during the system development, is to concentrate too much on reducing software development costs. What really needs to be reduced is software life cycle costs, and often you find that people make a lot of tradeoffs during software development to meet schedules, and many of those tradeoffs trade maintainability for speed of development. How much of the software effort does go into software maintenance? The best data that exist come from a Hoskyns survey[4] in Great Britian, which canvassed 905 installations there and found that almost 40 percent of the software effort in Great Britian goes into maintenance.

Figure 4 shows the distribution of installations by the relative amount of time they spend on software maintenance. The mode of the distribution is somewhere between 20 and 30 percent maintenance, but there are some installations that spend almost all of their time maintaining software. Air Force avionics software is much like this latter, and currently it costs something like $75 per instruction to develop the software, but the maintenance of the software has cost up to $4000 per instruction.[5]

WHAT FACTORS INFLUENCE SOFTWARE COSTS?

A later chapter in this book (by Wolverton) presents a number of valuable relationships for estimating software costs. A further step toward illumination of software cost factors was taken at a recent (October 1974) Air Force-Industry Workshop on Software

	Analysis and Design	Coding and Auditing	Test and Integration
Command-Control (SAGE, NTDS)	35%	17%	48%
Command-Control (TRW)	46%	20%	34%
Spaceborne (Gemini, Saturn)	34%	20%	46%
GP Executive (OS/360)	33%	17%	50%
Scientific (TRW)	44%	26%	30%
Business (Raytheon)	44%	28%	28%

Added documentation estimates: about 10%

Figure 3. Software Effort Distribution by Activity

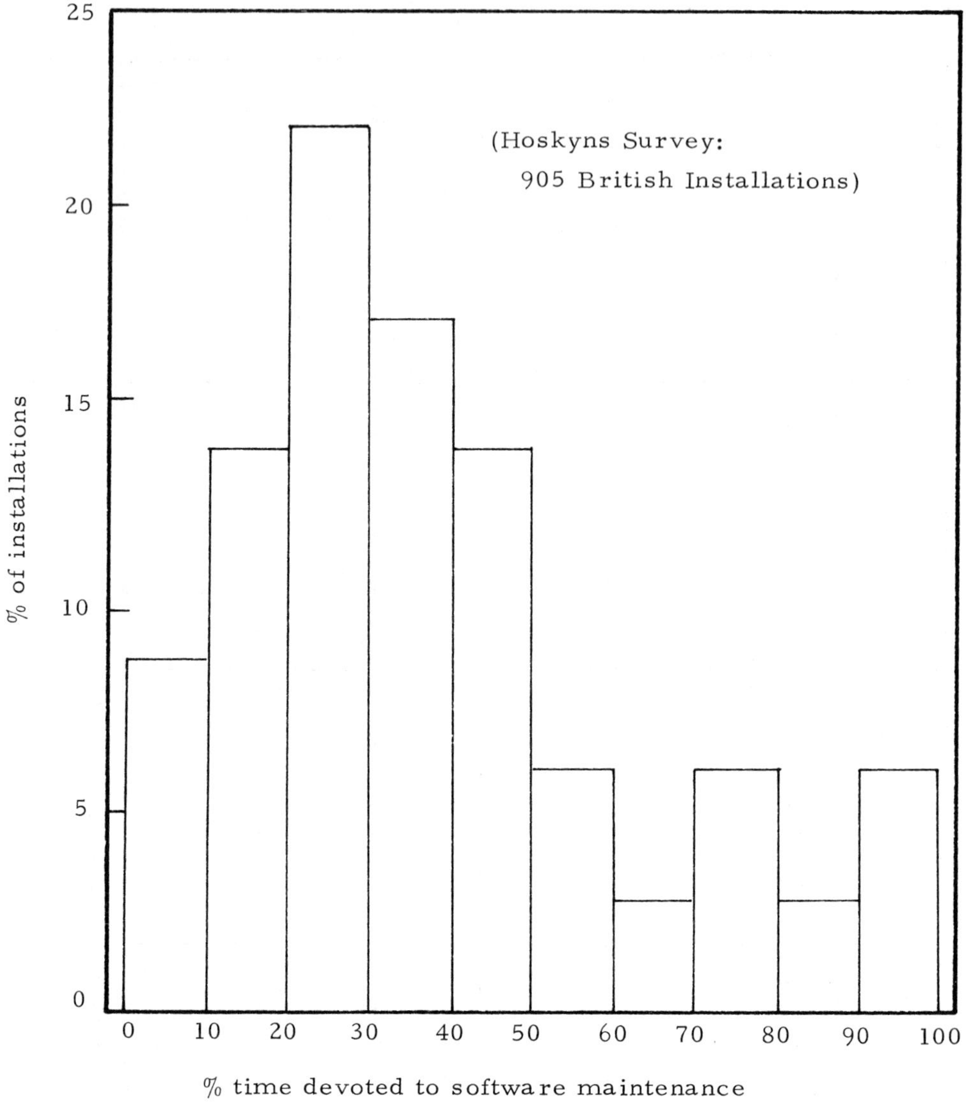

Figure 4. Software Maintenance

Costs held at USAF Electronics Systems Division. Table I summarizes the main factors identified in one of the working sessions; the text below provides further discussion of each item.

Number of delivered executable source instructions. This is currently the most widely used factor for cost estimation. "Delivered" implies "well checked out" and "documented;" also, it excludes such non delivered software as unit test driven programs. "Source instructions" excludes comments; it is generally considered a better estimation factor than object instructions.

Language. In general, participants' experience indicated that the cost per source instruction in assembly language or machine-oriented language (MOR) was about twice the cost per source instruction in a higher-order language such as COBOL or FORTRAN. The dollar figures were derived from an estimate of 15-30 HOL source instructions/day and the typical figure of $35,000 per burdened man-year for software manpower.

Real-time applications. These figures are derived from a rough consensus of experiences that the cost/instruction real time software was about five times that of nonreal time HOL programs.

Type. The operating system (OS) component of a system tends to cost about 2.5 times the cost per instruction of the applications or utility program components.

Point on learning curve. Participants' experience indicated that a generally experienced programming group would require another 50-100 percent more effort to develop an unfamiliar program as they would to develop a variant of a familiar program developed previously.

Application area. Another source of cost variation is whether the application involves a management information system (MIS), an avionics package, an industrial process control system, etc. Sometimes, another estimate of software cost can be made in terms of a percentage of the total system cost, but this must also be conditional with respect to the other factors.

Desired quality. Two major categories exist with respect to the degree of thoroughness of testing before a program goes operational. In the "man-rated" systems, where software errors may translate directly into the loss of human life, the fraction of the total effort devoted to testing has averaged about 40 percent; on other systems, it tends to be more like 15 percent.

Turnaround time. For the modern range of batch turnaround times (from 30 min to 1 working day), the length of the test period tends to be proportional to turnaround time. If testers have little useful to do while waiting for test runs to come back, then testing costs are also proportional to turnaround time. However, cost-reducing effects arise if testers can be documenting or eliminating errors by other means such as code scanning while they wait. For very short turnaround times including interactive systems, the relationship is much less predictable.

Amount of documentation. Experience indicates that documentation costs run about 10 percent of the total software development cost. For nonautomated documentation (e.g., excluding listings and automatically generated flow charts), typical costs are about $35-150 per page, depending primarily on the amount and complexity of the analysis involved.

Hardware constraints. The most useful relationship here is still that indicated in Figure 5, which shows the effect of hardware speed and memory size constraints on the relative cost of software. Although the data for the curve come from 34 airborne and spaceborne software projects, the same effect appears to hold for ground-based batch and real-time computing [6].

This software cost escalation effect becomes particularly crippling during the software maintenance phase, as the hardware is generally sized for production, leaving little capacity for fitting the test driver into core, expanding data areas, accommodating interactive modification aids, etc.

Schedule realism. Although the length of an "appropriate" schedule is as difficult to estimate as is cost, experience indicates that attempts to develop the software some percent faster than "appropriate" will usually increase cost by about that percentage.

Amount of previous software used. The best way to estimate the costs of adapting existing software into a new development appears to be to break it out separately, and subjectively estimate the costs of modifying it for the new application and of interfacing it to the new software.

Size and structure of the data base. This is recognized to be an extremely important parameter, especially on large-file oriented projects. So far, no counterpart to the cost-per-instruction factor has been established, although such a factor is much desired.

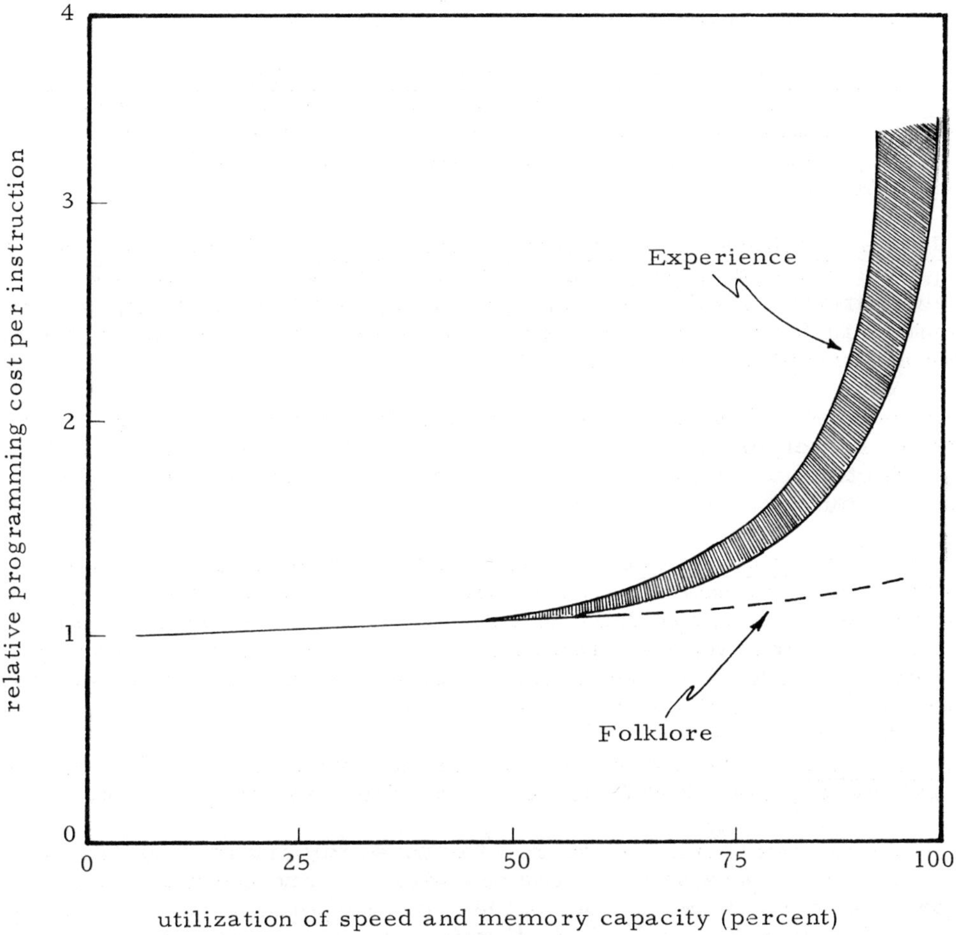

Figure 5. Hardware Strains Cause Major Software Impact

Complexity. This is another important factor which so far has eluded definition in such a way as to be used reliably in a cost formula. Some attempts have been made to correlate costs with such factors as number of interfaces, percentage of branch statements, number of paths through a program, and Halstead length, but so far without any highly reliable correlation.

Stability of requirements and stability of development environment. These factors are important determinants of software cost, but their influence can only be estimated subjectively. Their effect tends to be proportional to the length of time it takes to complete the project.

Representations of development environment. The added cost required to adapt software to actual operational conditions (different computer configuration, operating procedures, etc.) can be quite significant (up to 95 percent in some instances) but can only be estimated subjectively.

Personnel. This factor is considered by experienced estimators to be extremely important, but difficult to estimate other than subjectively. Productivity variations of 5:1 between individuals are common.

Development techniques. These include such things as using structured programming, top-down development, chief programmer teams, automated aids, and the like. No consensus was reached regarding the quantitative effect of using such techniques, except to agree that systematic approaches to software development are better than disorganized ones.

Management. Like personnel, this is another extremely important factor, but difficult to estimate other than subjectively.

These factors were considered the most important ones to account for in estimating software costs. There are many more possible factors (e.g., particular programming language, number of input and output quantities, frequency of operation, in-house versus contract, absolute hardware characteristics such as memory size and word size.) In general, such other factors tend to be less well correlated to cost than the factors above, although in particular situations (e.g., word size for avionics software) they may be both significant and clearly correlated with cost.

With respect to this book, the main point is that, for any particular project, some factors are not within our control while others are. The remaining chapters focus on those factors which usually are within our control (e.g., management, design techniques, and various development techniques) and point out how they may often be used both to reduce software costs and to improve its reliability.

TABLE 1

FACTORS INFLUENCING SOFTWARE COST

Factor	Relation to Cost
Number of delivered source instructions	Linear, modified by other factors
Language	HOL: \$6-12/source instruction MOL: \$12-24/source instruction
Real-time application	RT: \$30-60/source instruction
Type (OS, application, utility)	If OS, multiply by 1.5-2.0
Point on learning curve	If unfamiliar, multiply by 1.5-2.0
Application area (MIS, avionics)	Sometimes, as % of total system cost
Desired quality	"Man-rated:" test cost 40% of total Non-"Man-rated:" test cost 15% of total
Turnaround time	Approximate linear relation to testing cost
Amount of documentation	Approximately 10% of total; \$35-150/non-automated page
Hardware constraints	Asymptotic as approach to full capacity (Fig.
Schedule realism	% added cost = % of schedule acceleration
Amount of previous S/W used	Breakout + subjective
Size, structure of data base	Subjective
Complexity	Subjective

Stability of requirements	Subjective
Stability of development environment	Subjective
Representativeness of development environment	Subjective
Personnel	Subjective; approximately 5:1 variability
Development methods (e.g., structured programming)	Subjective; systematic approaches cheaper
Management	Subjective; high variability

REFERENCES

1. Information Processing/Data Automation Implication of Air Force Command and Control Requirements in the 1980's (CCIP-85), Volume I, Highlights, United States Air Force Report SAMSO/XRS-71-1, AD 900031L, April 1972.

2. Gilchrist, B. and K. E. Weber, "Employment of Trained Computer Personnel - A Quantitative Survey," Proceedings 1972 SJCC, pp. 641-648.

3. Boehm, B. W., "Keynote Address: The High Cost of Software," in Proceedings of a Symposium on the High Cost of Software, J. Goldberg (ed.), Stanford Research Institute, September 1973.

4. Implications of Using Modular Programming, John Hoskyns and Co., Ltd., Guide No. 1, Hoskyns Systems Research, Inc., 600 3rd Avenue, New York, New York, 1973.

5. Trainor, W. L., Software - From Satan to Savior, United States Air Force Avionics Laboratory, Wright-Patterson AFB, Ohio, presented at National Aerospace Electronics Conference, May 1973.

6. Boehm, B. W., "Software and Its Impact: A Quantative Assessment," Datamation, May 1973, pp. 48-59.

7. Proceedings, Government/Industry Workshop on Software Sizing and Costing, U. S. Air Force Electronics Systems Division (to appear).

CONSTRUCTION OF SOFTWARE: PROBLEMS AND PRACTICALITIES

Jules I. Schwartz

INTRODUCTION

Early Efforts

In the early 1950s, a small closely knit group of skilled programmers working with 256 words of immediate access storage and very limited file storage and peripherals, produced a computerized aircraft surveillance system which included a small set of radar input stations and tracked a few aircraft simultaneously. Based on this successful effort, this small, closely knit group, in cooperation with the U.S. Air Force, decided to produce a more complete system to permit automated tracking and interception of hostile airplanes. This system would consist of a number of duplex computers covering the entire United States, with communication between adjacent sectors, new radar equipment which would permit finer tracking, a number of additional functions, a wide variety of alphanumeric and vector displays and automatic backup between the various sectors as well as within the duplex computers. The capacity of the system was to be considerably larger than the prototype development, and the computer was to have 8000 words of core storage.

Any illusions that the original group had about retaining their past pleasant, intimate, technically exciting working relationship were soon shattered. Within a year approximately 1000 people were involved with the development of the SAGE system. People were recruited and trained from a variety of walks of life. Streetcar conductors, undertakers (with at least one year of training in calculus), school teachers, curtain cleaners, and others were hastily assembled, trained in programming for some number of weeks, and assigned parts in a very complex organization. The core storage of the computer was expanded to

64, 000 words. The originally hoped for capacities of the system were cut considerably. The system was first delivered over a year late at considerably more cost than was originally expected and not too long before people began to realize the threat of the manned bomber was beginning to decrease considerably as long-range missiles began to become a reality. So began the era of large-scale programming efforts.

Not too long after this reasonably successful start, another major effort was begun for an important military function. Those responsible for this one hired and transferred approximately 600 people within a very short time. After this first step was completed, the next problem was to determine what this system was to do. This took, to some people's chagrin several years. Man's ingenuity being what it is, however, a large number of these people were not wasted. They were put to work on the support (utility) system which was to assist the operational programmers when they got around to writing operational programs. The support system for SAGE had approximately 1, 000, 000 instructions and was actually very good, considering the time at which it was built, but for this new effort it was decided to improve upon the support system in many ways. It didn't make it. About two years later, the support system was not ready to handle the operational programs, which were finally being coded.

In 1961 a small group of highly skilled programmers produced at M. I. T. one of the first general purpose time sharing systems, called CTSS. This system evolved into one of the better known and highly successful time-sharing systems. Based on this experience, in 1964, ideas began to be formulated for a considerably advanced system called MULTICS. This was an ambitious effort, encompassing a number of new concepts, new hardware, and considerably more system programmers than were required for CTSS. I think it would be fair to state that this system did not proceed with the same feeling of pleasantness nor satisfaction that accompanied CTSS, although now about nine years later, it has resulted in a useful system.

These are a few of many experiences in system development which have taken place over the past 20 years. Very few of these have brought unanimous cheers from producers and customers because few were on time, met the original specification,stayed within the original hardware, and remained on budget (see [2]).

A Current Example

Within the past year, I had occasion to study the work of a small company which was attempting to produce an on-line system for an important sector of the commercial marketplace. In this case there were some key application oriented people who had done an excellent job of specifying the system requirements and overall design. They had done it to such great detail that it probably would have been a reasonably easy programming job for six or so COBOL programmers in a period of six to nine months. The programming team decided that straight programming was insufficient. They designed several languages, a syntax-directed compiler and a file-management system based on research papers they had read. Also they were utilizing program proving techniques to verify their design for some dynamic data allocation techniques which they were inventing, and were designing a very complex system for linking the various components of the operational program. Naturally all of this had to be completed before they could begin producing the application system. In sum, the budget for this tool-production effort was far more than the total programming job should have required, and the likelihood that the job would ever be finished, let alone finished on time, was very small.

This and numerous other examples seem to illustrate that things haven't changed very much in the past 20 years in the carrying out of programming projects.

Discussion

For the most part many of the papers in this book will present both new and existing technology which will assist the programmer and the manager in implementing programmed systems. Although I shall discuss some technology, my emphasis will be on another aspect of the production process. It will be more on the role of the manager and programmer in the system-building environments. I shall concentrate on the problems encountered in choosing the proper people, tools, schedules, and procedures, which if done improperly, will nullify the effects of the finest available technology or will result in using the wrong technology. There are a number of formal approaches to the management of programming efforts. These include rules for organization, sequential ordering of the steps necessary in a project, documentation requirements and standards, planning and tracking a project with such aides as PERT charts, GANTT charts, status reports, etc., personnel testing and rating, and other management techniques. Each one of these areas is important and deserves understanding on the part of all management personnel. However most of what I say here will assume that a formal management approach exists and I shall not emphasize these formal techniques to a significant extent. Instead, I shall try to discuss the problems of management from the viewpoint of the manager and his normal daily decision-making and problem-solving role.

I shall emphasize the peculiar problems faced in data processing management, and discuss practical (and impractical) solutions to problems. It is my belief that most people can master the ne necessary formalisms of project management, but that in data processing there are still enough ambiguities, misrepresentations, and variables that application of formal procedures without a clear understanding of the practicalities would not lead to successful project management. Thus I shall emphasize practical problems and guidelines of which every data-processing manager should be aware.

MAJOR STEPS OF THE PROGRAMMING PROCESS

There are essentially four major phases in the programmed system production process. These are:

- Requirements Specification
- System Design
- Programming (Coding)
- Checkout

In broad terms these phases can be defined as:

Requirements Specification - Translation of an operational (or application) requirement into a statement of the functions to be performed.

System Design - Translation of the requirements into a description of all the components necessary to implement the system.

Programming - Production of the code which will control the system and perform all required logic and computation.

Checkout - Verification that the coded and other components of the system satisfy the original requirements.

Regardless of how well or formally these steps are performed at any installation, there is probably no one who disagrees that these are necessary steps and no one who doesn't admit to performing them in some fashion on any programming effort, whether large or small. There is, then, <u>that</u> degree of understanding and agreement in the process of producing programmed systems. But the understanding and agreement almost seem to stop there. The main other area of agreement seems to be that the programmed system production process is a terrible problem, little understood, and fouled up with terrifying frequency.

ANALYZING THE PROBLEMS

Throughout the literature, there is a persistent exclamation of the difficulties encountered in managing the production of programmed systems and the general state of disarray in this field. Articles which deny problems exist are nonexistent although some maintain that the problems are not fundamental to data processing [11]. Those which claim to have some solutions for the problems are common, but the more reliable articles have (or should have) explicit or implicit disclaimers which limit the applicability of a technique or emphasize that it is useful "at present" for quite small or special kinds of programs, and not very representative of typical ones.

But there is a wealth of experience, and a number of ideas, techniques, and practices which can be used in managing these efforts. One must try to define what the problems are and develop solutions which can be used in terms of their actual applicability in real situations. The approach used in the following is to examine the problems and possible measures for each of the four major phases of the system development process. It is clear, though, that these phases are not independent. The problems in each phase can result from errors in others, and proper preparation in an early phase can make later work more manageable and accurate. Also, the total process is quite reiterative. However, there are distinct enough procedures in the different phases to make separate discussions worthwhile.

REQUIREMENTS

Let us first look at the requirements-specification phase. This is probably the least covered area in the literature. This step requires translation of a human, business, or government need into a statement of the functions to be performed by a software/hardware system. In many cases it seems trivial, but it probably is the part of the process which leads to more failures than any other. What are some of the major concerns?

A. <u>Typical Errors in Requirements Specification</u>

1. <u>Unclear Statements</u>

The requirements are vague, incomplete, subject to considerable interpretation. "The banking system of the future," "an automatic processor of insurance claims," are the kinds of statements which can be included in requirements which can lead to a very expensive catastrophe.

2. <u>Technical Infeasibility</u>

   Although the requirements may be clear, there is probably no possible way of implementing such a system. "An English-like universal retrieval language to permit clerks with no training Data Base Access," "an efficient network which will be optimal for a total range of problems." Although phrases of this type are outrageous, it is a certainty that people will be found who will volunteer to work on the problems in very real situations.

3. <u>Budget Infeasibility</u>

   Although the system may be ultimately feasible, its construction could never be done within the time, money, or manpower limitations. All jobs, easy or difficult, can fall into this category.

4. <u>Untimeliness</u>

   The requirements may specify today's need, but by the time the system is done, it will be insufficient, leading to many changes, delays, and increases in cost. The requirements may not take into account the enormous time and expense of transition from the current operation, which further delays its use.

B. <u>Importance of Communication between User and Producer</u>

During the requirements specification, there is (or should be) much interaction between the ultimate user and producer. They probably don't speak the same language. They probably don't have the same view of what's important, what's difficult, what computers are good (or bad) for, or anything else.

Although they seem to communicate, results can sometimes be ludicrous. I am acquainted with a number of examples of this kind. An interesting one concerns a major corporation where a process for handling their business was designed, based on long experience in the business and a considerable amount of analysis. The system, certainly amenable to automation, was basically a logical approach to currently manual procedures which the company had been using. The decision to automate was made and a group of programmers was assigned the task. Their interpretation of the task resulted in the specification of the requirements a language which could be used to "program" the company's functions, (although they did not use the word "program" in the requirements). By the time the initial specifications for the language were complete, the user representatives (noncomputer people) had no understanding of the "language" (it was in BNF) or, in fact, what was happening, but somehow had faith that their original ideas were being implemented.

As it turned out, the language which was designed was not comprehensible to anyone (including the language designers), could not be implemented at all, and, it is felt by some that if it had worked it would have been harder and more expensive to use than the manual techniques which were being employed at the time. But for three years, the company management and the programmers hung on, thinking that a set of requirements for the original problem had been developed. It hadn't been. After three years, the language and the original company-oriented approach, which at one time seemed quite reasonable, were dropped.

Although difficult, tedious, frustrating, and in spite of the fact that understanding by both sides may lead to the job not being done at all, one must pursue the dialogue. Management on both sides must ask questions, get answers, assure that all answers are clear and agreed upon. In other words, if the requirements are unclear, technically infeasible, out of the range of the budget, or specify procedures which will be obsolete, then customer satisfaction, even with the best tools and programmers available, will not result.

C. Major Questions to be Answered during the Requirements Process

To help prevent some of the possible wrong steps in this phase, the following (taken from [12]) are a good list of questions which one should answer as he develops requirements:

What should be produced?

Should it be produced?

Can it be produced?

1. What should be produced?

   a. Does it fill a need? Most situations have needs. These include requirements for more accurate accounting, better record keeping, quicker response to questions, better production methods, and more. But the solution may turn out not to include the use of a new computer system. Or the implementable system (rather than the hoped for one) may not fill the real need.

   b. For what market? (I know of one Data Management System which provided fast random access to small, nonchanging files. It was eventually called a "solution without a problem.")

c. What will be the advantages and disadvantages, efficiency and cost effectiveness of the new system? Remember to include production costs, use costs, durability, reliability, and maintainability.

d. Characteristics and side effects? The wrong system can make a very expensive computer seem like a step backward in time. A data-retrieval tool which requires clerks with an excellent grasp of linguistics or formal logic will work less well than a manual system.

2. Should it be produced?

a. Will it pay for itself? Remember optimism, conversion costs, transition, training, and disruption of current work are all possible bugaboos of any project. (Today people seem more concerned with this question, but they frequently want too much for their money.)

b. Will it be useful when introduced? Computer systems take a long time to build. During that time requirements can change.

c. Is it timely? Some systems are "before their time." The previously mentioned Data Management System was called this. The hardware wasn't ready. Neither people nor computers could utilize it effectively.

d. Make or buy? Given a reasonable price and confidence level, the use of existing tools, outside people or techniques may be much wiser than in-house creativity.

e. How to make the final decision? This is something which requires experience and willingness to honestly look for answers to difficult questions.

3. Can it be produced?

a. Is it possible at all? History tells us the answer is no in a large number of cases. A recurrent problem is overambition.

b. Are the resources adequate? Later we shall talk about estimation and the enormous expense of many projects. Some just run out of money, people, computer time, etc.

c. Are the production methods available? Deciding this and choosing the right methods are the subject of many other chapters in this volume.

D. Objectives of the Requirements Phase and Planning for It

The result of the requirements specification phase should include:

1. A clear, detailed functional description of the total system, including the user interface with the system.

2. A reasonably accurate statement of budget and schedules.

3. The resources available, required, and a plan for contingencies.

Actually, the requirements phase should take a relatively long period of time, although with a low level of manpower. Consequently, the results mentioned aren't all going to come out precisely at the end of the phase. For example, one needs some initial estimate of budget and schedule before beginning requirements. The type of system to be specified should be influenced by the magnitude of funds and time available to produce it. Also, some resources (at a minimum, some people) are needed during this phase. Ideally, one would like to fully determine the requirements, then establish a budget, then acquire resources. But it's not like that. However, during the requirements phase the budget is probably low because of low hardware and personnel costs. Two phase contracts are frequently wise. First, a smaller phase to develop requirements and then a second one to do the job.

E. Aides in Budgeting System Development Efforts

We would like quantitative methods to help the estimation process and to plan the schedule and budget. The facts available to assist in estimation are limited in preciseness, but they are based on much experience. Some maxims in the estimation are:

1. It is generally accepted today that software costs are more than hardware costs.

2. The dollar cost per ultimately delivered computer instruction is one measure. Estimates which vary from $1 to more than $50 an instruction are not unusual with $5 for average "fair" small jobs. Larger and more complicated jobs lead to higher potential costs.

3. Underestimation by a factor of 2.5 or more is not unusual. Overestimation is almost unheard of.

4. For tasks similar to ones performed previously by the same people, estimates within 10-30 percent are not uncommon (as shown in Figure 1). This figure, taken from [4] shows how the same team of people improved both their production capabil-

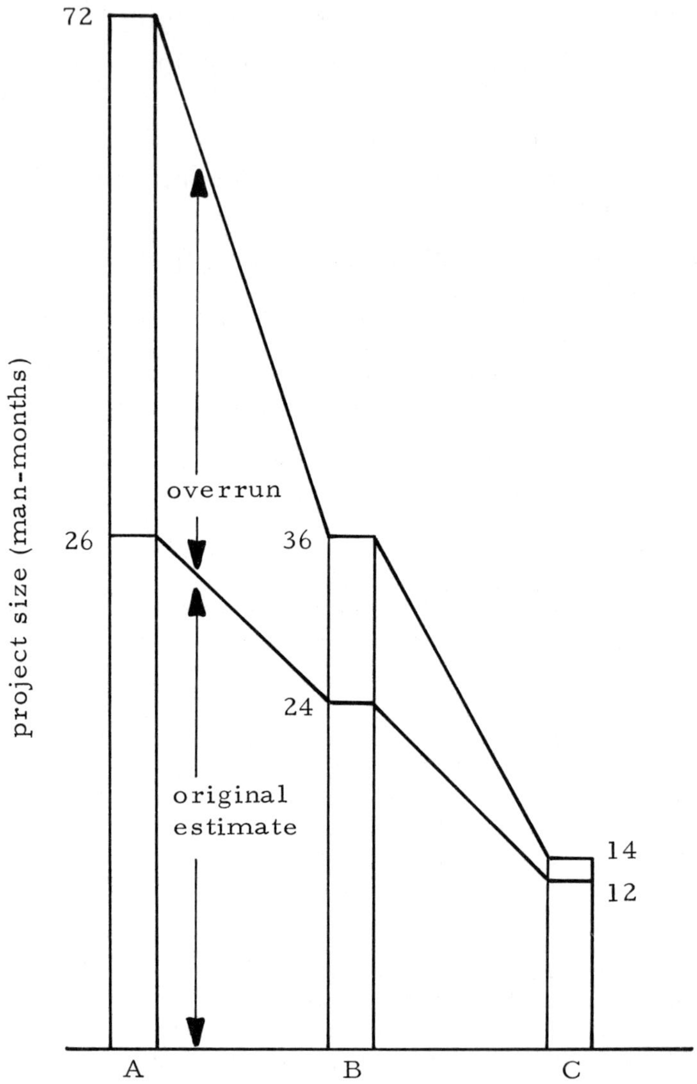

Figure 1. History of Three FORTRAN Compilers

ity and estimating techniques on the same job. (There are, of course, cases of people who make B or C's estimate and get A's result.)

5. Instructions/hour/man for some large systems can be around 3, or go as low as less than 1. For 100,000 instructions, this may mean at best 10-50 or more man years, for 1 million maybe at best 100-500 average man-years or more. Estimates of much more than this have been made for some efforts such as IBM's 0S/360, where some estimates state that 0.2 instructions/ hour were realized.

6. All estimates are functions of complexity, people newness, tools, size, hardware, programming language used, and other factors. The following figure (taken from [14]) shows one author's estimate of the effect of complexity (Figure 2). The definitions of the terms in Figure 2 are:

Easy	Few interactions with other elements; typically mathematical, logical routines. They interact only with the operational system, file-management system, and other supplied routines.
Medium	Some interactions; typically support programs; inculding compilers, I/O packages and some data management packages.
Hard	Many interactions; operating systems, real-time systems, and large applications.

7. Other quantitative values to the programming process have been given, (e.g., see [14]). One is that of the total time (after requirements) 30 percent is devoted to design, 40 percent to programming, and 30 percent to system testing. These are approximately equal to other estimates. (Programming includes initial checkout in this case.)

8. Management and support use half of the resources. In other words, for every programmer assume one other person, not a programmer, on the project.

9. During the last half or more of the project, computer time averages around 8 hours per month per man.

10. Averages are dangerous, as shown by the following curve (Figure 3) for computer use during a typical system development effort. Planning of computer time should be based on such a chart, (see [15]). To live by averages in this case is like saying the average temperature in a desert is 60° (0° for half the year, 120° for the rest).

Duration / Difficulty	6-12 Months	12-24 Months	More than 24 Months	
Easy	20	500	10,000	very few interactions
Medium	10	250	5,000	some interactions
Difficult	5	125	2,500	many interactions
Units	Instructions per Man-Day	Instructions per Man-Month	Instructions per Man-Year	

Figure 2. Instructions versus Complexity

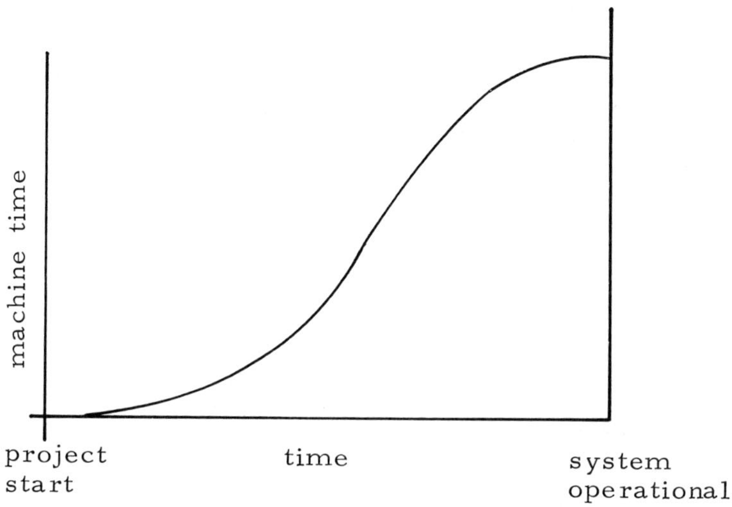

Figure 3. Use of Computer Time

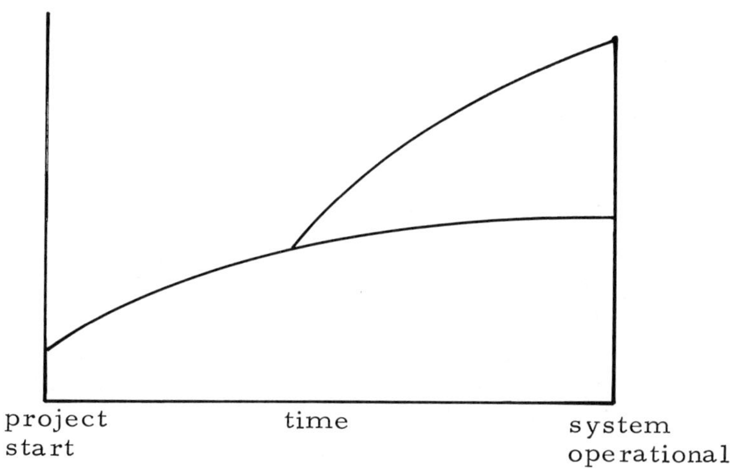

Figure 4. Costs over a Project's Lifetime

11. The rate of spending increases over time as seen in Figure 4.

12. There is a frequent desire to shorten elapsed time by various methods, such as adding more people. But one can compress schedules only so much. Also, paradoxically, estimates have been made that show that the same job done in a shorter time using more people costs more than one where more time is used, as shown in Figure 5 (taken from ref. [15]). Note also, that there is an area which will prove to be unfeasible. This area incidentally is one for which numerous projects have set their goals and had easily predictable results.

13. In reference [4] the following was proposed: Before undertaking a project to produce a new software system or component, read the following statements, checking all that apply. (Some have been slightly modified from original. Parenthesized remarked are mine.)

a. The new system will be substantially superior to its predecessor and to competitive systems. (A giant step forward.)

b. The new system corrects a basic philosophical defect in the previous system. (A new approach to an old problem.)

c. The specification is not yet complete, but it will be finished before any important programming decisions are made. (Early phase decisions will be made later.)

d. The specification is absolutely firm, unless, of course, the company signs a big order and requests some slight changes. (Tolerance.)

e. The programming team will be made up by selecting only the best programmers from other projects. (Belief that the whole company will pitch in.)

f. Because of expansion, a fresh team of programmers with applicable experience will be hired. (Faith in personnel department.)

g. The new computer is a great machine; the programmers will love it as soon as they can get their manuals. (Trust in the manufacturer and programmers.)

h. The programmers will, of course, have to share the machine with the hardware team checking out the new peripherals and the diagnostic package. (Belief that there are more than 24 hours/day.)

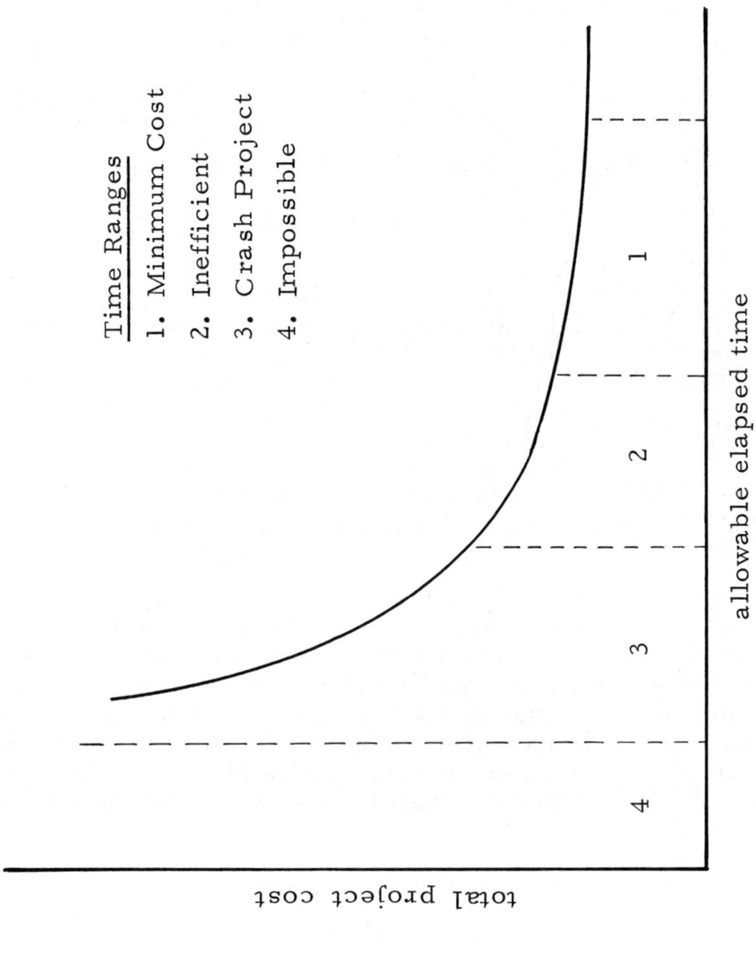

Figure 5. Shortening a Project versus Cost

i. Interfacing this system to the rest of the software is trivial and can be easily worked out later. (Leave some of the less interesting problems until later. Also, worry about error conditions later.)

j. Although the assembler (compiler, loader, file system, etc.) is not completely checked out, it will be ready long before coding is complete. (Trust in the tool-builders.)

k. The debug package isn't done but this system can easily be checked out at the console, hands-on, if necessary. (Belief that there are more than 24 hours/day.)

l. The budget is only preliminary but it's obviously conservative. (Use the rough budget approach.)

m. The project manager may have missed his budget on all previous projects, but he has learned his lession and won't miss this time. (Trust in people.)

For each statement checked on the preceding list, the original author suggests ten percent be added to the estimated cost and one month to the estimated time. If statement "f" is checked, add thirty percent and six months. The result should come much closer to the final result than the original estimate under the assumption that the original estimate was honestly made. I actually feel his estimates are low for the effect of these statements. This is a case where the error is very much a function of size and complexity of task. (A small project with "hands-on" debugging probably won't be terrible. But a large project would be. Expecting to hire many people is worse than hiring a few.)

14. Conclusion on quantitative aides. Clearly, these qualitative ideas don't provide a precise estimating capability. They give, for example, little quantitative help in deciding the "complexity" of the system, the quality of the requirements, the type of programmers, the quality and timeliness of the tools, etc. But they are based on experience, and they do counter the natural urge to be overoptimistic. They should not be ignored. Although they don't represent natural laws, they are statistically very accurate.

F. Summary of Requirements Development Principles

The requirements phase requires that the manager:

1. has patience, pays attention to detail, makes sure both he and the user understand every detail, and methodically agree on every point.

2. Doesn't underestimate. The manager should assume he is not that much smarter or luckier than others.

3. Makes sure that all assumptions as well as specifications are written down and are accounted for.

4. Keeps in mind that a foolish requirement will not be made intelligent by brilliant tools, techniques, or people.

V. DESIGN

The object of the design phase is the translation of the requirements into a statement of all components necessary to implement the system. The end result should be sufficient to permit programming to begin. The major components which will be described in the design phase are:

Program modules

Data base

System flow (Architecture)

Development and testing procedures

A. The Checkpoints of the Design Phase are to:

1. Make sure the requirements are satisfied.
2. Assure the design makes technical sense.
3. Make certain the documentation is clear and complete.
4. Provide a system which will lend itself to implementation, testing, and monitoring, during later phases.

B. Changes in Organization and Manager's Roles

It is during this phase that the project staff increases in size and complexity, and the problems of an organization with several levels of managers is likely to exist on larger projects. The managers at the top levels will get further from the details. If the higher level managers are highly computer- or detail-oriented, they might take on strange behavioral patterns.

Managers sometimes spend a disproportionate amount of time at lower levels, doing work that should be done several levels below. On the other side they might take casual interest in what's happening, spending much time meeting with their superiors. Finally, they might do what is really needed; that is, to see that proper management be performed at all levels. In any case, dependence on other people and procedures becomes a necessity during this phase and continues throughout the project.

C. People

Even with the best management techniques and technical tools, the programming profession remains largely people-oriented. One description of programmers was given in [10]:

"Although computer programming has not been around long enough for biological inbreeding to be considered a problem, the personality traits of the average programmer often reflect certain negative characteristics. For example, the average programmer is often excessively independent to the point of mild paranoia; he can be egocentric, slightly neurotic, and bordering upon a limited schizophrenia. The incidence of beards sandals, and other symbols of rugged individualism or nonconformity are notably greater among this demographic group, as any programming manager will testify. Two of the leaders of the Haight-Ashbury hippie movement were computer programmers."

We recall that the object is to produce a coordinated, implementable, well-documented, detailed description of a system to perform a probably complex operational function. If an individual with these qualities were permitted to go off and produce his own program, he sometimes might do an interesting (but probably unmaintainable) job. The undesirability of these traits for group efforts is obvious and in most cases the manager must make the programmer work in concert with a team.

My own summary of people in the system development process includes the following (see [2]):

1. They don't know the complete operational problem.

2. They communicate badly.

3. Within a group of programmers, there may be an order of magnitude or more difference in capability. This was described in quantitative terms (in [13]) where as much as a factor of 26 difference in ability was demonstrated within a small group of programmers.

4. Good programmers are creative. They are even creative in situations that may not require creativity. Some have a creativity compulsion. (Yet it has been pointed out to me that they are frequently conservative in many ways; e.g., in their attitudes concerning computers, languages, manufacturers, etc.)

5. Nonprogrammers involved in systems can't understand programmers.

6. It is extremely difficult to find out from people how a job is really progressing. Most programmers are optimistic by nature and most managers are gullible.

It is fairly obvious that people with these characteristics can wreak havoc with a system design if left to their own devices. Programmers are usually described as "professionals." The origin for this I don't know, but it has always intrigued me. I looked up the definition of "professional" to see how it would apply.

"Professional means (1) engaged in one of the learned professions or in an occupation requiring a high level of training and proficiency. (2) The man or woman expected to possess several distinctive qualifications. (3) Characterized by or conforming to the technical or ethical standards of a profession or occupation, manifesting fine artistry or workmanship based on sound knowledge and conscientiousness, reflecting the results of education, training, and experience. The word professional may also apply to a person participating for gain or livelihood in an activity or field often engaged in by amateurs."

In many ways, I guess programmers do qualify as professionals. Looking at some of the phrases as "requirement for training or proficiency," "distinctive," "manifesting fine artistry," "working for gain where amateurs are engaged," they do apply. We do need training and proficiency because developments come at a frightening rate. "Distinctive" capabilities are required, but not necessarily the kinds of distinctive traits which were previously described. The job does require "fine artistry" and we do "work for gain." One thing we do lack is the ability to qualify or disqualify "professionals."

D. The Need for Discipline during Design

The manager needs patience and understanding. He must know people's temperments and capability. He must know the good people and the weak ones. He must motivate them. He must take advantage of their creativity. But he must define standards, procedures, see that technical issues are decided, and instill some kind of control or discipline; an unpopular word in this field but essential if many of the potential problems are to be avoided.

But even discipline is also complicated. Without some other important concepts, it can be as catastrophic as the chaos possible without control. This is not a case for straight, unthinking discipline (not that I believe that could be achieved). First of all, we have not reached a stage where our first decisions are always right in these developments. Thus, after studying and listening, the manager may change some previous decisions, but conservatism may rule out changing others. Second, it is true that there is a wide range of problem difficulty as well as people capability within any system, so that the regimen with respect to different sections might have to be different. Third, it would be terribly wrong to characterize the program development process as a mechanical thing which could be legislated. There are numerous cases for flexibility. Even some of the major proponents of top-down programming admit that in practice there is a need for the design of some of the eventual lower-level modules early in the effort. Another example is that those who strongly believe in high-level languages will see areas where machine language programming should be used and vice versa. Also, one must recognize the value of new good techniques. But during the design and later phases, a great deal of data will be generated. This data, or information, must be uniformly described and well coordinated. To accomplish this, some level of control must be maintained throughout the design.

E. Technical Decisions

1. The Importance of Understanding the Level of Technology

So far we've discussed people and control during design. Implementation decisions will be made during this phase which will greatly affect the ultimate success or failure of the project. The first kind of decision is related to the techniques which will be used to produce the system, both in the application and support areas. One author [11] described a concept involved in the management of these kinds of developments which related to a very important part of the problem. He pointed out that programming has effectively three technological phases which are quite similar to those of other technologies. These are research, developmental and operational. The implications of a program in each of these stages is significant, in terms of what one can expect from the program, when to expect it, and how its development is to be managed.

If one is to develop an operational system within a typical time and budget available for most ventures, he had better plan on using application techniques which are operational. He also should plan on using support tools which are operational. "The failure to make the proper distinction will mean a failure to understand just what it is that is being managed. If this happens, the manager courts disaster." Many of the examples of failure in managing programming efforts are related to this phenomenon in some way. Thus there are very basic decisions concerning techniques to be used in the system to be produced and the support tools to be used in producing the system. Innovation and invention are important for progress. But one must understand that some new inventions in this field are frequently not very useful for practical applications. They frequently aren't useful at all except for lessons learned in using (or producing) them. Their schedules and costs are quite unpredictable, but our profession is replete with inventions. On the other hand, we clearly must recognize and use new techniques, where possible.

2. Aids Which Should (or Shouldn't be used in Measuring Technical Status

How is one to know what's practical within the scope of his project? A manager needs technical experience or at least someone in whom he can place technical trust. Reference material which could serve as a firm guide for the manager in selecting his tools and techniques as well as deciding on the scope of his own product is unfortunately unavailable in a single source. Instead there is such an enormous mass of material that no manager could read and evaluate it all even if he didn't have anything else to do. Also the type of material available is not at all helpful in the selection process. Let's examine the level of material available.

First, there are the actual system descriptions of announced or released systems. Today, even with these, a not uncommon reaction by those with experience to a new "operational" announcement is "it sounds good, but I'll let others try it for a year or so to get rid of the problems." This is said about products from quite respected and successful vendors. Of course, it is also taken for granted by these people that new releases will not be available on the announced publication date. An inexperienced manager could very well assume that when a vendor promises something will be working at a given time, he can use it on the critical path of his schedule. This, he will learn, is an assumption which requires considerably more investigation.

The second type of literature is the weekly or monthly trade papers and magazines. Although generally technical in nature, these are not considered at the same level of professionalism as some of the more learned proceedings and publications. They usually discuss issues or describe viewpoints and opinions as well a products and concepts. It should be remembered, however, that these are opinions, frequently by very enthusiastic and opinionated people who are quite impressed and actually believe that what they have done or are stating is a great step forward in data processing technology, or a solid argument against a step forward. Unfortunately, no verification of claims, or counterclaims, are made by anyone, and an attempt to rigidly follow advice or techniques in these publications can lead to some confusion. These publications do have the very positive characteristic that much of what they contain is negative – a valuable perspective in this field.

The fully professional publications describe concepts that are, in many cases, quite interesting. They usually represent a fair amount of study and sometimes some experience. For the manager interested in producing an operational system, however, they have some severe deficiencies. For example, they frequently fail to distinguish the state of technology of the concept being discussed. After describing a powerful, complex, Data Base Management System, the author may (or may not) just mention that so far this concept has only been used on data bases that fit in core memory or on one disk pack and that the extension to larger files (e.g., those that reside on many disk files) may be tried in the future. This extension might, of course, prove the undoing of the concept.

In the early 1960s, I attended a meeting of a number of governmental policy makers, contract monitors, and performance oriented personnel. The subject was the construction of a new major on-line operating system which would be available to military analysts for their work. It had seemed like a fairly rational meeting up to a point. Then the subject of interactive consoles began. When words like "teletype" and "typewriter" were mentioned, there was an immediate strong reaction from one of the important governmental representatives. He questioned why people were discussing the use of these limited types of consoles. When asked to clarify his objection, he very seriously stated that the system (to be produced around 1965) should permit users to communicate with the computer by handwriting. He had read some articles on the subject and felt that was the "only way to go." The only thing I remember about the meeting after that point was some incredulous expressions on the part of the more technically oriented people and the fact that it never seemed to get back on a rational course again.

Another thing that many articles don't usually describe adequately is who has used the system and what problems they had in actual use (if it has been used). After several years, a very difficult to use, slow, and maybe impractical system may appear to the developer to be quite natural. He forgets that even he might have had trouble getting used to some of the system's awkwardness. The reaction of the other real users (after the first one of incredulity) is usually quite less tolerant. Another thing these articles may neglect to mention, or at least not stress, is that the described system was designed to work in a very special environment of hardware and software. Thus any attempt to replicate it on a standard configuration which is used at the reader's installation is subject to great expense or time.

Having spent most of my working life in the computing profession, I don't know if publications in other fields are similar. My impression is that in at least some fields the distinction between research and operational status is clearer, and there are better defined steps which are necessary before any product is considered ready to be applied. This may not always be true, but I'm sure, for example, if literature in the medical profession were published and believed with the same abandon as in the programming profession, we would not have to worry about a population explosion. These comments are not made to disparage the publications, although I do feel that more technical commentary on status and actual value would be useful. The efforts and articles are necessary and certainly valuable in the long run. Papers on completed concepts only would not be of much interest. But I do believe that one must use great caution before planning to utilize concepts or tools he sees described in publications (or promotional material).

Finally, it should be pointed out that even reports on systems actually being used are subject to tremendous interpretation. Just recently, I was engaged in an informal lunchtime conversation with several people. All were acquainted with a recent acquisition of a compiler by a major aircraft manufacturer. The discussion centered on the quality and usefulness of the compiler. One presumably informed comment was that the compiler was excellent and was in current use. This brought out a surprised exclamation and a comment from another "well-informed" individual that the compiler was considered unacceptable, and the company was considering replacing it. I guess one could have laboriously tracked down the sources of these reports and found the truth (if it existed), but if my interest were in using that compiler, I wouldn't have been helped by that conversation. These differences may result from errors in communication, biases, or the transition of an organization in its view of a product over time (which, interestingly enough, can go from bad to good, or vice versa). I know of one organization which has outlawed structured programming. This is not to say that the concept is bad (see the Horowitz article) but the people situation can influence the use of a technique to a great extent.

3. Purchasing Software

For those looking for tools today, the purchase of software packages has become common. These packages certainly have advantages. They are probably much cheaper in the long run than a specially built system. They can be made available much sooner, more predictably, and they probably are more reliable. They may be better documented than a new development. If studied properly before purchase their operating and functional characteristics will be much better known than a new development. But here again, one must keep in mind that this is a software package, and the people providing the package have a major (and selfish) interest in providing it. Thus, the importance of really understanding it is paramount.

The area of Data Base Management packages is a good example. There are many (maybe hundreds) of systems labeled DBMS available. One can talk for hours on the differences among them and the wide range of requirements users have in this area. Thus a purchaser must carefully analyze his requirements and the properties of a DBMS before making a decision. The same is true in other areas as well.

F. Designing to Facilitate Better System Development

As we have seen, quantitative estimating techniques are approximate at best and require significant personal experience and subjectivity on the part of the estimators. It is obvious, therefore, the trouble doesn't stop at the original estimating step. Throughout the project's life cycle, the manager(s) must constantly be aware of where the project is, how far or close from the schedule each part is, what effects changes have had or will have, whether he should make personnel or technical changes, or whether he should announce budget or schedule overruns. Anyone who has had experience with noncommunicating, "independent to the point of paranoia" programmers knows that determining the answers to these questions during any project can be a terrifying problem. Thus one should attempt to make the system design help the manager monitor the status throughout the rest of the project.

1. Greater Complexity Leads to More People Dependence

The goundwork for a system which lends itself to accurate monitoring and control (as well as successful technical operation) is laid during design. It is here that the pieces of the system are described. If the pieces are large, multifunctioned, redundant, and intersecting, it is clear that not only will they be difficult to produce but their status will be almost impossible to measure.

The manager will have to place his faith and future down the hall with the noncommunicative, overly optimistic programmers. It may turn out that these people don't know what they are doing and in fact may be doing something which has little value to the project.

2. The Necessity of Modularity and Independence

What can a manager do to prevent this period of mystery and uncertainty from developing? There is a basic precept that is commonly accepted, if not universally observed, as the major solution for this problem. It is the foundation for many programming concepts which are being discussed widely today. The key words in this precept are modularity and independence. The object is to have a design in which all the pieces have a status that is easily measured. This implies that modules are small, have well-defined and simple interfaces, and have realms of responsibility which are nonredundant. During the system design, the modules can be precisely defined in terms of their expected function and timing requirements. Then during the programming and checkout period the status can be accurately measured. This is the heart of all of the currently described techniques for producing software: top-down, structured programming, levels of abstraction, and many of the defined management approaches. These techniques will be discussed in later sections. But their underlying idea is that systems should be constructed from well-defined modules.

G. Summary of Design

The problems during the design phase are: technical decisions, people, and architecture. In sum, the key words to be observed during the design phase are discipline, caution, and modularity. A mixture of experience, technical competence, and constant care are needed to get the system development started in a fashion which will make successful completion and delivery possible.

VI. PROGRAMMING PHASE

A. Lack of Visibility

It is during this period that the visibility of the system development effort can decrease to a point of nonexistence. During the requirements phase the technical discussions are at a reasonably high level, the participants are relatively few, and the amount of documentation is limited. During design, if pursued properly, the individual pieces can be well-defined and fairly easily understood, and most of the descriptions are in English. But while programmers are writing code, the amount of detail and the nature of most programming languages require a strict conformance with management procedures to assure that things are proceeding satisfactorily. If modules are large and very complex, the manager's job is essentially hopeless. He might as well take a vacation, or he can spend most of his time briefing upper management or selling new jobs (which many managers do). On the other hand, if the programmed units are small and well-defined, the chance of ongoing inspection exists as well as the possibility of observation of excesses in schedule or size.

B. Technical Aids

1. Programming Languages

Here is an area where there has been a great deal of technology developed over the years. The major contribution is, of course, in the area of programming languages. It is now generally accepted practice to use some higher level language on most major system developments. Over the years the arguments for and against the use of these languages have tended to be fairly consistent in qualitative terms, although quantitatively there has generally been a decrease in claims. That is, they're probably not as valuable for programming as once claimed, nor are well-developed compilers as bad in producing efficient code as once claimed. Factors of 2 and 3 improvement in programming time and the same or less in efficiency decrease are generally accepted today with established compiler languages.

2. Basic Support Tools

The major issues today in support tools concern the previously mentioned organization and construction. In general, a large percentage of the basic software (compilers, operating system, debugging routines, Input/Output, etc.) is supplied by the computer manufacturer or other software supplier. Relatively rarely are programmers permitted to invent these kinds of support tools as part of a system construction process. One of the more common areas of interest today is the selection of the Data Base Management System. This is natural since many systems today have as a basic function the manipulation of large quantities of data. The choice of a DBMS is in itself a subject of considerable magnitude. Although many systems are labeled DBMS, they actually have quite different characteristics. Both the system needs and the DBMS capabilities have to be studied very carefully before one is chosen.

3. Need for Experts in Different Technical Areas

The emphasis on data base problems is an example of another kind of phenomenon which is not unusual in most current system developments. In the past, programmers were generally divided into two categories – software builders and application programmers. Today, we have a variety of specialties. Some of them are:

a. Data Base Definition

b. Data Base Use

c. DBMS

d. Teleprocessing

e. Job Control Language

f. Operating System (and generation)

g. Application System (and its subdivisions)

When one considers that it can take a person a long time to become expert in any of these areas on a particular computer, it is not difficult to see why managers must think carefully before choosing systems and people. Here is where we see the intersection of a number of managerial problems. Remember, there is a considerable difference among programmers' capabilities. With the great variety in specialization necessary, two things are clear. The manager will not be expert in everything. Also, he will not have many experts in any particular area. Thus he is quite dependent on one or a few people in certain areas. These are areas where technical expertise is required to select the correct approach and execute it. It is not an area which can benefit very much by systematized approaches of management. Thus if the wrong individual is placed in a key technical position the manager may not be able to detect it very soon, and it might cause considerable damage to the development effort. Here is where selection of systems and people is one of the critical managerial choices. New systems will probably have fewer experts and more problems and questions leading to higher start-up and maintenance costs. Extreme care in screening experts to handle support systems must be used. As in all cases, if the choice of either system or people seems to be wrong, the manager must make the decision of whether and what to change early.

C. Continued Managerial Attention to Detail

In general, then, the programming phase is not one in which the manager can relax, waiting for more obvious signals to appear when the programs run on the computer. Programs must be examined as they are developed. Problem areas can't be ignored. Close attention should be paid to all technological areas. One must keep very much on the alert for weak people in all areas. They can cause considerable damage. In a recent article on structured programming, there was a description of a very successful effort using this management technique along with the "chief programmer" concept. This article would have been more convincing in favor of this technique if it hadn't mentioned that the project was done with a small team of very good people. It is generally felt that a small team of very good people is perhaps an ideal way to do all projects using almost any technique.

At a seminar on system development which was once held at M. I. T., one of the guest speakers was the man who had been responsible for the programming of the SAGE System which I mentioned at the beginning of this paper. He went into detail about how the project mushroomed from a relatively small, well-controlled, reasonably intellectual affair into a massive conglomeration of many hundreds of people, roomfuls of documents and budget and schedule overruns. When asked what he would do differently if he had it to do over again, he thought for a while, then said that the only thing he could think of would be to hire only 12 good people and do the whole job with them. This is certainly an exaggeration. First of all there is a diversity of knowledge needed in these developments. Also there are documentation, training, installation, and numerous other support requirements. Generally, it is assumed that for every programmer on a project there is at least one support or management person. Therefore having very small teams for very large projects is not very realistic. In addition, with small teams, the criticality of all individuals is very high. Turnover can be catastrophic, and has in fact severely damaged some projects. Also the definition of very good people is itself subject to question. Thus, although one should feel blessed when he succeeds in getting a good small team and a reasonably small project, there probably is no team of more than one person for whom some management practices are not necessary. But the quality of the people is a critically important factor to the difficulty of managing it and the value of the product. In summary the problems during the programming phase are: lack of visibility, choice of languages and other tools, and the need for a variety of specialists. The manager must continue to pay attention to details and monitor the progress.

VII. TESTING

A. Renewed Visibility

The program and system checkout phase of system development is one which has received a great deal of attention. For one thing, it is the phase during which schedule slippages become obvious, although the reasons for slippage may stem from earlier phases. It is the phase in which the rate of progress frequently slows down perceptively; in fact it can go negative as when a 90 percent completed projected becomes 80 percent complete with the passage of time. It is also the point of no return in system development. It is not unusual that when schedules are clearly slipping in the early phases of system development to assume that the time will be made up during the test period. But, of course, there are no more significant periods in which to make up slack once the test phase is reached, not that they could in fact have been made up by sacrificing test time anyway. Thus slippages detected during the test phase result in one (or more) of the following: (1) people work tremendously long hours, (2) system capabilities are reduced, usually leading to the definition of new releases, (3) a system full of problems is delivered, and (4) a confession of slipped schedules is made, and system release is postponed.

Of course, the difficulties encountered in testing aren't due exclusively to the technology of testing. It is at this point that all previous errors in system scheduling, management, and technical concepts surface, although they surface in the form of a test schedule which can't be met. Up until this point, errors of many kinds are hard to detect without considerable effort. If two documents describe procedures which are actually incompatible, would lead to impossibly slow execution, or are not possible to program, only careful examination will find it out in many cases. But during testing, these problems will be quite visible.

B. Some Clear Signposts to Problems during Testing

A proper system development effort prior to testing will help lessen the number of traumas which occur during testing. Sometimes at this point there is a review of the course of history on the project. The manager might look at the original schedule which described what <u>may</u> have seemed like a reasonable set of milestones, manning, and computer requirements and wonder what went wrong. Well, a large number of things might have gone wrong. Let's review some, briefly.

- Key people left the project.
- Certain people turned out badly.
- Impossible-to-implement technical choices were made.
- Changes to original requirements were made without any change in schedule or budget.
- Hardware was late or unreliable.
- Delivered software was late or unreliable.
- Someone forgot to account for vacations, illness, etc., during the project scheduling.
- Original manpower buildup did not keep up with the plan.
- Key people spent a very large portion of their time making presentations to higher management, customers, or prospective customers.
- Working conditions turned out to be worse than anyone could have guessed.
- A disproportionately large part of the job rested in a few people's hands and this led to the avoidance of a methodical, controlled approach in those areas.
- A bad choice was made in such packages as DBMS, Teleprocessing, etc.
- Design problems were left unresolved.
- Nobody paid attention to the size and timing of the system as it was being developed.
- No preparation for testing was done during earlier phases.

With the exception of those events which are completely technical, there are none on this list which would not be immediately apparent to even the most naive manager. In addition, there are none which don't obviously have a severe impact on schedule and budget. Yet, until the point in the testing phase had been reached where tragedy is quite clear, nobody may have considered that the system schedule had slipped or at least noted that the occurrence of some events required stern measures during the system development efforts. More likely, people will feel that the testing techniques must be modified or the amount of computer and working time available should be increased.

C. Effectiveness of Techniques and Tools for Testing

Of course, testing is frequently done badly. The literature describes many techniques which are supposed to improve the situation. There has been some controversy at times over the value of these methods. One of the techniques which has been presented on the range from orders of magnitude better to inferior for program debugging is the use of interactive checkout. The early proponents of time-sharing helped fuel this particular controversy by making quite extravagant claims regarding the virtues of on-line programming. Since prior to that time the major part of the data-processing profession had become used to and were producing large batch-processing systems, there was, of course, a skeptical group within the community. As usual in the computing world, most arguments were based on intuition and prejudice. There was no quantitative data to back up either side.

In the middle 1960s, a few people decided to try to "prove" the case for or against on-line programming. This generally included controlled experiments where a number of individuals were given a small set of programs to produce and check out using both on-line and off-line techniques. Attempts were made to account statistically for programmer differences, experience, and to isolate the experiments to the checkout process. In general these experiments did show that checkout elapsed time was less using interactive techniques than otherwise and also showed that the use of computer time for interactive checkout was more than for noninteractive debugging. But the differences in both cases tended to be small ratios (2 to 4) rather than the order of magnitude some expected. Also, it turned out that these experiments didn't seem to make many people happy. Everybody with opinions on the subject seemed to find fault with the methodology or the results.

It turns out that many claims for new system development concepts would have similar quantitative results, if measured. The initial claims are based largely on intuition and features of the system which aim toward solving specific faults of the current technology. In the majority of cases, it probably turns out that there is some accuracy in the value of the new ideas. But it also turns out that in the majority of cases the quantitative results are not nearly as great as predicted, and a number of issues arise in practice which dampen considerably the original hopes.

In '54-'55, I was involved with the development of one of the original automatic programming languages, PACT. By today's standards, it was a very small step into higher level languages. Yet, I recall that several members of the original team seriously discussed the possibility of stopping the project, because it might eliminate the need for programmers. Well, it's probably true that an enormous majority of people never heard of this language, and it is absolutely true its existence and the existence of all the languages which have come since seem to have had little effect on the growth of the programmer population.

So again we see that the manager does not easily find a remedy for his possible problems. He should be aware of new techniques, and where they are operational apply them or else realize they're not if he does use them. But he should never assume that any technique will permit him to abrogate his responsibility. That responsibility being to manage as he wants a doctor and hospital to manage the healing of a member of his family or himself during a serious illness. Among other things, this would include very close attention, no unwarranted assumptions, careful planning, and the institution of reasonable measures when problems are first detected.

Throughout this discussion, the appearance of conservatism which I mentioned before, seems very strong. In a field which has shown such remarkable growth in a relatively short period of time, this may seem quite paradoxical, particularly from a person who has been involved in many of these developments. In fact, a strict adherence to the "stick with the old approach" is clearly as unwarranted as a philosophy which assumes that nothing should be done using the same approach as previously. But one should examine the approach and carefully evaluate its reasonableness for the task and schedule at hand. One must understand the things and people he's dealing with.

D. General Approaches to Testing

In testing, a number of approaches are currently available for examination, some closer to practicality than others. Techniques exist which, although not obviously oriented to testing, have as their basic idea the improvement of the testing phase. Higher level languages certainly fall into this category. They not only provide a means for producing code faster, they should reduce the number of coding errors as well. In addition, they should assist in the documentation problem, which in turn aids the testing and maintenance functions. The concepts of structured programming are also clearly aimed towards making the testing period more precise and less costly. Hetzel [3] described the six basic principles of testing. These are:

1. Modularity — This consists of the previously described construction of a system in modules and testing it in that fashion. Typically, a design is done in decreasing levels of subdivision while testing is done in increasing levels of integration. However, a total top-down approach would actually have the system checked out in the same order as the development, where the lower-level modules are represented by dummy or simulated routines during the higher level checkout.

2. Design for Testing - This includes three areas:

a. Testing Specifications

These could be accomplished either through developing formal specification languages which can be compared against the coded programs or coding directly from the specifications (which is more typical). For the former, little has actually been done in a practical way. For the latter, the major problem is assuring that the specifications are correct and somehow making certain that the code is actually following the specifications.

b. Putting in Testing Aids during Development

This must be done in a way which does not adversely affect the eventual running of the system. It is frequently overlooked in the midst of system building pressures, and in fact, few people use testability as a design criterion in practice.

c. Structuring Logic for Testing

This is included in the ideas of top-down, structured, functional programming and others which regiment the size and function of each module and the order of producing them.

3. Simulation — Included in this area is the construction of driver programs or hardware, or simulation routines which act in concert with the routine being tested. Here one must develop realism, which is not easy, and the building and testing of the simulation routines can be as difficult as the development of the system being tested (see the article by Royce).

4. Sampling — The technique which is probably used in practice more than any other is the use of sampling. This is the running of the program against data inputs, which actually are a small sample of the total possible set, and observe the results. Unfortunately, it seems highly unlikely that statistically valid samples will ever be possible to choose for this kind of testing. It is clearly one of the reasons that there is a general agreement that no program is ever checked out except those that will never run again. To assist in the input of sample

data there are programs called Test Data Generators. These can be very generally oriented or oriented to a specific problem area. However, the former probably do not really help the confidence in validation very much, and the latter are very rare. For very standard products, such as COBOL compilers, there have been reasonably useful sets of test cases. Typically of course, the most significant sample testing is done in conjunction with users, presumably in field or pilot test mode, but unfortunately it is frequently in the guise of a released package.

5. Logical Reduction — One of the difficulties in achieving confidence that a program is checked out is the incredible complexity of programs. Reference [7] points out quite graphically the effect of high connectivity of different modules as they are being checked out. Most management techniques are oriented towards lowering this complexity. One theoretical aid is a technique which, either manually or automatically, will reduce the logical complexity of a given program. Some practical tools, (see for example [8]), have been developed to show which portions of programs have been exercised during an execution, (see articles by Brown and Stucki). Many such aids have been suggested and this logical reduction is the basis for program-proving techniques. Although these seem as if they will ultimately be the real solution to program testing problems, they are currently of very limited value. Various articles provide an overview of this field (e.g., [9]). Most point out the theoretical value but not the practical limitation of these techniques.

6. Standardization — One of the practical techniques for developing testable systems is the establishment of standards in the programming effort. These can include such things as the programming language, macros, subsets of languages, general programming conventions, module size with entry and exit sequence, and documentation. All of these things assist in making program checkout easier to observe, help the support system be less costly, make programmer transfer easier, and control wild creativity on the part of some programmers. They can have the side effect of limiting the operating efficiency of a system or actually make some things harder to do than would otherwise be the case. However, these are techniques for instilling discipline in the implementation task which, as stated before, is an extremely important management requirement.

In sum, all of these techniques, whether manual or automatic, have some validity. The key is to understand which are applicable, what sorts of problems they apply to, and what the set of existing aides is, along with their limitations. Whatever the technique used, or the strength or weaknesses of the previous system development, the testing phase does have one major advantage. This advantage is the visibility of the product. For the first time in the system's development one can see the output or see that no output is being produced. Thus he can get an actual view of the system's timing patterns. The key point is to have structured the system so that this visibility is useful. That is, the outputs seen can be clearly measured against the inputs, and a reasonable sample of input-output combinations for a routine can provide a feeling of confidence of the routine's validity. At all levels, tests for system integration should have been prepared with precision. Above all, tests should be prepared ahead of time. As much attention should be given to test design as is given to program design, and, as stated before, program design should be oriented to the period of testing. Thus, the key words for the testing phase are preparation, choice of technique(s), precision, analysis and review.

VII. CONCLUSIONS

The preceding discussion shows that there are at least six major areas of concern of which one should be aware in the production of programmed systems. They are:

- Planning
- Budgeting
- Techniques and Tool Selection
- People
- System Architecture
- Attention to Detail

Under each we can list the following major points:

A. Planning

1. The step from a small prototype effort to a full scale operational one can be enormous.
2. Don't try to make spectacular technological or philosophical advances in producing an operational system.
3. In planning to build a system, one should make sure the following questions are satisfactorily answered.
   - What should be produced?
   - Should it be produced?
   - Can it be produced?

4. In planning a project, use the following rules:
   - Small technical steps.
   - Assure specifications are complete and agreed upon.
   - Be realistic in people acquisition plans. (There should not be too many new ones. They won't all be comparable and they won't all have relevant experience.)
   - Choose tools according to their current capability.
   - Choose management properly.
5. Requirements must be clear, technically feasible, realistic budget-wise, and timely.

B. Budgeting

1. A minimum amount of budgeting is necessary before a project begins, but complete budgeting and manning should not take place until the requirements are clear.
2. Plan on true state-of-the-art techniques. If you don't, admit that you don't and budget and schedule accordingly.
3. Our current estimation techniques lead to the following conclusions:
   - System building is expensive.
   - Underestimation is universally the rule.
   - Repetition decreases the cost of a project and increases the confidence in the estimate.
   - Cost is a function of many factors (newness, complexity, people, hardware, understanding, etc.).
   - There are some schedules which no budget would make feasible.
4. There are three levels of technical capability of any hardware/software system; research, development, operation. Know which one you have.

C. Techniques and Tool Selection

1. There is some substance in most technological claims. However, the quantitative payoff is probably not so high and negative side effects can be expected with most innovations.

2. Where questions exist concerning applicability of a tool or techniques, skepticism is probably the correct approach. Learn what to look for in technical statements, written or verbal

and what to look further into. Who has used it? What results did they get? What machine and operating system did they have? What was the configuration? What are its complete operating characteristics? What doesn't it do? Who can learn to use it and how?

D. People

1. Since system users and system producer don't normally speak the same language or have the same kinds of knowledge, particular attention must be given to communication between them. No implicit assumptions should be made by either party.

2. Programmers tend to have a variety of characteristics. Foremost among them is independence, whether creative or conservative. They have a tremendous range in capability.

3. Discipline tempered by technical understanding is essential to any project.

4. Wherever possible, small highly skilled, cooperative team efforts are preferred. But one must apply realism when trying to restrict size.

E. Architecture

1. Systems should be constructed out of well-defined and independent modules.

2. There are various approaches to testing. However, the one that remains most practical is running test cases with sample data. Thus testable modules are important.

3. Preparation for testing through system design and test planning is of critical importance.

F. Attention to Detail

1. One cannot make up for lost time in the testing phase.
2. When events occur which can affect schedule or budget, they should be handled immediately either by taking an effective measure, or slipping the schedule. Some effective measures are:

   - Changing effort
   - Changing scope
   - Replacing people
   - Replacing technique
   - Buying something
   - Modifying schedule

3. In managing programming efforts, never assume they will go well, are going well, or have been going well. Treat each effort as if it is a developing disaster, and maybe you won't have one.

REFERENCES

1. Baumgartner, J. S., Project Management, Richard D. Irwin, Inc., Homewood, Illinois, December 1963 (first printing).
2. Report on a Conference Sponsored by the NATO Science Committee, J. N. Buxton and B. Randall (eds.), Rome, Italy, October 27-31, 1969, Software Engineering Committee, The Kynoch Press, Birmingham, England, April 1970.
3. Hetzel, W. C., Program Test Methods, based on Proceedings of the Computer Program Test Methods Symposium held at the University of North Carolina, Chapel Hill, June 21-23, 1972, Prentice-Hall, Englewood Cliffs, N. J., 1973.
4. Report on a Conference Sponsored by the NATO Science Committee, P. Naur and B. Randall (eds.), Garmisch, Germany, October 7-11, 1968, Software Engineering Committee, Scientific Affairs Division, NATO, Brussels 31, Belgium, January 1969.
5. Tsou, J. T., Proceedings from the Third Symposium on Computer and Information Sciences, Miami Beach, Florida, December 1969, Software Engineering, Coins III, Vol. I, Academic Press, New York, 1970.
6. Weinwurm, G. F., On the Management of Computer Programming, Auerbach, Inc., Philadelphia, 1970.
7. Haney, F. M., "Module connection analysis – a tool for scheduling software debugging activities, Proc. NCC, 1973.
8. Brown, J. R. and R. F. Hoffman, "Evaluating the effectiveness of software verification – practical experience with an automated tool," Proc. NCC, 1973.
9. Linden, F. A., "A summary of progress toward proving program correctness," Proc. NCC, 1973.
10. Brandon, R. H., "The economics of computer programming," On the Management of Computer Programming, Auerbach, Inc., Philadelphia, 1970, pp. 35-42.

11. Reynolds, C.H., "What's wrong with computer programming management?" On the Management of Computer Programming, Auerbach, Inc., Philadelphia, 1970, pp. 35-42.

12. Bemer, R.W., "Manageable software engineering," Proc. 3rd Symposium on Computer and Information Sciences, Academic Press, New York, 1970, pp. 121-138.

13. Sackman, H., W.J. Erickson, and E.E. Grant, "Exploratory experimental studies comparing online and offline programming performance," C.ACM, 1963, pp. 3-10.

14. Aron, J.D., "Estimating resources for large programming systems," Report on a Conference Sponsored by the NATO Science Committee, Rome, Italy, Software Engineering Committee, Kynoch Press, Birmingham, England, April 1970.

15. Pietrasanta, A.M., "Resource analysis of computer program system development," On the Management of Computer Programming, Auerbach, Inc., Philadelphia, 1970, pp. 67-87.

2 Requirements Analysis

Requirements specification and analysis is the translation of a user (person, business, government) need into a statement of the functions to be accomplished by an automated system, followed by an analysis of the cost and size of that projected system. This first phase of the software cycle is subject to substantial error because it intrinsically relies upon subjective human judgments. Moreover there is scant factual information on which such decisions can be based. Too often requirements analysis is simply bypassed and this is the main subject of the paper by Winston Royce. In it, he strongly advocates a carefully done requirements analysis and delineates all of the potential difficulties if his advice is not followed. He persuasively points out why a pure top-down analysis is impossible, since accurate requirements analysis implies a consideration of many of the low-level parts of the proposed application. This must be done before the design phase is begun. The second aspect of his paper is concerned with the merits of simulation as applied to validating requirements. He points out its value as a tool for analyzing the completeness, consistency, and traceability of a requirements set. He then compares simulation with several alternatives.

The article by Ray Wolverton draws upon an available data base at TRW. Two large command and control systems were studied with respect to predicting the size and cost of the latter extrapolating from the statistics of the former. Wolverton first breaks down the software cycle into checkable phases; i.e., at each point validation of progress can be measured. He then describes in detail how costing figures are obtained for these phase points. The ratio estimator approach is combined with both top-down and bottom-up estimation. Competitive bidding within the development group is an integral activity. An automated system keeps a history and allows for continual changing of parameters. Though keyed to his aerospace applications, several interesting curves are given relating module cost to number of instructions, percentage of time spent in various development phases, and cost distribution by activity. This article is an edited version of [42] in the bibliography which should be consulted for more detailed information.

SOFTWARE REQUIREMENTS ANALYSIS: SIZING AND COSTING

Winston W. Royce

INTRODUCTION

Often the difference between success and failure of a large software project lies in the consistency and completeness with which the system requirements have been specified, and in the fidelity with which these requirements have been translated into estimates of the cost, schedule, and hardware required to support the application.

Some large software projects have been scrapped completely because they were not responsive to user requirements. Others, [1] have had up to 95 percent of their originally delivered code rewritten in order to satisfy user requirements. I will begin by describing the usual causes and symptoms of such requirements mismatches, and will provide some recommendations for avoiding them in future projects.

Other projects have encountered difficulties because of an inability to infer the scale of hardware resources necessary to satisfy the requirements. For example, the Univac-United Airlines reservations system was scrapped when it was found that, among other things, the original estimates of 9,000 instructions executed per transaction had escalated to 146,000 [2]. Some capabilities are becoming available to help; as pointed out in the papers to follow, they involve including a minidesign activity in the requirements process. Analytic models of computer systems [3-4] are very helpful, to the extent that their assumptions (e.g., inputs have normal, uniform, stationary, independent, etc. distribution) are justified in the application. They can be quickly developed and extended, and their analytic structure facilitates sensitivity studies. When such simplifying conditions cannot be assumed, simulation models [5-6] can be used. They can be built to cover more general situations, but generally take longer to develop and require more effort to perform sensitivity studies. Later on I will describe the use of modeling and simulation in relating requirements analysis to computer sizing in several TRW projects.

Another difficulty involves the translation of requirements into an estimate of the cost of developing software and of the distribution of costs over the various project functions and phases. Countless software projects have overrun their estimates manyfold, to the extent that a prevailing rule of thumb is to multiply any initial software cost estimate by two before using it.

The most significant early work in the software costing area was done by System Development Corporation for the Air Force Electronic Systems Division and the Navy Command Support Activity [7-8]. This work primarily involved the collection and analysis of summary information on a large number of software projects in order to derive multivariate linear prediction formulas for estimating overall software project costs, durations, and computer usage requirements. Although the analyses provided a number of insights, the actual formulas were of limited practical value: the 13-parameter estimator for project size had a mean of 40 man-months and a standard deviation of 62 man-months.

Subsequent work and practice involved primarily determining the number of instructions to be written and using cost-per-instruction factors to estimate software costs [9]. Only rough estimates were generally made on cost breakdown by phase and function, although some papers give indicators that more detailed procedures were being evolved [10]. Thus later on I will describe the structure and use a set of capabilities used to relate software requirements to cost at TRW. These involve detailed phase and function breakdown and guidelines [11] for modifhying cost-per-instruction estimates for each element to reflect its relative complexity and any special circumstances.

WHAT IS REQUIREMENTS ANALYSIS?

The single most important function of requirements analysis is to define the problem. It should provide a well-reasoned substantiation of a nonconflicting and complete set of requirements. The requirements set that results must be specific in describing both end product performance and production methods but nonspecific as to design approach.

This conflicting duality in the use of language, in which performance and construction methods are specifically stated and design approach is unstated, is one of the prime difficulties in creating a good requirements set.

Requirements also serve as a means for describing the common goals of all participants to the procurment. The language of requirements has the semantic qualities needed to best achieve agreement among all participants even if they are in disagreement about particular design features or operational modes.

Requirements analysis continues throughout the life of a procurement. It is the predominant activity in the beginning and continues on as a major activity late into the development cycle.

It is possible to discern three quite different phases. In the beginning as the first step of the procurement an original set of requirements is created based on certain axiomatic, primordial circumstances. This first step is the most important and the most difficult of the three. The second phase follows immediately; it corresponds to the downward allocation of requirements in progressively greater detail to the lower level system components. It is at this stage that detailed software requirements first arise. Finally, when design begins, an iterative upward modification in requirements takes place on conformance with the realities of the design, code, and test processes.

This paper is concerned primarily with the first two phases: the creation of the original requirements set and the downward allocation to the lower level system components. In our judgment the single most important cause of poor management of software projects is the inability to successfully accomplish these first two phases of requirements analysis.

WHAT HAPPENS WHEN REQUIREMENTS ANALYSIS IS DONE POORLY?

There are four kinds of problems that arise when one fails to do adequate requirements analysis: a) top-down design is impossible, b) testing is impossible, c) the user is frozen out, and d) management is not in control. (In effect the problems are a rudimentary kind of "requirements analysis" for doing requirements analysis.) Although these problems are lumped under various headings to simplify discussion, they are actually all variations of one theme – poor management. Good project management of software procurements is impossible without some form of explicit and governing requirements.

If the stated requirements are vague, then many decisions will be made by the designers. In order to deploy the designers it is first necessary to split up the design into a number of parts equal to the number of designers; if this is not done formally it will be done informally by the designers. Each designer as he proceeds with conceptual, preliminary, and final design will make literally hundreds of decisions based on his own narrow perception of his design area. Finally, when these individual parts are made to work together, generally by brutal force-fit techniques, the result is a design which has evolved from bottom-up synthesis. Perhaps with the application of enough money and schedule, and with the tolerant realization of some of the unwritten requirements this bottom-up process can be made to work. It often can be difficult.

Software synthesized from a purely bottom-up approach is invariably deficient in the following respects. There is a high degree of undirected milling around and in consequence lowered productivity. Certain functions are wastefully duplicated (design overlap). Certain necessary functions go unrecognized until late in the development cycle (design underlap).

Another consequence of loosely stated requirements is that test personnel must themselves then do the requirements analysis before testing can proceed. It is far better to do requirements analysis using systems analysts in the beginning rather than using software test specialists late in the program.

Requirements analysis has everything to do with software management. The requirements set that emerges is the principal device which project management uses to achieve direction and control. Without a proper set of requirements, project management is faced with the following real-life situations.

Incipient cost and schedule overruns are unrecognizable because their diagnosis is dependent on a self-judgment by the designers as to their progress – a judgment which is invariably optimistic. If the designer must describe how he is responding to requirements, then a more objective judgment of progress is possible.

Without an existing set of requirements, the user is frozen out. He can only visualize the evolving design based on what the designer says it will contain. He is pretty much at the mercy of the software designer who may not be competent at forecasting operational problems and thus fail to provide the right solutions. The consequences of failing to predict operational problems are generally that late in the procurement cycle, possibly so late as to require a retrofit in the field, a major redesign is required to make the software work. Work-arounds must be invented which compromise operations away from best practice. Unforseen events stress the system and it fails.

All of this can probably be prevented if the user can get his hands on a comprehensive set of requirements and reshape them into something he can live with. He has great incentive to do this since, of all parties to the procurement, he is likely to suffer the most if the design is faulty.

In conclusion a requirements set is the common language by which all parties to the procurement communicate and, hopefully, achieve agreement on the principal technical issues.

A coordinated set of requirements is the best way for procurement agency, the using agencies, and the contractor to set down their mutual expectations. The language of requirements is just detailed enough to give the necessary cost and schedule protection and just vague enough to permit the selection of a better design approach. Without a requirements set, the agreement between the contractor, the procurement agency, and the using agencies is a struggle.

HUMAN FACTORS

Since the absence of requirements analysis is so clearly fatal to success, why is it not always done routinely? Requirements analysis is very hard work. It is an activity which is judgmental, intuitive, heuristic, unrigorous. Rarely are there opportunities for deductive reasoning or mathematical demonstration.

Many engineers characterize it as unsubstantial, mushy guesswork. Given a choice they will rush into design whose principles are firmly based on the physical sciences and mathematical laws rather than struggle with requirements analysis. Because of this viewpoint they are invariably drawn into a bottom-up approach.

Another reason requirements analysis deflects people from doing it is that it is not really a necessary step. Only design and production are truly necessary. Like testing, which is included only because people make mistakes, requirements analysis is included because it is a means of establishing technical goals toward which everyone will work. It provides direction and control. Theoretically if the designers and builders were skillful enough, they would not need this external direction and control.

To apply the preceding argument to a complex software system is absurd and no one really subscribes to it. However, it is true that if one skips requirements and jumps into design, there is usually an early momentary feeling of success based on an unusual degree of apparent progress. The design start-up transient seems to be smoothly done without benefit of requirements. This phenomenon traps people into believing they are on their way to doing the design without paying the price of requirements analysis.

IMPROVING THE PROCESS

Requirements analysis can be improved by the use of tools which help human beings cope with its judgmental, subjective qualities. These qualities cannot be eliminated since they are intrinsic to the process. However, there are two major possibilities for improvement. One is to quantify the process while the other is to test the requirements before committing oneself to the final design.

Another problem with requirements is ensuring that they are current and that their provisions are being incorporated within the design. The answer here is to force compliance.

Let me now expand on these points.

Requirements analysis is primarily concerned with the interaction between five phenomena: cost, schedule, performance, implementation methods, implementation risk. The interaction between these five phenomena form a closed mathematical system in which each parameter is functionally dependent on the others.

$$f(\text{cost, schedule, performance, implementation methods, implementation risk}) = 0.$$

This formulation implies two things: first that we can solve for any one in terms of the other four, and second that all other phenomena can be safely disregarded insofar as they affect requirements analysis.

How can we use this equation to quantify requirements analysis? Ideally we would like to determine the function, f, for each system under study. Except for the simplest kinds of systems, none of which are ever encountered in practice, a direct solution is impractical. Instead we must simplify the modeling of the interactions.

To do this, first of all recognize that the sum of the performance plus implementation methods is by our definition just requirements.

Next consider implementation risk. Ordinarily this is very difficult to quantify in a front-end, conceptual study typical of requirements analysis. It is too dependent on system details. Furthermore of all the phenomena it is the one for which the most disagreement occurs. Generally what is done is simply to assume sufficient schedule and costs to reduce the implementation risk to some acceptable, agreed upon standard and transfer it from a derived variable to an input variable.

Exactly the same approach; i. e., treating as an input variable rather than a derived variable, is also applied to schedule. This seems quite shocking on first consideration because schedule unlike risk is a primary, first-order concern of all systems. However, there is a fairly convincing argument justifying this simplification. Assume that the best schedule has been assigned to a system for development. Imagine variations about this best schedule both shorter and longer. If shorter a greater rate of application of resources will get the job done at approximately the same cost. Similarly for a longer schedule a lesser rate will suffice, again, at approximately the same cost. Only if the deviation from the best schedule is large in either direction will the costs change and (in both cases) increase. To first order for quite large deviations in schedule about the point of best schedule (i. e., minimum cost) the cost is independent of schedule.

By introducing these simplifications we get

$$f(\text{cost, requirements; schedule, implementation risk}) = 0$$

where items following the semi-colon denote input parameters whose influence is secondary. Solving for cost the relationship we are after takes the form

$$\text{cost} = g(\text{requirement, schedule, implementation risk}).$$

This is the simplest form which still retains enough fidelity to be of value in requirements analysis. Simple as it is, it is very difficult to achieve in a form which is broadly applicable to a wide variety of systems. For software systems, however, there is some chance of obtaining such a relationship because there is a high degree of uniformity between software systems even for widely differing applications.

INCLUDING DESIGN IN REQUIREMENTS ANALYSIS

Costs result from the actions required to produce a design. Therefore, if we are to obtain the desired quantification by linking costs with requirements we must do the design. But then we are faced with a dilemma.

Up to this point we have strongly urged that requirements come first before design. To quantify and improve the process of generating requirements we are now suggesting that design come first; hence the dilemma.

We extract ourselves from this dilemma in two ways: first by letting some bottom-up design creep into requirements analysis, and second, by calibrating costs to a limited number of system sizing parameters.

The best approach to high technology software development generally cannot be based purely on a top-down approach. If there exist complicating design features which are intrinsically new and outside the experience of the systems analysts doing the requirements analysis, then there is a need to do some selected bottom-up, early, nondeliverable prototype design if for no other reason that to establish costs.

For all other aspects of the design, namely those aspects that are not critical or are within the prior experience of the system analysts, it is possible to bridge the gap between requirements and cost without actually doing the design.

RELEVANT PARAMETERS

To strengthen the process of requirements generation and also to minimize the extent of concurrent prototype development, it is necessary to find a set of parameters which are common to all information systems and upon which the majority of costs depend. Given that such parameters exist, then the costing of requirements separates into two subprocesses.

First, there is system sizing which is the process of going from requirements to an estimate of these critical system parameters. Second, costs are then estimated from a previous calibration of system size with cost. This second process assumes that calibration data exist from experience and that it has been properly updated and applied to account for both inflationary factors and modified development risks.

For information systems the irreducible minimum set of parameters is three: register speed, storage volume, and number of software instructions to be coded. These are the system parameters that directly or indirectly accrue costs. To eliminate one of these parameters would jumble the costing process. To add more parameters would perhaps improve the fidelity of cost modeling but at the price of more awkward usage.

The relation between number of software instructions and cost has been the subject of several studies. See the article by Schwartz for further elaboration. There is some existing data but not nearly enough to build a really comprehensive model. The biggest problem is that of making people keep accurate records as to instructions delivered, difficulty, and the attributable costs.

The relationships between register speed, storage volume, and costs is largely unexplored.

VALIDATION OF REQUIREMENTS

The capability of testing performance requirements, both during the synthesis stage and before releasing in a final compliance version, is perhaps the most necessary step in substantiating requirements. As a result better methods to substantiate requirements are one of the most sought after capabilities today in the field of software requirements analysis.

The predominant approach is to use simulation wherein the system is modeled with respect to its main operational features. With the aid of the simulation the system is subjected to experimental test over a wide range of performance parameters which have in turn been derived from the various candidate sets of requirements. If there is sufficient fidelity in the simulation, the analyst can directly see the operational consequences of these input requirements and precisely select the best set of requirements to govern the system.

There are basically five approaches to validating requirements. Listing them in the order of increasing fidelity and cost to implement, they are: estimation, off-the-shelf simulation, new simulation, prototype development, and do-it-twice.

Estimation is the cheapest and least reliable method. It is the method of last resort when there is no other alternative.

The next two methods are that of simulation but a distinction is made between existing simulations and new simulations. The distinction is important since the construction of a new simulation tailored exactly to a new system incurs costs and uses schedule. When the simulation must be built, operated, and its results factored into a requirements analysis, the front-end schedule pressures can be enormous. In this situation an off-the-shelf simulation may be the only alternative.

Improved fidelity (as well as greater costs – usually) over a simulation can be achieved by recognizing the critical design problems and building a prototype version for each. Software is well suited to this approach. It represents both a means for arriving at accurate costs, and as a means of accurately estimating performance.

Finally there is the possibility of doing the job twice. By this we mean building the entire product, delivering it and allowing the users to operate it in the real world for an extended period. Then those who built it, those who procured it, and those who operate it get together and produce a set of requirements for a new, improved version which is then produced. For some reason the principal software design problems are much more tractable for human beings the second time around. (This argument does not extend to the third or fourth version; after building it a second time there is little to be gained in producing subsequent versions.) The reason this approach is so little used is obvious: it is far and away the biggest user of cost and schedule.

One last point on methods for synthesis and validation of requirements. If the method is any good at all for bolstering requirements analysis it is then also valuable as a design tool and a test tool. In assessing the cost and schedule consequences of a requirements analysis tool it is important to factor the usefulness of this tool in the other development phases.

PROS AND CONS OF SIMULATION

Simulation is highly flexible and is almost always the best solution for requirements validation. Over a tremendous range of cost, schedule, and fidelity constraints, simulation will do the job. To ensure that simulation is effective it is necessary that its implementation be based on a simulation-oriented language and skilled personnel. Without at least these two ingredients the effectiveness of simulation as a requirements analysis tool will deteriorate.

If the simulation schedule is short-fused or if critical elements of the design are so little understood that no one knows how to simulate them,then some augmented approach is required. For short-schedule situations the analyst should be prepared to use existing simulations for brand new poorly understood designs, prototype development is in order.

Simulation is probably the most widespread technique in use today for synthesis and validation of software requirements. There is a reason for this. The principal content of a software requirement specification should address the following phenomena: function, throughput, input/output, data management system support, and operating system support. Except in rare instances, none of these phenomena is derivable from either physical or mathematical considerations. (Contrast this with hardware systems where the principal mission requirements are invariably derivable from some underlying physical or mathematical arguments.)

To substantiate software requirements the analyst then must turn to something else – usually it is some form of simulation. From the analyst's viewpoint the best alternative is to solve the system consequences in terms of the five listed critical software phenomena. The software requirement analyst feels fairly comfortable about making judgments in these areas. As a result the analyst selects and substantiates requirements by judging their performance consequences.

The most effective mechanism for directly linking requirements with their performance consequences is simulation. It is for this reason that simulation techniques have become so widespread.

Simulation has broad applicability to most problems of requirements analysis. It has universal appeal to system analysts as an effective problem-solving tool. Like all powerful methods in widespread use it can be overdone. There are four circumstances which are good examples of how or when simulation ought not to be applied.

Simulation construction ought to be based on a simulation-oriented language if it is to be really cost and schedule effective.

When building a simulation for requirements analysis there is a natural tendency of the designer to build in too much fidelity. This means extra instructions to be designed, coded, and debugged as well as extra instructions to execute uselessly when operating the simulation. If too much of this is allowed, the simulation is uneconomic to use. Make sure that the simulation designer does not burden the simulation with unwanted fidelity. (There is an important exception to this "too-high fidelity" argument. When using a simulation as a design or test tool, accuracy is the primary goal and generally all the fidelity possible should be built into the simulation. Economic usage is a lesser consideration since there are fewer parameter variations to study.)

The purpose of a simulation is to produce useful output which cannot be otherwise derived. If however the input to the simulation requires as much guesswork as the output (if there were no simulation), then nothing has been gained. We have just transferred the guesswork from the output to the input. For a simulation to be justified the human mind must be better capable of estimating the input to the simulation than the output derived from the simulation.

If a closed form solution is available, don't simulate. A closed form solution gives one insight into a problem that a simulation cannot touch even after executing to exhaustion.

CONCLUSION

It is perfectly possible to produce a solid set of requirements and find that they are ignored. To prevent this there must be a mechanism which forces allocation of requirements downward to the system components and traceability in both directions between all levels of requirements and the system components. This is particularly necessary for requirements which govern software throughput, coding standards, setting and using data, and interfacing with the operating system.

It is perfectly possible to produce initially a bad set of requirements and rigidly enforce unyielding compliance until the product is either doomed or, more commonly, burdened with some silly features. It is important that there be a mechanism for evaluating the benefits of change and undoing any damaging requirements unwittingly applied in the beginning. The provisions of MIL-STD's 483, 490, and 1521 (military standard) which among other things govern change control through the use of a Configuration Control Board (CCB), Interface Control Working Group (ICWG), and three design reviews (SDR, PDR, CDR) plus a series of final reviews (PCA/FCA, FOR) are very workable in practice. They serve as a good example of how to control requirements.

It is possible to produce a solid set of requirements which are adhered to in the beginning but quickly go out of date because of design iterations and thus eventually are ignored. The half-life of a requirements document on a typical 20-month duration software project is at best four months. There must be a simple, quick-reaction updating mechanism to keep the requirements current. During the early stages, a turnaround time of 30 days is tolerable for putting a new requirement on contract and disseminating to the designers. During the later stages of coding and during the test phase this turnaround time should not exceed three days and one day is preferable. This requires that an authorized arm of the CCB be in almost continuous session during these critical phases; further that the documentation update cycle should not exceed 4 to 8 hours. These numbers seem extreme but they are not. With the right kind of commitment and planning they can be achieved.

In summary four techniques for strengthening requirements analysis have been identified.

1. There should be an automated tool for analyzing the completeness, consistency, allocation, and traceability of a requirements set. The technology is simple – it is hardly much more than a sort and list operation with some special formatting. In spite of its simplicity it is not widely used. The reason for this is probably because of the way requirements are written, namely long prose text set off in numbered paragraphs. The format is difficult to convert to machine-readable and processable format. Furthermore the relationships among requirements, particularly those that overlap or jointly apply, are never spelled out. The inputter to any automated requirements analysis tool must work all this out by deduction and inference as he loads the program. None of this is terribly difficult but it is generally not done.

2. Improved methods for designless costing to quantify requirements selection are required. We need better models of the interaction between cost, schedule, risk, and system parameters which govern performance. We need better data to input to these models.

3. In order to cope with short-scheduled, low-cost fire drills, we need off-the-shelf simulations which require no additional design or coding but, through data base control, can be tailored to the problem at hand. Right now one of the biggest deficiencies in the industry is a generalized simulation which can do really effective computer sizing.

4. Simulation building requires a simulation-oriented language to be effective. There are several languages that are quite advanced in their capabilities for handling complex simulations. Improved language features which serve to broaden their application are required.

Note that these four techniques do not automate requirements analysis; they serve only as tools which aid the process. Requirements analysis is fundamentally a process which depends on human intuition for success.

The most important management function is to ensure that requirements analysis is done. Furthermore, it should be done as the first step in the procurement.

The other four management disciplines cited are also important but not nearly so important as the first one. The inability to produce a governing requirements set as the first step is the most common failing of unsuccessful software projects.

REFERENCES

1. Information Processing/Data Automation Implications of Air Force Command-Control Requirements in the 1980s (CCIP-85), U.S. Air Force, SAMSO/XRS-71-1, April 1972.
2. "United drops UNIVAC contract for $56 million data system," Aviation Week, February 9, 1970, p. 31.
3. Kimbleton, S., An Analytic Framework for Computer System Sizing and Tuning, RAND P-5162, January 1974.
4. Denning, P. J. and R. R. Muntz, "Queueing theoretic models," Proceedings 1973 ACM/NBS Workshop on Computer Performance Evaluation.
5. Boehm, B. W., D. W. Kosy and N. R. Neilsen, "Simulation aids for designing integrated information systems: the ECSS language," Astronautics and Aeronautics, November 1972.
6. Katz, E. V. and R. F. Jewett, "Functional simulation of on-line computer systems," Proceedings AIAA Integrated Information Systems Conference, February 1961.
7. Nelson, E. A., Management Handbook for the Estimation of Computer Programming Costs, SDC, TM-3224, Oct. 1966.
8. Weinwurm, G. F., ed., On the Management of Computer Programming, Auerbach, Inc., New York, 1970.
9. Fried, L., "Estimating the cost of system implementation – part II," Data Processing Magazine, April 1969, pp. 24-28.
10. Aron, J. D., "Estimating resources of large programming systems," Software Engineering Techniques, NATO Science Committee, April 1970.

11. Wolverton, R. W., "The cost of developing large-scale software," paper in this volume.

THE COST OF DEVELOPING LARGE SCALE SOFTWARE

Roy W. Wolverton

INTRODUCTION

Estimating the cost of a large-scale computer program has traditionally been a risky undertaking. Now that software has been with us for nearly two decades it is reasonable to hope that we have learned something that would make our predictions less unreliable. At TRW we have been motivated to make a serious effort toward improving our software estimating methods for large-scale software systems, for a set of very compelling reasons.

1. Our customers have shown a growing unwillingness to accept cost and schedule overruns unless the penalties were increasingly borne by the software developer.

2. Partly as a consequence of 1, we have entered into software development contracts where both adherence to predicted costs and on-time delivery were incentivized. That means we made more money if we could predict accurately the cost and the time it would take to do the job.

3. We found that we could improve our estimates only by improving our understanding of exactly what steps and processes were involved in software development, and this understanding enabled us to manage the effort better. The better management, in turn, improved our estimates.

This paper presents the essential results of our efforts to improve our software cost estimating techniques. It should be understood that the specific contracts that are used here were government contracts whose particular provisions shaped those efforts to some degree. Nevertheless, we feel that much of what we learned is of general interest and can be applied or adapted to nearly any software development program of any size.

We can start with a review of some of the ways in which software differs from hardware development, and which have traditionally contributed to the problem of estimating software costs. One of these ways is the problem of managing the people. The nature of programmers is such that interesting work gets done at the expense of dull work, and documentation is dull work. Doing the job in a clever way tends to be a more important consideration than getting it done adequately, on time, and at resonable cost. Programmers tend to be optimistic, not realistic, and their time estimates for task completion reflect this tendency. The software engineer, the mathematician, and the programmer have trouble communicating. Visible signs of programming progress are almost totally lacking.

Another set of difficulties arises from the nature of the product. There are virtually no objective standards or measures by which to evaluate the progress of computer program development. Software characteristics are often in conflict, requiring frequent tradeoffs among such factors as core storage requirement versus tight code, fast execution time, external storage to minimize I/O time, maintainability by the evenutal user, flexiblity or adaptability to new needs, accuracy and reliability, and self-check and fail-safe modes of operation. The applications software developer finds himself in a dynamically evolving and constantly changing environment.

Software planning has problems stemming from the natural desire to get going, which means taking shortcuts. What are the steps that should precede the start of coding, and how does the knowledgeable manager allocate his limited resources? Planning also is made difficult by the problem of translating the customer's functional requirements into software requirements, and later defining the procedures by which you determine that those original customer requirements have been met. It is not always easy to determine when you are through and whether you have delivered what you said you were going to deliver.

The overall approach we have developed for dealing with these problems and producing reasonably reliable cost estimates for large-scale software systems consists of the following basic elements, which will be discussed in detail in the remainder of this paper.

1. Understanding exactly what the software development process consists of over its life cycle.
2. Conduct technical reviews against predetermined acceptance criteria to the end that, upon customer approval, predetermined baselines are established.
3. Control software physical media (tapes, disks, decks) to assure use of a known configuration in testing, demonstration, certification, and delivery.
4. Apply software configuration management controls and procedures to assure that required changes to baselines are implemented, tested, fully documented and understood.
5. Provide a data reporting, repository, and control system to assure that all problems, deficiencies, change proposals, and software configuration data are analyzed, supported, recoverable, and available to all project and user personnel when and where needed.

Technical reviews are required during the software development life cycle. Reviews ensure that the resulting software products meet the requirements established for that level of completeness and understanding. A "baseline" is established at designated points in time during the software development cycle when the requirements (or design) have been defined, documented, reviewed, and approved. From that time forward, that baseline serves as the reference point for evaluating and managing any changes in scope, price, or schedule.

In the specific cases to be discussed, certain of these principles were incorporated in government software procurement policies applied to the contract, but no manager of a large software development should ignore them whether they are required by his customer or not. For example, without software configuration management – configuration identification, configuration control, configuration status accounting, and verification – the software development manager will spend much of his time solving problems that need not have arisen. Software is controlled through control of documentation within a structured software development process.

There are several ways of analyzing the software development process, but the one we have chosen leads to the definition of seven phases, or steps, each ending in a discrete event or document. The steps are basically sequential, but in practice there are iterations between adjacent steps and even between any of the steps. The seven steps are as follows.

Step 1 – Performance and Design Requirements: This document establishes the requirements for performance, design, test and qualification of the software at the system level.

Step 2 – Implementation Concept and Test Plan: This document provides, at an early date, the preliminary design concepts that meet the requirements, and identifies the preferred approaches, design tradeoffs, and alternatives, and leaves no high-risk technology area unresolved.

Step 3 – Interface and Data Requirements Specification: This document defines the interfaces between subsystems and major elements within subsystems, including presentation of table and file structure, data origin, destination and update characteristics.

Step 4 – Detailed Design Specification: This document provides, in precise detail, the complete design and acceptance specifications for the software at the routine level, which includes detailed flow charts, equations, and logic. It is the source material from which the program is coded.

Step 5 – Coding and Debugging: Upon design review and approval of the Step 4 documentation package, which may be staggered in time and organized into volumes dealing with a single computer program module, the coding of the software can begin. This step is devoted to coding and debugging (and amending documentation), using debugging aids and desk check of the first compilations. The phase terminates for a given module when it has passed the development-level verification tests imposed by the designer, and he turns the module over for assembly onto the master tape for the beginning of independent system validation testing.

Step 6 – System Validation Testing: As the software modules are released by the design group for assembly onto the master tape, the buildup of the software package into successively more complex interfaces and capabilities can commence. When two or more modules are assembled, the first stages of "system testing" can get underway according to the test plan started at Step 2 and upgraded in level of detail at Step 4 to include test procedures and quantitative acceptance criteria. The phase terminates when all modules have been successfully tested against the predetermined acceptance criteria at the system level.

Step 7 – Certification and Acceptance Demonstration: This final step is devoted to formal acceptance of the software system by subjecting it to previously defined acceptance and test specification procedures, which are executed in as near an operational environment and host computer configuration as possible. The phase terminates with successful "operational demonstration," witnessed by the customer and his quality assurance team. The software packages are then ready for installation, integration, and checkout in the operational environment.

The final step in the software development life cycle is the forerunner of the operations and maintenance phase, strictly speaking, Step 8. This phase is concerned with installation, integration, and checkout in the full operational configuration. The software contractor assists in any way required to integrate the software products of the development, or acquisition, phase into an operational software package that meets the original (and updated) performance and design requirements, the product of Step 1 and subsequent updates. The activities of this phase will also include training, rehearsal support, software problem reporting, fault isolation and correction, formal problem closure and documentation update, and finally, first mission operations support. Because this is not part of the software development effort, we cost it differently — usually as a level of effort.

PRICING PITFALLS

Pricing is the complete process by which we arrive at a price that we quote to the customer. Cost estimating is a major part of that process, although it frequently has to be done several times before a final price is arrived at. The general principles involved in pricing large R & D efforts of any kind have been defined by Beveridge [1], and apply to large software developments as well. Beveridge's discussion centers around the preparation of a proposal in response to a government Request for Proposal (RFP), but his common-sense principles are applicable to any complex pricing exercise where many individuals are involved.

There is a general tendency on the part of designers to goldplate their individual parts of any system, but in the sense of software the tendency is both stronger and more difficult to control than in the case of hardware. A major task of management is to make certain that the design coding proposed (and priced) does meet the customer's need and that each individual component design can be traced to a specific need, while at the same time it does not provide more (more speed, more accuracy, etc.) than the customer needs or wants. Anything being offered a customer beyond what he has asked for should be clearly identified (and priced) as an option. That is what is meant by the "fixed-price attitude:" What is the absolute minimum I can do to satisfy the needs stated in the RFP?

SOFTWARE COST ESTIMATING METHODS

The software industry is young, growing, and marked for rapid change in technology and application. It is not surprising, then, that the ability to estimate costs is still relatively underdeveloped. Even though many organizations are trying to devise more scientific and objective means for estimating costs of large software systems, the present state of the art is largely judgmental. We will, however, discuss certain important exceptions shortly. A review of other firms and agencies confirm that we are facing a problem common to all [2]-[5].

Estimating the cost of producing computer software relies heavily on the judgment of experienced performers. The software analyst, or estimator, normally breaks the total job into elements that are estimated separately and then summarized into an estimate for the total job. The estimating analysis and synthesis may appear as a mental process or may involve an explicit algorithm [6].

In either case, an empirical data base is used as an objective reference, and the estimator uses his judgment to account for differences. Pieces of information used in the comparisons and adjustments for differences include: a) analysis of initial requirements; b) allocation of requirements to software modules; c) estimates of number of object instructions per modles; d) complexity and technological risk; e) user environment and characteristics of the customer; f) computer of choice and interchangeability among other user sites; g) higher order language of choice or criteria for use of assembly language; h) type of software to be developed; i) whether software is to be delivered to an operational user; j) technical experience for that type of job; k) capabilities of the member of the technical staff who probably will do the work; l) type of code and its incentive structure; m) length of development time; n) single-model multiple-release versus multiple-model single-release development concept; o) performance record of other large-scale systems (AWAC, SAGE, etc.) and the number of instructions and development man-months; and p) management factors to do with productivity rates, error rates, work environment, availability of computer time, and many other variables.

Most estimators use a logical sequence in establishing their estimates. The logic uses exchange coefficients between some measurable parameter and its cost and adjustment factors derived from experience. One of the pitfalls is that estimating ratios should be directly traceable to recorded cost facts (not hearsay), and even the factual data can contain varying and unstated allowances for risk (we may have assumed a 40-h workweek, our records show we charged that rate, but our records do not show that most personnel worked 45-50 h/week or more). Our long-term objective at TRW has been to create a systematic software development estimation system that can significantly reduce statistical variances between estimated costs and actual costs, and is not only accurate in that sense but also simple, fast, and convenient. We will briefly look at estimation methods in general, and two in particular that have been developed and reduced to practice at TRW.

General Logic Followed in Estimating

Traditional cost estimating procedures start with fixing the size of each activity, its start date, and duration. When necessary, adjustments are made to account for the caliber of performer personnel to be assigned, risk, complexity, uncertainties in requirements, and so on. Finally, the amount and type of manpower (man-months per month) and computing resources (hours per month) are converted to dollar costs by applying bid rates. Other direct changes (documentation costs, travel, etc.) are added, and summaries are made through the pricing system. Traditional methods can be classified as one or more of the techniques described below.

1. Top-down Estimating: The estimator relies on the total cost or the cost of large portions of previous projects that have been completed to estimate the cost of all or large portions of the project to be estimated. History coupled with informed opinion (or intuition) is used to allocate costs between packages. Among its many pitfalls is the substantial risk of overlooking special or difficult technical problems that may be buried in the project tasks, and the lack of details needed for cost justification.

2. Similarities and Differences Estimating: The estimator breaks down the jobs to be accomplished to a level of detail where the similarities to and differences from previous projects are most evident. Work units that cannot be compared are estimated separately by some other method.

3. Ratio Estimation: The estimator relies on sensitivity coefficients or exchange ratios that are invariant (within limits) to the details of design. The software analyst estimates the size of a module by its number of object instructions, classifies it by type, and evaluates its relative complexity. An appropriate cost matrix is constructed from a cost data base in terms of cost per instruction, for that type of software, at that relative complexity level. Other ratios, empirically derived, can be used in the total estimation process, for instance, computer usage rate based on central processing unit (CPU) time per instruction, peripheral usage to CPU usage, engineers per secretary, and so forth. The method is simple, fast, convenient, and useful in the proposal environment and beyond. It suffers, as do all methods, from the need for a valid cost data base for many estimating situations (business versus scientific, real-time versus nonreal-time, operational versus nonoperational).

4. Standards Estimating: The estimator relies on standards of performance that have been systematically developed. These standards then become stable reference points from which new tasks can be calibrated. Many mature industries, such as manufacturing and construction, use this method routinely. The method is accurate only when the same operations have been performed repeatedly and good records are available. The pitfall is that custom software development is not "performed repeatedly."

5. Bottom-up Estimating: This is the technique most commonly used in estimating government research and development contracts. The total job is broken down into relatively small work packages and work units. The work breakdown is continued until it is reasonably clear what steps and talents are involved in doing each task. Each task is then estimated and the costs are pyramided to form the total project cost. An advantage of this technique is that the job of estimating can be distributed to the people who will do the work. A difficulty is the lack of immediate perspective of the most important parameter of all: the total cost of the project. In doing detailed estimates, the estimator is not sensitive to the reasonableness of the total cost of the software package. Therefore, top-down estimation is used as a check on the bottom-up method.

The estimation process is nearly always a combination of two or more of the basic classifications given above. We will briefly discuss two methods that have been used in estimating the cost of developing large-scale software at TRW: a method we used in June 1969 which we will call "smoothing and extrapolation," and the current method we used beginning in October 1970, which we will call "a software estimation algorithm."

A Systems Approach to Software Cost Estimation

To be as free as possible to deal with the cost estimating method, we will use hypothetical or normalized numbers where numbers are necessary. Assume the software development and test life cycle consists of the seven steps previously defined except that the starting point at contract go-ahead is immediately on completion of Step 2. We need to understand this assumption clearly, since it establishes the remaining milestone events which are included in the cost which was negotiated with the customer. In other words, the proposal was at a level of detail such that it was, by itself, the implementation concept and test plan, Step 2. The RFP package, together with the bidder's briefing, was very detailed, technically complete, and was, by itself, the performance and design requirements, Step 1.

Our reference project for the most recent past successful software project was identified, and its case history was laid out in terms of the actual events, costs start dates, and durations. The normalized period of performance is shown in Figure 1. We will call this case history A. The cost distribution by development activity, that is, the actions that characterize the intervals between discrete milestone events, is shown in Figure 2. Using case history A we can identify similarities and differences with respect to our cost estimating for our new project. The basic cost method, smoothing and extrapolation, is a combination of earlier methods plus some new ideas for the new project. We will call the new project case history B.

A major development cycle difference was that case A has a baseline design specification deliverable under contract, which accounted for about 12 percent of the total cost as shown by "analysis," and also had the implementation concept and test plan deliverable under contract, which accounted for another 18 percent as shown by "design" (see Figure 2). Even though the software development cycle was different, we had exact data on the manpower assigned to the balance of the milestone events, which are similar. We now are in a position to extrapolate from case A to case B. Furthermore, since case A has been produced on time and under cost, we were in a strong position for proving demonstrated cost performance on a previous project.

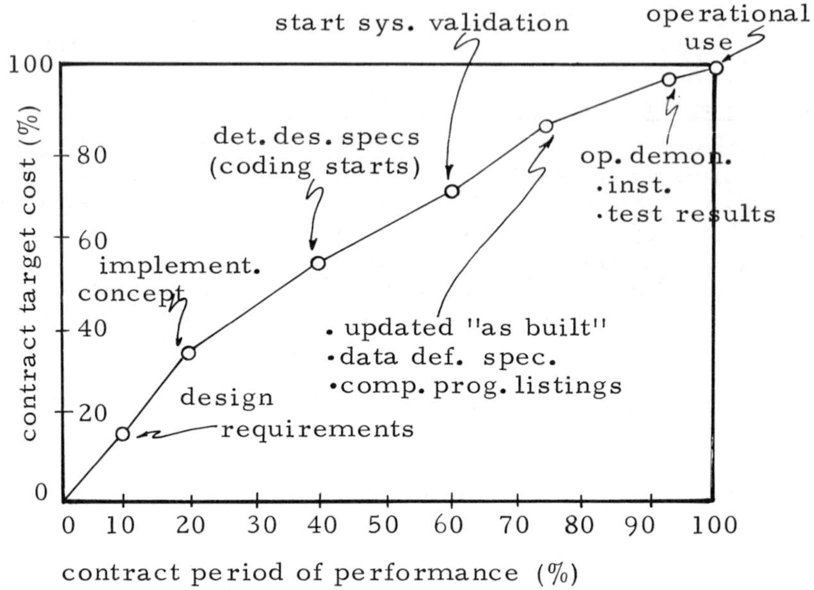

Figure 1. Typical Software Development Cost Experience (case history A)

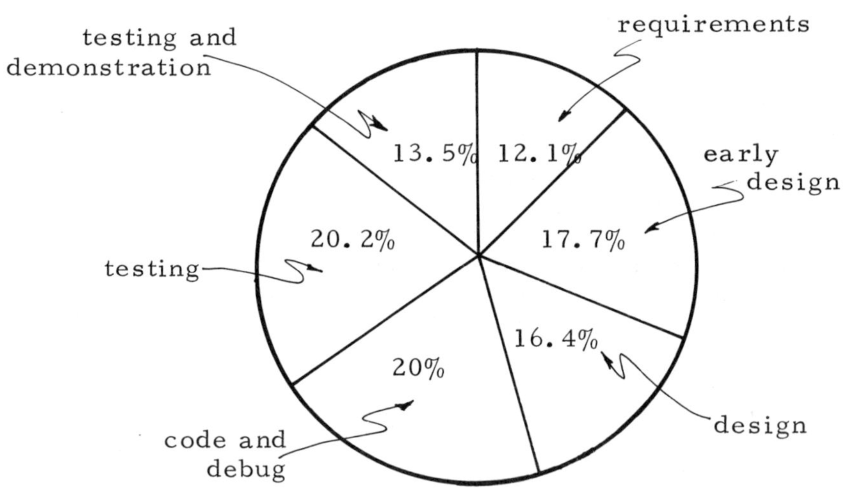

Figure 2. Cost Distribution by Activity during Full Period of Performance (case history A). All Activities Include Documentation and Travel Costs

A major functional difference was that case B represented a unified communication, command, and control software system, whereas case A did not have the command function. Immediately, greater attention was given to the analysis and design of that new technology area and its interfaces. Even here, important similarities were identified in the history file because in case A the "similar" command function was the responsibility of another associate contractor. We concentrated on improving the information transfer by having full control of the interface, and by approaching the solution from an entirely new direction. We decided the technical risk was somewhat higher for case B because the command algorithm design, coding, and testing were innovative. We developed the overall system block diagram, and allocated statement of work tasks to software functions. We were in a position for a first rough cut target cost.

The whole idea in this case was a) to price the total software system from the top down using the experience of the system concept group, b) to price each work package from the bottom up using the experience of each of the five work package managers, and c) to conduct a mock negotiation between the system concept group and each work package group taken one at a time. Differences were derived, costs were traced back to source authority requirements in the customer's statement of work, and adjustments made between the cost, probable risk, and scope of work.

In both methods the basic unit of estimation was the "man-month" for a given task or element. The distribution of the work (man-months per month) was driven by two critical variables: initial operational capability (IOC) and full operational capability (FOC). Software configurations were required by the RFP.

The distribution, or manpower spread over the proposed period of performance, was initially determined by the system concept group using one new idea. That idea was first to assume that the total development manpower resource was 1000 man-months, and then to determine the shape of the manpower distribution over time that maximized the fee incentive with least risk, such that the area under the curve remained constant (namely, 1000 man-months). This curve would serve to generate the master schedule for IOC and FOC events. The amplitude of the curve would be the primary focus in the separate negotiations with the five work package managers.

The amplitude represented the number of man-months per month for any given time slice. The sum of the manpower estimates of each of the five work packages at any time point determined that month's manpower requirements, and the sum of those over all time determined the total IOC/FOC manpower requirements, hence total cost. Of the five initial estimates, four were judged too high in the internal first cut negotiations, and one was judged too low.

To be effective, the basic incentive structure must be simple, even though it is necessary in the contract to address the major contingencies and allowable options. If the basic incentive structure is not simple it will not readily be grasped by the many people at all levels of the contractor's plant whose work affects the chance of success. If they do not understand it, they will not do anything differently because of the incentive structure. If they do not, the incentive contract will have failed to achieve its fundamental purpose: the people who work on all aspects of the entire undertaking must be conscious of the incentive and must do their work with more care and quality because of it.

The entire incentive approach presumes that the contractor will take specific internal implementing action. It should include some tangible internal management actions that place an additional incentive on the work quality. A clear explanation of the essential features of the incentive structure should be given to all who work in any manner on the software, keyed to the contribution each one can make to affect the fee that can be realized by his company.

	Number of Object Instructions	Man-Months	Rate
	(I)	(M)	(I/M)
Case History A	102 400	570	180
Case History B			
IOC	160 000[a]	945	170
FOC	215 000[a]	630[b]	340

[a] IOC activities included design and production of a prototype software package of an additional 20,000-object instructions. A slightly modified version was made during FOC.

[b] Learning curve phenomenon has been verified by empirical data and controlled tests in other industries [8], but not systematically for the software industry.

The normalized contract cost as a function of the normalized period of performance is shown in Figure 3 for case history B. The normalized cost distribution by development activity over the software life cycle for both IOC and FOC is shown in Figure 4. In estimating the cost of large software systems, we treat "operations and maintenance" (O&M) as a level of effort commencing immediately after selloff of the system in its operational environment. In the multimodel software development, O&M of the first model overlaps the purely development activities of the second model. To avoid any misinterpretation of the development costs, the O&M amounted to 15 percent of the total contract value. Comparison of case history A and B in size and cost (man-months), excluding O&M is given on the previous page.

A Software Cost Estimation Algorithm

TRW has developed a cost estimation algorithm based on the assumption that costs vary proportionally with the number of instructions. For each identified routine, the procedure combines an estimate of the number of object instructions, category, relative degree of difficulty, and historic data is dollars per instruction from the cost data base to give a trial estimate of the total cost. The design group estimates the first three software parameters. The system concept group provides the appropriate cost data base used by all designers, as well as the allocation of resources to each phase of the software development cycle, the schedule for each milestone event, and the labor mix. The procedure then spreads the total cost over the period of performance according to these input parameters, gives the man-months per month by labor category, the cost associated with each development activity, and the computer usage by month for checkout and test activities. The output may be considered a "trial estimate" in the sense that the proposal team must be satisfied with the resulting estimate when tested against any conventional method of cost estimating.

The first step in the method is to categorize the software routines that are being considered in the preliminary design. The software categories have been selected based on experience, and are those functionally different kinds of software entities for which a significant cost per instruction (CPI) is expected. Categories that have stood the test of usage in several proposal and preliminary design activities are: a) control routine, which controls execution flow and is nontime-critical, b) input/output routine, which transfers data into or out of the computer, c) pre- or postalgorithm processor, which manipulates data for subsequent processing or output, d) algorithm

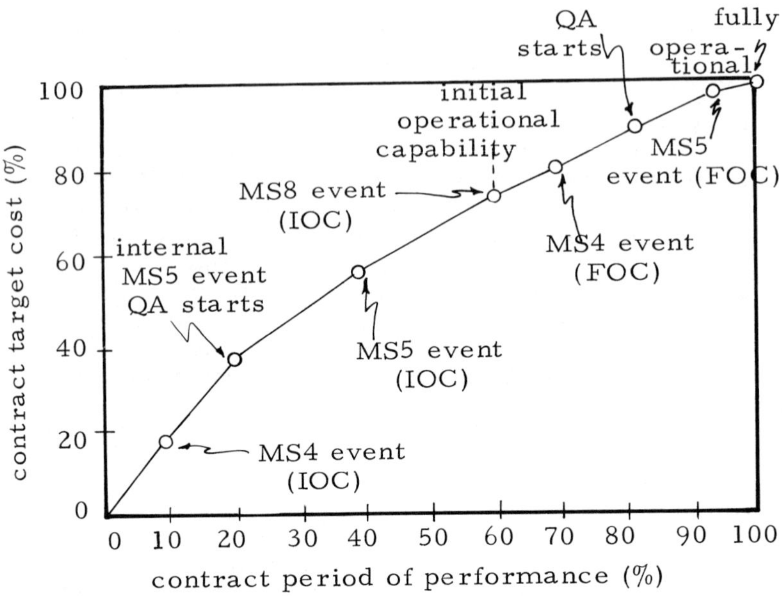

Figure 3. Typical Software Development Cost Experience (case history B - multimodel development)

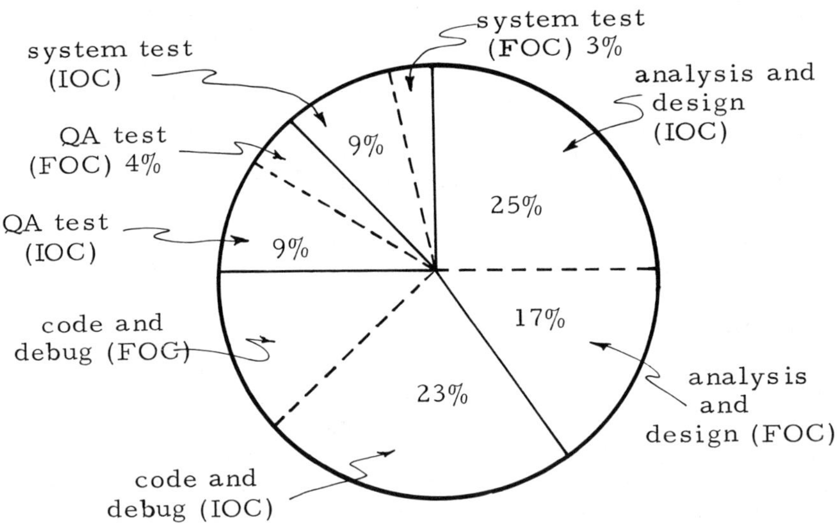

Figure 4. Cost Distribution by Activity During full Period of Performance (case history B - multimodel development). All Activities Include Documentation and Travel Costs. Distribution excludes O&M costs.

which performs logical or mathematical operations, e) data management routine, which manages data transfer within the computer, and f) time-critical processor, which is a highly optimized machine dependent code.

The next step is size and complexity estimates by routine, or subprogram, by the designer. To balance cost and risk, the designer may decide to use software elements that are available to him from a software library and need only some degree of modification or adaptation. At the other extreme, a new technique may be required and be estimated as a high technological risk. To account for the degree of difficulty of a given kind of routine, the designer estimates a risk or complexity factor. This is the most crucial step in the estimating process, for it establishes the cost of the routine with all direct and indirect charges amortized against it. The other steps basically determine how the total cost will be spread over the development cycle.

Two consultants have different views of how software parameters should be estimated, in general. Brandon says a single individual should establish a complexity rating scale and make a "standard estimate" for each job based on: a) complexity rating of each job; b) machine used; c) language used; and d) estimated number of instructions. Brandon uses equations fitted to historical data to get standards, and he measures performance against the standard [9].

Lecht believes the estimator should interview the member of the technical staff who will do the job, and negotiate personal agreement on effort. Historical cost data reinforce the estimator's judgment where similar jobs can be found. The estimate is based on: a) similarity with previous modules; b) person doing the job; c) machine used; d) languages used; and e) estimated number of instructions. Lecht does not believe meaningful performance standards can be set for software [10].

The simplest technique for narrowing down the many subjective choices early in the estimation process is to ask, is the routine new or old, and is it easy, medium, or hard. A complexity rating coefficient can be applied continuously from 1 to 20 as a multiplier, if preferred. The important consideration is allowing sufficient degree of freedom to accommodate a learning experience and individual differences in performance in the effort to obtain a realistic cost. For our present purposes of early preliminary design, we will allow the designer four choices to account for six levels of difficulty for each routine. They are:

	Easy	Medium	Hard
Old	OE	OM	OH
New	NE	NM	NH

The only parameter that changes as a function of degree of difficulty (OE through NH) is cost per instruction. Override control is available to the designer. Sample data sets will be given in the section of Software Cost Data Base.

The next step is to identify the various development and test phases for producing the software from the conceptual stage to delivery of the operational software to the ultimate user. For our present purposes, the seven steps given in the section entitled The Software Development Cycle will be adopted, but they could be any other steps tailored to the needs of the particular application. For each phase an estimate is required for the fraction of the total amount to be allocated to it. In the case of manpower allocation for distribution of 1000 man-months over the development cycle, it was functionally allocated as 424 man-months to design and analysis, 210 man-months to code and debug, and 366 man-months to check out and test. This distribution of 42-21-37 percent at this level of detail has been borne out in practice by several other researchers, as will be demonstrated shortly.

The fourth step is to define the activities in each development phase by means of an activity array and associated cost matrix. The activities as a function of development phase is a 25 x 7 matrix: that is 25 activities are identified for each of 7 phases. In turn subsets of the activities may be summed to "super activity" levels, and the makeup may vary from phase to phase.

The final step in setting up the initial conditions for the cost estimation algorithm is to provide schedule data based on the customer's statement of work, or other management considerations. Schedule data are input as man-months from go-ahead for each of the milestone periods.

Burden rates are input for projected overhead rates, general and administrative, and so forth. Labor mix is designated and unburdened bid rates for the labor grades desired for the phase are defined. Selective cost cuts are under management control by the override capability. The other direct charges are input, which for software is typically travel as a percentage of direct labor costs, such costs as 3 percent and documentation at 10 percent.

Computer usage data for a machine in the CDC 6500 class with time-shared central processor unit based on sampled data from a programming department by month have been given in [11].

Number of MTS	Total Number of Processor Units Used	Number of Processor Hours per Man-Month	Peripheral Hours per Man-Month
36	55.6	2.20	7.6
35	31.0	1.27	4.4
33	30.0	1.30	4.5
33	46.5	2.02	7.0

Following for slightly less power in a 370/155 computer, for instance, a figure of 3 h/month/programmer man-month would be reasonable. At an average productivity of 1 object instruction/h, this is equivalent to 156 instructions/man-month, or 1.2 min/instruction. The data in the third column are based on 1.42 processor units corresponding to 1 h of computing time.

The summary output from the cost estimation algorithm, SPREAD, includes: a) cost per routine based on other historic burden rates or proposed burden rates; b) average cost per instruction, number of instructions, and category; c) total number of development computer hours per routine; d) simple graphic display of schedule and events; e) cost breakdown by development phase per routine in total dollars and percent; f) cost breakdown by activity, by routine, and summed over all routines in the software, such as management, review, documentation, specifications, design, coding, and testing; and finally, g) manloading and cost summary by management showing for each month the labor breakdown for senior staff, staff, technical, clerical; also computer hours by month, other direct charges, cost by month, and cumulative cost.

The outputs from the cost estimation algorithm are considered a "trial set" for the cost estimation group. The trial set is used in combination with all other sources of data to test that cost position against the project objectives. The approved trial set, which contains the best judgmental and quantitative measures of cost per software element and per activity, becomes the input to the official pricing computer run. Necessary translation of the data set to exactly match the customer's work breakdown structure (WBS) or other appropriate cost elements is made for the final pricing run. The official cost figures are produced by cost guidelines, approved rates, and procedures that have been established by the in-house pricing group and approved by the government auditor. The results of the software cost estimation algorithm are retained as cost backup data and for possible use in later cost justification. The official cost figures from the pricing computer run show man-loading and costs collected and aggregated against the customer's WBS.

The cost estimation approach has the following advantages.

a) The amount of data required to obtain a cost estimate is minimal.

b) The software designer immediately sees the cost consequences of his preliminary design.

c) To the extent that the routine is directly traceable to a requirement, the requirement is directly traceable to a total cost.

d) Comparisons of alternate schedules on resource allocation can be made rapidly.

e) A cost justification is produced that can stand the test of government audit.

SOFTWARE COST DATA BASE

Sensitivity coefficients or exchange ratios used by the cost estimation algorithm reside in the data base. The objective in cost estimating is to realize greater accuracy and precision while anticipating risk and its impact on profit. The greater the risk, for a given confidence level, the greater the allowance on the part of the estimator for this uncertainty. The more uncertain the estimate, the less competitive is the cost proposal. Further, an estimate of cost backed by relevant cost experience facts gives confidence to negotiator, management, and the customer. Cost justification is demanded by the customer, and is usually provided in the form of lower level backup data.

Valid data based on proven experience are required for any cost estimation process. Producing good operational software is dependent on the many activities of good people properly directed and motivated. The process is difficult to measure and apply widely beyond the technology center for which the performance measures were derived. There is no universal model. Applying "average productivity rates" without knowledge of the development steps that were used in deriving the rates is wrong.

Averages based on large samples are useful in comparison of a local variable against a global variable, if the estimator is reasonably certain he is comparing truly equivalent measures. Metzelaar has studied the problem of industry-wide productivity rates in terms of program size and complexity [12].

The activities that productively occupy the analyst's time along with the plant overhead and other direct charges, largely determine the price to the customer. It is in the company's best interest to agree on measurable activities that should be available in the software cost data base for cost justification and estimation of new work. The activities that have been identified in this regard are given below [2].

1. Learning and Orientation (L),
2. Analysis and Design (A),
3. Coding (C),
4. Test and Checkout (T),
5. Verify/Quality (V),
6. System Integration and Test (I), and
7. Documentation.

In late 1971, TRW compiles in-house data on a wide variety of software development characteristics, which in turn were independently analyzed by Lulejian and Associates under contract to the U.S. Air Force [13], [14]. The variables of particular interest for our present purposes were analyzed by Lulejian and Associates for a package of 88 routines developed by TRW. A brief interpretation of four of the analyses that bear on the cost of developing software is presented next.

Consider Figure 5. This is a plot of cost versus number of instructions for the 88 routines. Two conclusions can be drawn, either by direct observation or by regression analysis.

a) There is a general trend in the data – larger routines cost more.

b) A linear fit to the data is not very good.

If one attempts to predict costs from routine size alone, one can expect errors of about 50 percent in the predicted cost. The prediction is better than nothing, but not much better. Figure 6 shows the same data plotted another way – cost per 1000 instructions versus number of instructions. If the cost of the routine can be estimated by a fixed cost per 1000 instructions,

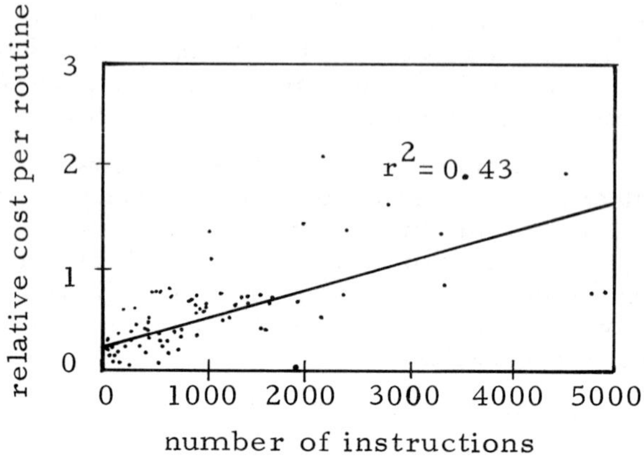

Figure 5. Relative Cost per Routine versus Number of Instructions

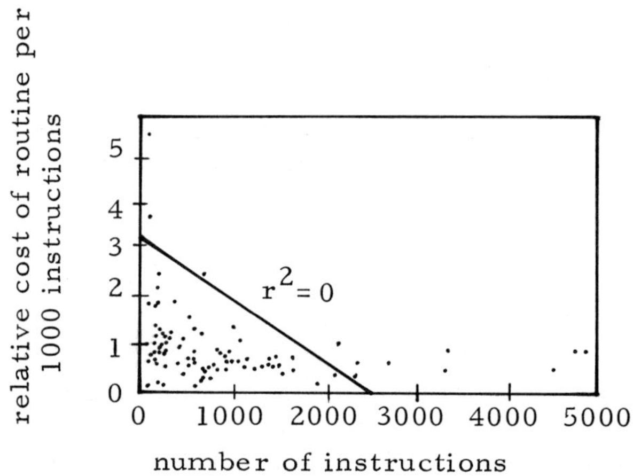

Figure 6. Routine Unit Cost versus Number of Instructions

one would expect this data to show constant cost. It appears to be constant, with a large error, especially for small routines. Again one concludes that cost can be predicted from number of instructions provided that one is willing to accept fairly large errors.

The conclusion is that there are no simple universal rules for costing software accurately. It is necessary to understand the nature of the individual program and the individual routines within the program.

RESOURCE ALLOCATION

Various researchers have separately discovered by empirical methods a rule of thumb, namely, that analysis and design account for 40 percent, coding and debugging account for 20 percent of the total resource (cost) spent for software development, the 40-20-40 rule. If the cost of "modeling" of physical systems is to be borne by the software development group, as contrasted to modeling analysis from raw data by technology centers within the company (such as thermal, attitude control and pointing, propulsion, electrical power, and so forth) an extra 30 percent typically would be required in addition to the software development by itself. In other words, the deriving of equations of motion or physical behavior of other physical systems from raw data is not included in the software development resource allocation. Similarly, the cost of computing time is not covered in the resource allocation. Experience has consistently shown that computer costs add an additional 20 to 25 percent of the total cost of the project; that is, a $5 million/year software development contract will cost the government in additional $1 million for GFE computing time to the developer. Boehm discusses his views on resource allocation in [15]; his findings are presented in Table II.

TABLE II

COMPUTER PROGRAM DEVELOPMENT BREAKDOWN

	Analysis & Design	Coding & Auditing	Checkout & Test
SAGE	39%	14%	47%
NTDS	30%	20%	50%
Gemini	36%	17%	47%
Saturn V	32%	24%	44%

TOPICS FOR FURTHER WORK

The topics that were originally identified for discussion will be summarized, together with key issues that influence cost estimating of large software systems and that need further work and study.

1. What is the typical code production rate per programmer man-month? A working standard may be inferred from the data given of 1 object instruation/man-hour, which is equivalent to 156 instructions/man-month, or 1870 instructions/man-year, or 6.4 man-months/1000 object instructions for nontime-critical software.

If a burdened man-month varies between \$4300 and \$4900 in 1972 dollars for a typical programming department's labor mix, on the average this working standard translates to \$27.50-\$31.50 as the cost per instruction. Both case history A and B correlate strongly with these standards. They are characterized as large software jobs whose development is firmly structured and controlled. But what about the R&D work, not well-structured and controlled, and which therefore does not lend itself to estimation by extrapolation from a historical cost data base?

The underlying question is whether we have identified all the right parameters to capture and quanitfy in our cost data base. Do we understand the causal relationships, and can they be isolated from their effects or symptoms?

2. How does code production rate vary with problem complexity? With more sophisticated physical systems being brought under software command and control, a corresponding increase in technological riskand complexity causes an increase in a responsible cost estimate. Reliable estimates place this increase in cost right now from 3 to 5.5 times the average of our historical cost data base. The leading causes of these predicted increases need serious attention and study, and effective management methods to detect and deal with them. For example, we have already observed in two cases that the cost of producing real-time (or time-critical) software is three times more costly than nonreal-time software. Should the development dollar be spent on highly optimized machine-dependent code by the applications programmer or on more efficient compilers and assemblers?

Cost tradeoffs are needed between the crucial parameters that define the problem complexity and the cost benefits. A marginal utility theory is needed for the economics of software development. Parameters that are crucial in defining problem complexity include degree and time phasing of simulation, extent of prototype code, parallel development of different formulations of key algorithms, new computer hardware/software, assembly language coding, multisite operations and interchangeability, growth requirements, critical timing and throughput, hardware/software interfaces, fault-tolerant computing, core occupancy constraints, reliability, and safety [16]-[18].

3. How does this rate vary as a function of computer availability? accessiblity? configuration? The President's Blue Ribbon Defense Panel reported in June 1970 in its staff report on automatic data processing that because of the government's method of selection and procurement of computer systems, multiple computers in the same geographical area can result in costs that are as much as five time larger than would be necessary if a few large computers were used in a shared operating mode. The underlying problem here is that of data privacy and protection (security) for enabling the use of remote terminals by government agencies for both classified and unclassified work. An independent evaluation by E. C. Nelson of TRW is that a dedicated computer installation costs three to five times as much to operate as if it were a time-shared installation with proper remote terminals. If private industry can enjoy these benefits of cost effectiveness by use of remote terminals (three to five times less expensive), it would seem that some, if not a large part, of government installations could enjoy the same benefits if the problems of data privacy and protection were solved to everybody's satisfaction.

A management goal is to do the difficult parts of the software twice – once to produce prototype code early in the development cycle using perhaps 8-20 percent of the resources and an improved version with the technological task eliminated for the operational version. One pitfall is that the risk is highest in procurements where a new computer and its operating system are being developed concurrently with advanced applications software, so just when computer time is needed the most, it is available the least. More planning to reduce the computer selection and procurement time is needed.

Furthermore, in some operational systems, the computer configurations available to the user is significantly different from the computer configuration available to the computer program associate contractor. Such a working environment requires an integrating contractor to maintain system-level configuration control. This may add 10 percent to the total cost and is viewed as an insurance policy. To eliminate such occurrences, standards for computer configuration control is needed by the associate contractor and, equally importantly, by the user.

4. What are the pieces of information required to make a realistic prediction of software development cost? We have identified the activities that occupy the analyst's time. However, it is one thing to identify significant activities for allocation of resources, and it is another thing to hold the right set of individuals accountable for the expenditure of those resources for those things over the life cycle of the software development, which spans 12-24 months or longer. The purpose of a cost-estimating system is to reduce the variance between estimates of what a software development should cost and what it actually does cost. The cost history data file is a key element in an improved cost estimating system. Further work is needed in maintaining cost control over the actual performance period considering the following.

a) Recording and displaying of both individual and aggregate programmer activities, such as previously defined by L, A, C, T, V, I, and D, by easy-to-use automated project control and prediction tools.

b) Fast computation of project cost-and time-to-complete predictions by current and look-ahead activity statistics, including uncompensated overtime, as is now feasible through automated cost control tools.

c) Provision for storing, retrieving, and tracing of project statement of work deliverables to their cost estimate and cost estimate to actual cost, by activity, over the useful life of the software through cost control tools.

5. How does code production rate vary as a function of programmer quality? quality requirements on the final product? The point to be made here is that we have seen convincing evidence of the validity of the 40-20-40 rule. For a $5 million project, $2 million will be spent on checkout and test to the extent the rule applies. A management objective is to check out every logic path in the software to deliver an error-free program. This is a high-quality final product insofar as being error-free is a measure of quality. Achieving this objective may add significantly to the development cost but reduce even more significantly the operations and maintenance cost. With improved test tools, considerable improvement in efficiency of more branches checked per computer hour becomes realizable. From the analysis given for one software system, the quality of the programmer in years experience and supervisor's rating seemed to make

no difference in the cost in terms of the goodness of fit. As R. J. Hatter says, some of the signs exhibit counter-intuitive behavior.

Technical performance standards and criteria are needed in the software development process. A wrong standard is better than no standard because at least it gives a sense of direction to the effort. A technical performance measurement system is needed for applying to the software development process, and which is understood and applied to all management and performer levels over the life cycle. Since software development is more process oriented than product oriented, such standards become measures of group productivity if not individual productivity. In some organizations it may be interpreted to be against company policy to measure and report on a productivity index of an individual member of the professional staff, such as code production rate, or error rates (as measured, for instance, by software problem reports). Producing quality custom software is a profit-motivated business and more businesslike procedures are being applied as the product lines mature [19].

6. <u>How does cost vary with completeness of problem formulation?</u> Using the 40-20-40 rule again, but this time dealing with the "analysis and design" 40 percent, we have evidence that analysis and design takes the lion's share of the software development dollar. A management goal that has proven effective in the past is to produce superior documentation which is reviewed with a knowledgeable technical staff in the customer's complex. Thorough and continuous involvement of the customer in the development process has been a reality of several large software developments. Nothing takes the place of competence and communication when it comes to understanding the customer's or sponsor's requirements. Translating total system requirements which may not be well understood even by the customer, to the software system requirements is a crucial first step. In the requirements definition and preliminary design phase, there is typically a lack of data but lots of leverage (influence on the ultimate design outcome), in contrast to the operational phase where there are lots of data but little, if any, leverage. This is a significant area for cost- and performance-effective improvement.

7. <u>What is the role of "design-to-cost" in the development of large-scale software?</u> The DOD joint logistics commanders have recently entered into an agreement concerning the acquisition and ownership of major weapon systems based on the concept of "design-to-cost" [20]. The term "design-to-cost"

is defined as a process utilizing unit cost goals as thresholds for managers and as design parameters for engineers. Cost parameters (goals) are to be established that translate into "design to" requirements. In the past, the order of priorities for major weapon system acquisition and ownership has been: a) performance, b) availability, and c) cost. Today, under the design-to-cost doctrine, the order is: a) cost, b) performance, and c) availability. The applicability of the design-to-cost concept to hardware is now beginning to emerge and is being reduced to practice. The relationship of the design-to-cost concept to software is not now understood.

In the 1975-1980 era, this reordering of priorities of major weapon systems, of which software is generally an integral part, is expected to have a sizeable influence on both hardware and software life cycle acquisition and ownership, particularly in the sense that the unit cost requirement will become a driving parameter in the design of large-scale software. System development will be continuously evaluated against the unit cost requirements with the same rigor as now applied to technical requirements. Practical tradeoffs must be made between system capability, cost, and schedule. Traceability of estimates and costing factors, including those for economic escalation, will have to be maintained.

REFERENCES

1. J.M. Beveridge, The Anatomy of a Win, J.M. Beveridge and Associates, Inc., Playa del Rey, California, 1970.
2. W.C. Lynam, P.N. Metzelaar, and D.H. Hibsman, "S&ISD cost estimating system final report," TRW Systems Group, Redondo Beach, California, November 13, 1970.
3. S. Stimler, Real-Time Data Processing Systems: A Methodology for Design and Cost/Performance Analysis, Columbia University Press, New York, 1969.
4. W.F. Sharpe, The Economics of Computers, Columbia University Press, New York, 1969.
5. G.F. Weinwurm, et al., On the Management of Computer Programming, Auerbach, Inc., Philadelphia, 1970.
6. W.W. Royce and E.A. Rollin, "A Software Cost Estimation Technique," TRW Systems Group, Redondo Beach, California, October 27, 1970.

7. J. L. Martin, Jr., "A specialized incentive contract structure for satellite projects," Space and Missile Systems Office, Los Angeles, California, April 18, 1969.

8. H. E. Boren and H. G. Campbell, "Learning curve tables," RAND Corporation, Santa Monica California, Rep. RM-1691-PR, April 1970.

9. R. H. Brandon, Management Standards for Data Processing, Van Nostrand, New York, 1963.

10. C. P. Lecht, The Management of Computer Programming Projects, Amer. Management Assoc., New York, 1967.

11. F. J. Mullin, "Computing Time Usage," TRW Systems Group, Redondo Beach, California, May 18, 1971.

12. P. N. Metzelaar, "Cost Estimation Graph," TRW Systems Group, Redondo Beach, California, April 30, 1971.

13. C. A. Bosch and B. W. Boehm, "Software Development Characteristics CCIP-85 Study Group," TRW Systems Group, Redondo Beach, California, October 8, 1971.

14. R. J. Hatter, "CCIP Study Regarding Analysis of TRW Software Analysis Data (Excerpt)," Lulejian and Assoc., Inc., Redondo Beach, California, November 29, 1971.

15. B. W. Boehm, "Some Information Processing Implications of Air Force Space Missions: 1970-1980," RAND Corporation, Santa Monica, California, January 1970.

16. H. Hecht, Figure of merit for fault-tolerant space computers," IEEE Trans. Comput. (Special Issue on Fault-Tolerant Computing), vol. C-22, pp. 246-251, March 1973.

17. G. J. Schick and R. W. Wolverton, "Assessment of Software Reliability," presented at the 11th Annual Meeting German Operations Res. Soc., Hamburg, Germany, September 6-8, 1972.

18. J. R. Brown and H. N. Buchanan, "The Quantitative Measurement of Software Safety and Reliability," TRW Systems Group, Redondo Beach, California, Site Defense Program Rep. SDP 1776, August 24, 1973.

19. E. R. Mangold, Software Development and Configuration Management Manual, Software Produce Assurance, TRW Systems Group, Redondo Beach, California, October 1973.

20. H. A. Miley, Jr., I. C. Kidd, Jr., J. J. Catton and S. C. Phillips, "Joint Design-to-Cost Guide: A Conceptual Approach for Major Weapon System Acquisition," presented at the Soc. American Value Engineers Conf. Practice of Design-to-Cost, Long Beach, California, October 21, 1974.

21. V. LaBolle, "Cost estimating for computer programming," Proc. IEEE 1972 Int. Conv. Exposition, New York, March 20-23, 1973. (Contains large bibliography of 99 annotated references, pp. 28-30.)

22. B. W. Boehm, D. W. Kosy and N. R. Nielsen, "ECSS: a prospective design tool for integrated information systems," presented at the American Institute of Aeronautics and Astronautics, Integrated Information Systems Conf., Palo Alto, California, February 17-19, 1971, paper 71-228.

3

Design

One of the main results that came out of the week-long seminar was that the design phase is one of the high leverage points in the software development process. Statistics from several studies concur that almost 50 percent of the errors detected at testing time were traceable back to an initial error made in design. Thus, if we can improve our effectiveness at this stage it will have a maximum impact over the entire effort. It seems improbable that the design of software will ever be completely formalized. Intrinsically, design is a creative process accomplished by the proper synthesis of computing structures. But, by delineating relevant parameters and considering various methodologies we can come far closer to perfecting this art.

The article by Barry Boehm on software design reviews the major design philosophies including: bottom-up, top-down using stubs or problem statements, structured design (programming) and model-driven design. For all of them he carefully outlines their applicability. This includes a complete list of their respective advantages and disadvantages in a variety of circumstances. His main effort is spent in describing his own concept of model-driven design. This is an amalgam of several of the foregoing procedures. It consists of both process and properties submodels which help to focus on the control and data flow of a developing system. The article represents a nice summary of design strategies.

SOFTWARE DESIGN AND STRUCTURING

Barry W. Boehm

INTRODUCTION

In 1974, the major leverage point in the software process is at the software design and structuring stage. This stage begins with a statement of software requirements. Properly done, the software design and structuring process can identify the weak spots and mismatches in the requirements statement which are the main sources of unresponsiveness of delivered software. Once these weak spots slip by the design phase, they will generally stay until during or after delivery, where only costly retrofits can make the software responsive to operational needs.

The software design and structuring phase ends with a detailed specification of the code that is to be produced, a plan for testing the code, and a draft set of users' manuals describing how the product is going to be used. Software costs and problems result from allowing coding to begin on a piece of software before its design aspects have been thoroughly worked out, verified, and validated. Figure 1 illustrates this quite well. It summarizes an analysis of 220 types of software errors found during a large, generally good (on-cost, on-schedule delivery) TRW software project [19, 20]. The great majority of the types of errors found in testing the code had originated in the design phase. Even more significantly, the design errors are generally not found until later in the test process. Of the 54 percent of the error types which were typically not found until during or after the acceptance test phase, only 9 percent were coding errors. The other 45 percent were design errors.

A particularly important stage is design verification and validation. Many of the design errors could have been caught before

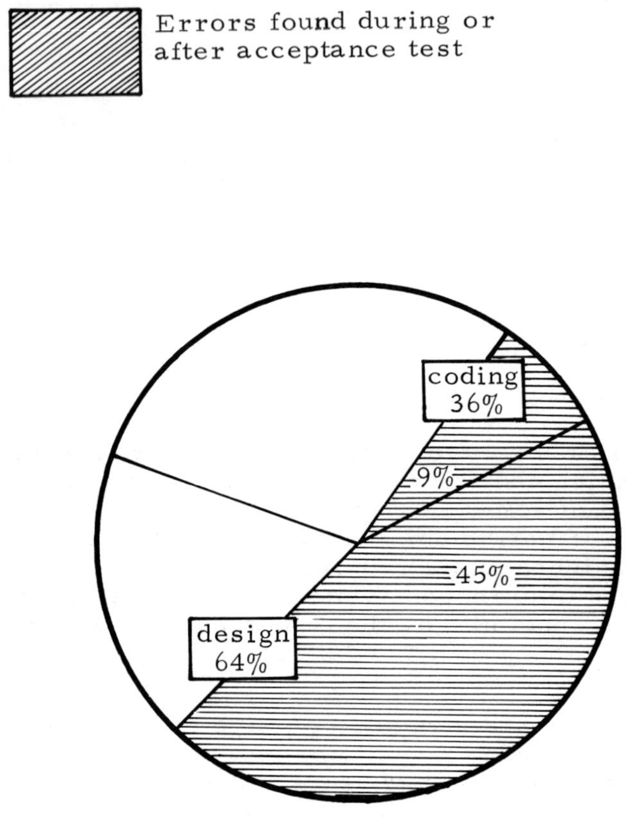

Figure 1. Software Error Sources

the coding phase by using better design review procedures or better tools for design consistency checking – some of which are now under development at TRW [20, 21].

Figure 2 provides another perspective on the importance of thorough software design specification and review. It shows data collected on a 24,000-instruction Navy command and control software project which was analyzed for the CCIP-85 study [22]. Here, conceptual errors accounted for 61 percent of the total number of errors detected.

The most significant correlation, though, is the following. On the "Executive" components of the project, only 37 percent of the time was spent on analysis and design, and the ratio of conceptual to clerical errors was 4:1. The other two components of the project spent 54 percent and 59 percent of their time in analysis and design; their ratios of conceptual errors to clerical errors were 0.6 and 0.5.

Some of the difference is probably due to the fact that executive software is conceptually more difficult. However, there can be little doubt that if more time had been spent on validating the design of the executive prior to coding, many of the conceptual errors would not have been committed to code. Similarly, better design tools and techniques should catch or avoid many of the design errors early without increasing the cost of the design phase.

An increasing number of techniques for improving the design process are now becoming available. It is becoming harder and harder to sort out just what each technique does and does not provide.

This paper provides a classification of software design and structuring techniques into a few main categories which can currently be considered as software design alternatives. For each alternative, it presents a short description and a balance sheet indicating the advantages and difficulties in using the technique.

In an overall comparison of the alternative techniques, none of them provides positive assurance of satisfying all the criteria, but each criterion is satisfied by at least one of the techniques. This would lead one to believe that an appropriate synthesis of the techniques might prove successful.

The following major design and structuring alternatives will be described and evaluated: Bottom-up, Top-down stub, Top-down/Problem Statement, Structured Programming, and Model-driven Design.

Figure 2. Distribution of Software Error Causes

Causes of Error	Hardware Diagnostics (%)	Executive (%)	User Programs (%)	Total (%)
Unexpected side effects to changes	5	25	10	19
Logical flaws in design original design	5	10	2	8
changes	5	15	8	12
Inconsistencies between design and implementation	5	30	10	22
Total: conceptual errors	20	80	30	61
Clerical errors	40	20	50	28
Inconsistencies in hardware	40	--	20	11
	100	100	100	100
Total errors detected 3 year sample	36	108	18	162
Number of instructions	4 K	10 K	10 K	24 K
% Analysis and design	59	37	54	

Most software design and structuring techniques fall generally within one of these categories. Some other variations exist, such as iterative multilevel modeling and prototyping; these will be discussed below in the context of the other concepts.

BOTTOM-UP

The typical bottom-up software development begins with the development of several computational routines whose function is considered important to the application. Sometimes the process involves modification of related previously existing computational routines in an attempt to avoid duplication of effort (Phase I in Figure 3).

Once these are developed, the need is seen for a test driver to support testing of the modules and their interfaces, a control program to determine the sequence in which the computational routines are called, and some input-output routines to service both. These are then built in Phase II.

Once they are built, the need is seen for an input-output control capability to sequence the input and output routines, perform initializations, conversions, error checks, etc. Also needed is an executive to moderate the interfaces between the input-output sector and the computational sector, and a test driver to test the entire system. These are then built, and the entire system tested and subsequently modified as errors are detected in Phase III.

Advantages

High-risk Components. These are low-level component tasks for which there is a high risk as to whether or not they can be performed as specified; e.g., processing sensor data in real-time, automating human discrimination functions. They are well-handled since the bottom-up process generally begins by concentrating on them.

Reusable Modules. Being component-oriented, the bottom-up approach tends to do well here, but often at the expense of other considerations.

Disadvantages

Integration, Verification, and Validation. These tend to be very costly because of the lack of early attention to interface problems and overall system requirements.

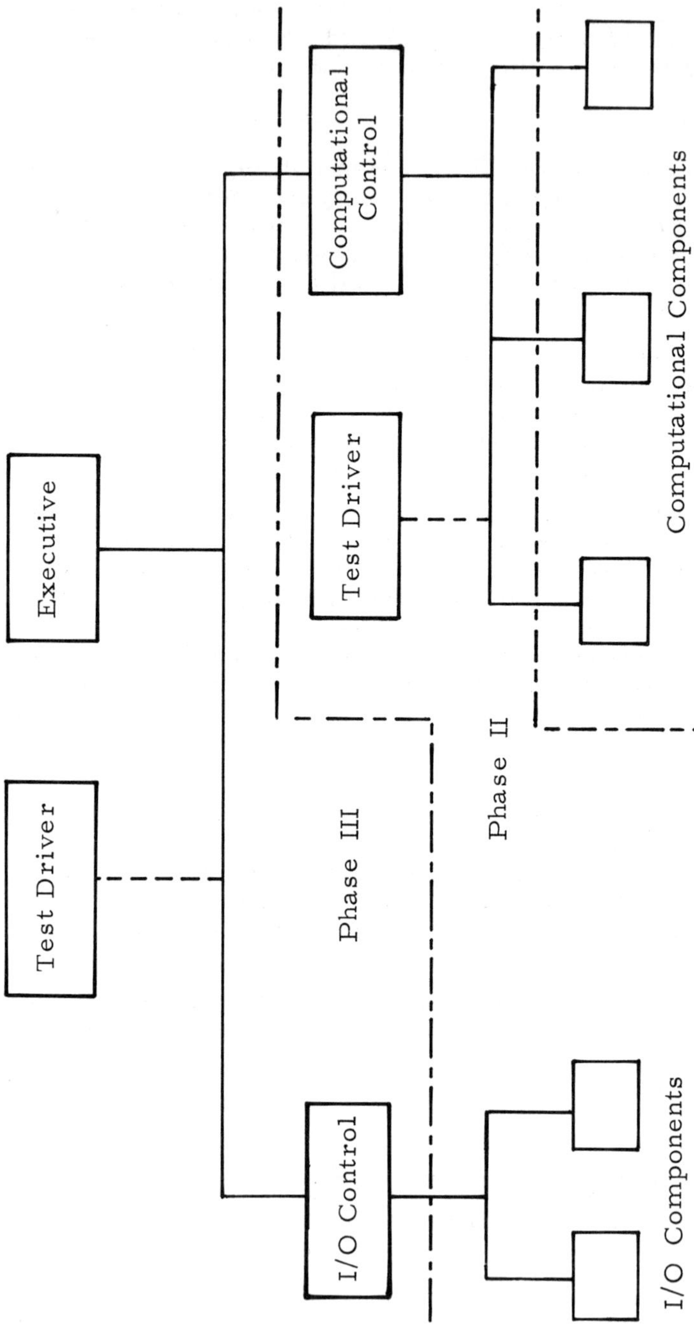

Figure 3. Typical Bottom-Up Approach

Visibility and Tracking. Tracking the progress of individual components is straightforward, but the lack of well-defined overall user requirements and system interfaces makes overall visibility difficult.

Maintainability. Often, different assumptions made during the development of individual bottom-level components lead to a higher-level control structure and a data structure which are simply "kludged-up" to make the components work together in their current form. Such constructs are very difficult to modify to meet changing requirements.

User, Data Structuring Issues. The lack of early attention to overall system requirements mentioned above, and the generally "kludged-up" data structures are the sources of these difficulties.

TOP-DOWN STUB

The top-down/stub approach, as described in references [1] and [2], proceeds as follows. The designer begins by determining what overall functions will be performed by the software system, in what order and under what conditions. He then proceeds to develop a working top-level computer program, containing all the logic controlling the sequencing between functions, but inserting dummy programs or "stubs" for the functions. He then proceeds to test this top-level program thoroughly before proceeding to the next step.

The succeeding steps consist of fleshing out the stubs into a lower-level sequence of control logic, computation and subfunctions, each of which is again represented by a stub. Each subprogram is developed to replace a stub, it can be tested immediately, not only by itself, but also as a part of the software subsystem and system it joins by replacing the stub.

The top-down/stub approach to software design is often enhanced by several optional aids. One is the HIPO (Hierarchial Input-Process-Output) technique [3], which provides designs with a standard way to represent the inputs, processes, and outputs of each module and the module's relationship to the overall control hierarchy. Currently, no automated aids are available for developing or checking HIPO descriptions. Another is the walk-through, an element of "egoless programming" [4, 5] in which the designer-programmer presents his design and its underlying rationale to his team leader and a group of peers to eliminate as many bugs as possible before coding begins. Another is the chief programmer team [6], a management approach in which a single indivudual (aided by a backup) produces the bulk of the design, writes a good deal of the code, and reviews all of it personally. Another is structured programming, to be discussed in more detail later.

In top-down/stub design, changes to the software are first worked out at the highest level affected, and then propagated downward as appropriate. The process thus concludes with not only a completed design but a completed and tested program, in which the lower levels of the control structure were not designed until the upper levels were programmed and tested.

Advantages

Early Integration. Committing the top-level design early to testable code focuses attention on interface problems at a stage where they are relatively easy to resolve. (It also creates a useful additional deterrent to arbitrary changes of scope.)

Parallel Testing. Testing can proceed much faster when one can immediately test his program at the unit, subsystem, and system levels. (Experience has shown that one must prepare to handle an overload of test shots at this stage while somehow preserving good turnaround time.)

Visibility and Tracking. The well-defined interfaces and stub organization make it relatively easy to track progress and isolate trouble spots.

Maintainability. Traceability from high level requirements to low level code is maintained at least partially through the hierarchical control structure.

Disadvantages

High-risk Components. Proceeding in strictly top-down fashion can lead to a large investment in top-level structure before discovering that a low-level component can't do its job; e.g., to process inputs in real-time, to automatically discriminate friend from foe, at which point one must virtually start another top-down design from scratch.

Common or Reusable Components. Particularly when several designers get into the act, people have found that several branches of the control hierarchy terminate with a requirement for a similar capability, say, for sorting, but that a great deal of rework must be done at the higher levels to accommodate the requirement with a single routine.

Machine-dependence. As it begins by developing an executing version of the top-level control structure, the top-down/stub approach unfortunately commits the project to a specific hardware system right away before the hardware implications of various design decisions are completely understood. One may avoid this difficulty by using the top-down/stub approach more as a programming technique than as the complete design process.

User and Data-structuring Issues. The top-down/stub approach is a formalism for organizing a program's control structure. If the user's requirements are poorly understood, or if the data structure implications are not also considered in advance, the delivered software may be unresponsive or hard to maintain. With an experienced, thoughtful designer, these will generally not be problems. But if considered as a "cookbook" approach by inexperienced designers, the top-down/stub approach can lead to problems: one group using it for the first time had an 83 percent overrun on a job budgeted at 450 man-hours.

TOP-DOWN PROBLEM STATEMENT

Several variants exist on the problem statement approach, but in general, each attempts to define a special problem domain and establish for it a set of constructs and capabilities for expressing, analyzing, and ideally generating programs within the problem domain. In the domain of business system problems, ISDOS and its Problem Statement Language epitomize the problem statement approach [7]; a good review of business problem statement languages is Ref. [8].

Another variant involves the use of iteratively refined simulations as successive problem statements which drive program design and development, as in Iterative Multilevel Modeling [9], SODAS [10], and DES [11]. Another is Glaser's LOGOS approach, centered around the problem domain of computer operating systems [12].

In the ballistic missile defense problem area, TRW has evolved a set of problem statement capabilities currently being used in the design and development of the large Site Defense of Minuteman (SDM) software project. These capabilities allow a designer to specify a top-down control structure via a hierarchical set of Functional Sequence Diagrams (FSD's). The FSD's are specially structured time-sequenced flow charts whose elements may be expanded into attribute descriptions via a Functional Properties Matrix, which may identify the various categories of activity (data handling, control, report, test, etc.) as a function of mode (preoperational, operational, or postoperational). Another associated design and data-structuring construct is the N-square chart, which indicates the flow of data to and from the component elements of the system.

Another design and development aid on the SDM project is a process construction language. This language is designed to be able to drive both a simulation of the SDM system and the building of the program itself. Thus, in one mode, the command "PERFORM RADAR SCHEDULING..." will call out a simulation of the radar-scheduling activity; in the other mode, the actual radar-scheduling code will be assembled for execution.

Advantages

Early Integration. This is provided by the emphasis on early specification of the sequence of functions and their interactions via data, and of a simulation model of the system to be developed.

Data Structuring. Most of these approaches provide explicit capabilities for assessing data implications and some degree of data structuring.

Maintainability. In general, the problem statement provides very good traceability from requirements to code, and a natural way of specifying modifications.

Visibility and Tracking. The problem statement provides a well-understood context within which software development can be monitored.

Disadvantages

Limited Applications Context. The price generally paid for the implicit contextual framework provided by the problem statement approach is a restriction to the problem domain for which such a framework is relevant. Specifying BMD software via ISDOS would be extremely awkward, as would the use of FSD's to specify a personnel-payroll data processing system.

Machine-dependent Support Software. Although the problem statements are generally machine-independent, at the present time the programs which operate on them generally are not.

STRUCTURED PROGRAMMING

Structured programming [13, 14] is strictly more of a program-organization discipline than a design technique, but it can be used to significantly enhance most of the available design techniques. It is basically a set of standards for organizing the control structure of a set of computer programs. The key ideas in structured programming are:

1. Only "proper programs" having one flow of control in and out of each unit should be developed.
2. Only three basic control structures are allowed: DOWHILE, IFTHENELSE, and SEQUENCE. These three structures are sufficient to express any proper program [15]. Two additional structures are optional, the DOUNTIL and the CASE.
3. Programs are organized according to a hierarchical, modular block structure.
4. Additional standards are imposed on the size of modules, the formatting of instructions and declarations, program commentary, etc.

Advantages

The modularity, standard control structure, and format conventions of structured programming generally make programs easier to understand. Organizing programs in this way also generally requires more careful thought; this leads to many advantages, particularly in reducing the incidence of errors. Also, the structuring and limited number of logic components makes it easier to develop automated software development, test, and documentation tools. Enforcing any sort of programming standard generally leads to fewer interface problems. These factors combine to produce the following main advantages:

- Visibility and Tracking
- Maintainability
- Testing and Reliability
- Support of Early Integration

Disadvantages

Asynchronous Control and Error Exits. The natural way to handle these types of program control involves the use of nonproper program logic. To express an interrupt capability with structured

	Bottom-Up	Top-Down/Stub	Top-Down/Problem Statement	Structured Programming	Model Driven
Universality	VG	VG	C	G	G
User RQTS Refinement	P	C	G	C	G
Design Validation	P	G	G	G	VG
Early Integration	P	VG	VG	G	VG
Data Structuring	C	C	G	C	G
High-Risk Components	VG	C	G	C	VG
Machine-Independence	C	P	C	VG	VG
Reusable Modules	VG	C	G	C	G
Efficiency	C	C	G	C	G
V&V Assurance	P	G	G	G	G
Maintainability	P	G	VG	VG	VG
Visibility & Tracking	P	VG	VG	G	VG

VG = very good G = good C = caution P = problem source

Figure 4. Comparison of Alternative Design Techniques

programming, for example, would require IFTHENELSE for each type of interrupt after every statement in the program.

Common or Reusable Components. Structured programming strictly leads to the use of duplicated segments of in-line code to handle many functions usually performed by common multi-purpose components.

User and Data-structuring Issues. Structured programming does not address these. It is strictly a formalism for organizing the control aspects of a program.

Figure 4 summarizes and extends the balance sheets given on the previous pages. For each of the approaches described, it provides an assessment for each of several software criteria or characteristics. Most of the ratings are straightforward; the "caution" rating implies either that the approach can lead the designer astray under some conditions, or that the approach says virtually nothing about how to achieve the characteristic.

As seen in the figure, none of the techniques described provide positive assurance of satisfying all the criteria, but each criterion is satisfied at least to the "good" level by one of the approaches. This would lead one to believe that an appropriate synthesis of the techniques might prove successful. The concept of Model-driven Design evolving at TRW gives promise to provide such a synthesis. A rating of the near-term objectives for Model-driven Design is given in the rightmost column. The concept is summarized in the pages to follow.

MODEL-DRIVEN DESIGN

Model-driven Software Design (see Figure 5) begins with two models which are independent of the specific software capabilities to be designed. One is a "process model" of the software design and development process, best illustrated by such documents as the recent TRW Software Development and Configuration Management Manual [16]. The other is a "properties manual" of the characteristics of a good software product, best illustrated by such documents as the recent TRW report for NBS on Characteristics of Quality Software [17].

The process model specifies the overall sequence of activities, which begins with the specification of another model, this time a specific-project-oriented model of the functions to be performed by the software. This model is checked for completeness via checklists derived from the properties model, using techniques along the lines of the Requirements/Properties

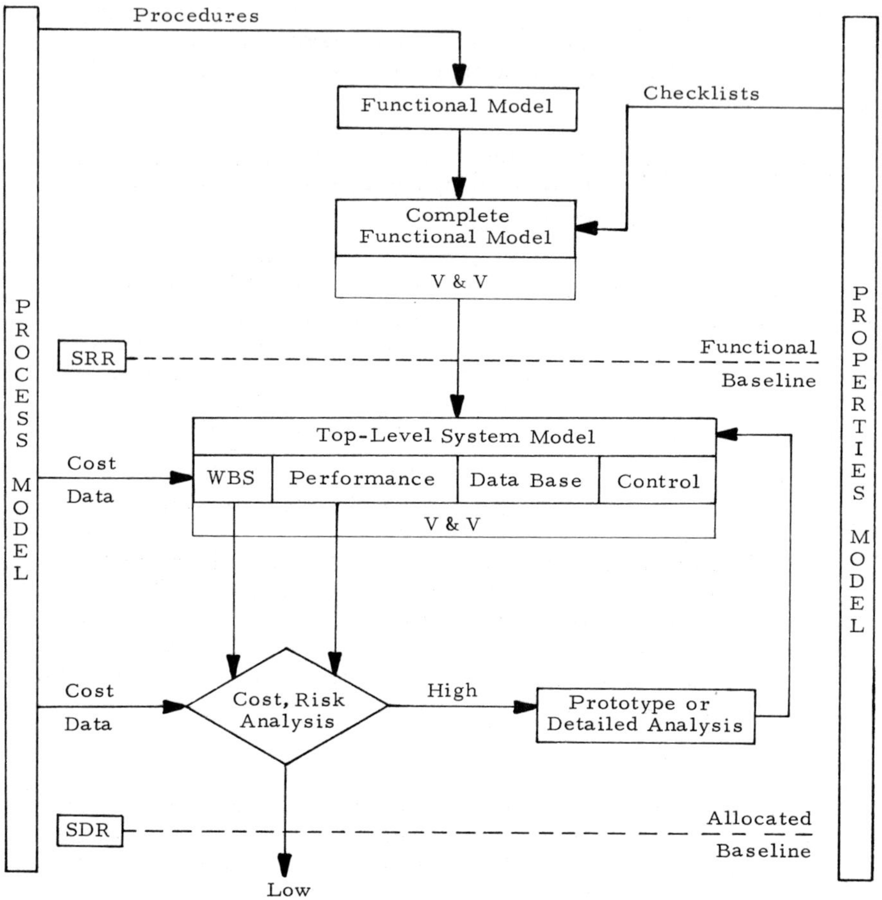

Figure 5. Model-Driven Software Design

Matrix formalism being developed at TRW [18]. Additional walk-throughs or protocols are worked out with the prospective user to provide design verification and validation (V & V) followed by an official System Requirements Review and establishment of a functional baseline for the system.

The resulting functional model is then used to generate a top-level system model with four complementary components:

- a model of the overall control structure, using an enhanced version of Functional Sequence Diagrams,
- a model of the data base, using the N-square formalism and additional data structure models appropriate to the application (batch, on-line, real-time random/sequence access, etc.)
- a model of system performance or processing efficiency (generally a rough analytic model will do at this stage, but more detail may be appropriate for performance-critical systems)
- a rough model of the work breakdown structure (WBS), cost, and schedule required to develop the software, based on experimental data which form a part of the process model.

After these models are checked for consistency, the WBS and performance models are exercised to determine whether there are any high-risk components within the software to be developed. If not, the design can proceed top-down. If so, however, some detailed simulation or bottom-level prototyping is needed to determine the right approach to be taken for the critical components. A good conceptual model for this process is given by statistical theory: an example is given in the appendix which shows how this kind of risk analysis helps determine the appropriate sequence of design activities in a system involving real-time sensor data processing.

It is important that such risk analysis and design sequence activities have strong participation from the user, as both the risk assessments and the resulting design decisions generally involve assumptions about the user's need and priorities. Thus, even though the system design phase is culminated by a thorough Systems Design Review by the user, this fact should not lead either the user or the developer to succumb to the temptation to avoid user-developed interaction during this or other design phases. In fact, many successful software projects owe a good deal of their success to having been designed by a joint user-developer team –

an option which deserves consideration for the future government software procurements.

The preliminary software design (see Figure 6) begins with a thorough description of the information processing system to be developed (the allocated baseline) and an understanding of the residual risks involved in developing it. Sometimes these risks are extremely low, in which case the allocated baseline can indeed be a basis for a firm determination of the resources required to complete the project; e.g., a fixed-price type contract. However in most cases even the detailed analysis or prototyping activities described above will not eliminate a good deal of cost uncertainty which can only be resolved by proceeding to the next step or preliminary software design.

Often, then, the preliminary design step will involve a continuing refinement of the cost and risk models, and their supporting WBS and performance models. These are developed in conjunction with a top-down refinement of the models of the data and control structures. This process generally begins with a more detailed layout of the data structure, which then provides a general context for the refinement of the control structure. For large projects, this latter process can be assisted by a machine readable but machine-independent description of the inputs and outputs of each module, along the lines of the HIPO technique, but extended to accommodate automated consistency checking of the attributes of the inputs and outputs.

The preliminary design phase, and the detailed design phase to follow, are similarly characterized by:

- continuous user involvement;
- explicit planning for and performance of design verification and validation activities;
- explicit consideration of risk and uncertainty resolution;
- thorough reviews to assure firm resolution of issues in each phase before proceeding to the next.

The detailed design phase concludes not only with a build-to coding specification, but also a thorough test plan and draft user's manuals so that the user has an accurate picture of how his product will work.

Some additional points on model-driven preliminary and detailed design are:

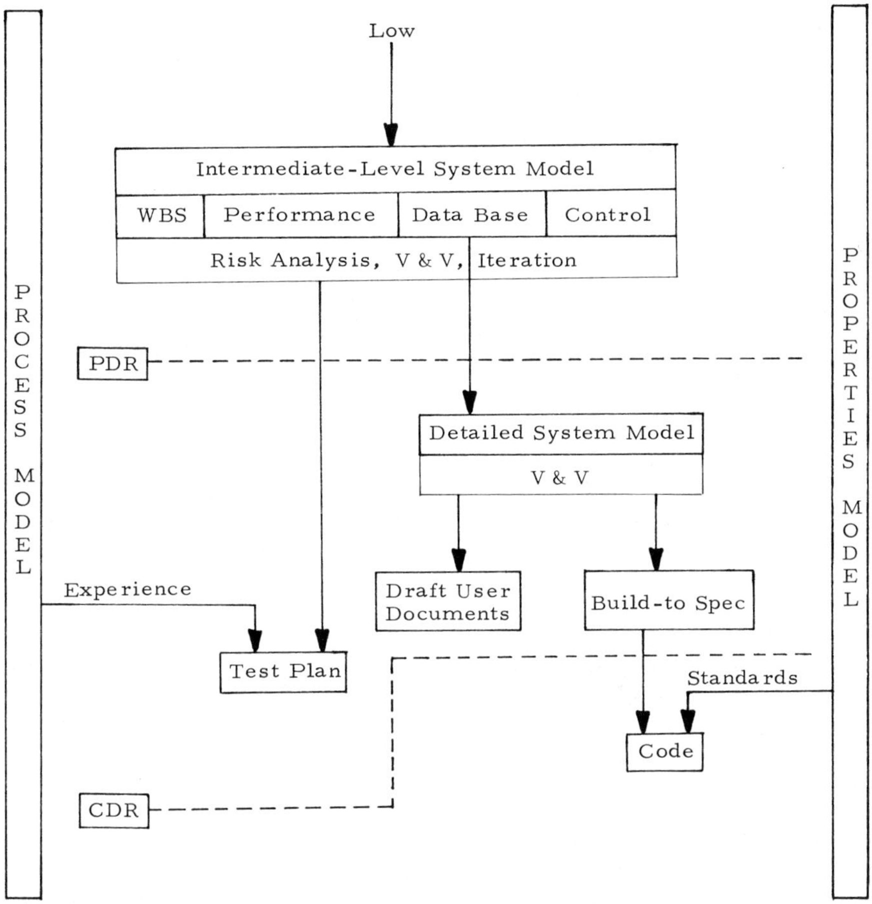

Figure 6. Model-Driven Software: Preliminary & Detailed Design

- In order that user considerations rather than hardware constraints continue to be the major detriment of the design, a commitment to a specific hardware configuration should be delayed until as late as possible.
- At some point, the result of a risk analysis may be to factor the development into two or more phased development activities (five "loops" in the TRW Site Defense project), in which the actual performance in the earlier developments can be used to guide the design of successive development portions.

Advantages

Emphasizes Design Validation. Model-driven design makes explicit provisions for design test planning and performance before proceeding to subsequent phases. The several models provide reference information which can be used to support design consistency and completeness checking.

Emphasizes Early Integration. Greater assurance of design integrity at early stages of development results from the formulation and cross-checking of successively more detailed models of control structure, data structure, performance, and work breakdown structure.

Avoids Premature Hardware Commitment. Model-driven design is basically a "software-first" approach. The performance model and optional prototyping activities provide the capability of resolving many of the hardware-software tradeoff issues before committing the project to a particular hardware configuration.

Explicit Risk Analysis for Design Decision. In general, the objective of model-driven design is to avoid building up a large inventory of code or detailed design specifications when there is a high risk that they may have to be scrapped as nonresponsive or expensively retrofitted. The explicit assessments of risk, and the options to proceed in high-risk situations via higher-level design analysis or quick disposable prototypts, both support this objective.

No Major Weak Spots. Although model-driven design has been synthesized from other design approaches to fulfill this objective, its full performance in practice has yet to be demonstrated. Currently, the Site Defense project at TRW is the closest approximation to complete model-driven design and, though performance to date is highly satisfactory, it has not reached its culmination. The major potential problem area is that inexperienced or model-happy designers will use model building as an alternative to thinking about and resolving design development issues, rather than a means to stimulate thinking about and resolving such issues. Thus, "model-driven software development" should admit to both of the following interpretations:

- The software development activities are driven by the formulation, analysis, and iterations of preliminary models;
- The model development activities are driven by the overall objective of producing a cost-effective software product.

Disadvantages

Exists Only for Limited Problem Domains. At the current time, the model-driven approach can be applied to real-time software projects with characteristics somewhat similar to ballistic missile defense. Some additional capabilities in the performance and data modeling areas in particular need to be provided to make it generally applicable.

Extension Requires New Developments. The main capabilities needed to provide general model-driven facilities are:

- A language for expressing software requirements design specifications, and performance characteristics for simulation;
- A set of formal and automated aids for checking the completeness and consistency of software requirements and designs;
- A set of capabilities for top-down data structuring.

Requirements/Design/Simulation Language. A language is needed for specifying the components and characteristics of software systems in ways which support performance analysis, automated aids to consisistency checking and traceability of requirements into design and code specifications, completeness checklists, and — most importantly — a clean and common understanding among the software builders, buyers, and users of what is to be built. Components of such a language would include:

- Precise terminology (Are response time, reaction time, turnaround time, port-to-port time, and delay time the same or different concepts?)
- A taxonomy of elementary information processing functions (Send, receive, store, query, sort, process, tally, etc.)
- A means of describing performance or specifying a performance or specifying a performance model
- Facilities to characterize software via inputs and outputs, via properties, or via data structures and dynamics

Requirements Analysis and Design Verification and Validation Aids. These include completeness checklists and capabilities for consistency checking of software designs, such as the module description consistency checker being built at TRW along the lines described in Reference [17].

Hierarchy of Performance Modeling and Simulation Tools. Capabilities are needed to support smooth evolution of performance models to levels of greater detail or of higher aggregation; e.g., along the spectrum from analytic models through semianalytic simulations to bit-level simulations.

Top-down Data Structuring. Capabilities are needed to accumulate a number of statements of data usage (existing files, required outputs and response times, access control, etc.) and organize them in ways to support data structuring and performance analysis. ISDOS [7] is a good step in this direction.

Structured Programming Extensions. Language features are needed which extend the constructs of structured programming in ways which accommodate asynchronous control. Existing languages should be extended to easily accommodate structured programming.

On-line Analysis and Design Aids. Providing such capabilities would not only reduce design concurrency problems on multiperson efforts but would also assure that the design is in machine-readable form for easier analysis.

REFERENCES

1. R.C. McHenry, "Management concepts for top down structured programming," IBM Corporation Technical Report No. FSC 73-0001, February 1973 revision.

2. H. Mills, "Top down programming in large systems," Debugging Techniques in Large Systems, Randall Rustin (ed.), Prentice-Hall, Inc., Englewood Cliffs, N.Y., 1971, pp. 41-55.

3. "HIPO: Design aid and documentation tool," IBM Corporation, Armonk, New York, SR20-9413.

4. G.F. Weinberg, The Psychology of Computer Programming, Van Nostrand Reinhold, 1971.

5. "Structured walk-through: A project management tool," IBM Corporation, Bethesda, Maryland, August 1973.

6. F.T. Baker, "Chief programmer team management of production programming," IBM Systems Journal, vol. 11, no. 1, 1972.

7. D. Teichroew and H. Sayari, "Automation of system building," Datamation, August 17, 1971, pp. 25-30.

8. J.D. Cougar, "Evolution of business system analysis techniques," ACM Computing Surveys, September 1973, pp 167-198.

9. F.W. Zurcher and B. Randell, Iterative Multilevel Modeling — A Methodology for Computer System Design, IFIP Congress, Edinburgh, 1968.

10. D.L. Parnas, "More on simulation languages and design methodology for computer systems," Proceedings Spring Joint Computer Conference, 1969, pp. 739-743.

11. R.M. Graham, G.L. Clancy and D.B. DeVaney, "A software design and evaluation system," ACM Communications, February 1973, pp. 110-116.

12. E.L. Glaser, et al, "The LOGOS project," Digest of Papers 72; Innovative Architecture Compcon 72, IEEE, Catalog No. 72-CH0659-3C, 1972, pp. 175-192.

13. E.W. Dijkstra, "Notes on structured programming," Structured Programming, Dahl, Dijkstra and Hoare (eds.), Academic Press, London, 1972.

14. H.D. Mills, "Structured programming in large systems," IBM/FSD, Gaithersberg, November 1970.

15. C. Bohm and G. Jacopini, "Flow diagrams, Turing machines and languages with only two formation rules," ACM Communications, vol. 9, no. 5, May 1968, pp. 366-371.

16. Software Development and Configuration Management Manual, TRW Systems Group, Redondo Beach, California, 28 December 1973.

17. "Characteristics of software quality," TRW Document No. 25201-6001-RU-00, TRW Systems Group, Redondo Beach, California, 28 December 1973.

18. B. W. Boehm, "Some steps toware formal and automated aids to software requirements analysis and design," TRW Systems Group, Redondo Beach, California, November 1972.

19. "Information processing/data automation implications of Air Force command and control requirements in the 1980's," U.S. Air Force, SAMSO/XRS-71-1, April 1972.

20. "Characteristics of software quality," TRW Document No. 25201-60001-RU-00, December 28, 1973

21. B. W. Boehm, "Some steps toward formal and automated aids to software requirements analysis and design," to be presented at IFIP Congress 1974.

22. J. McGonagle, A Study of a Software Development Project, J.D. Anderson and Associates, October 1971.

APPENDIX

SOFTWARE SYSTEM DESIGN AND DEVELOPMENT: TOP-DOWN, BOTTOM-UP, OR PROTOTYPE?

One difficulty which may occure in using the top-down structured programming approach to software development is that of high-risk modules. If one proceeds too routinely through a top-down structuring of a program, he may at times find himself with a fifth-level module which is supposed to "understand natural-language queries," "process a megabit of sensor information in two milliseconds," or something equally impossible. And, in coming up with an acceptable compromise for handling this module's task, he may have to rework all of the structure that was painstakingly worked out at levels 1, 2, 3, and 4. It is such practical difficulties that have led some people to consciously reject the top-down approach in favor of the bottom-up approach, and led others to advocate building a throw-away prototype before proceeding to develop the production-engineered software system. However, in straightforward programming projects with no high-risk elements, the prototype approach would generally result in duplicated effort.

There is a formalism which can help determine how much bottom-up prototyping should precede the top-down specification of the overall program structure. This is the statistical decision theory approach, which takes explicit account of risk aspects. It is illustrated below by an example.

The Statistical Decision Theory Approach: An Example

Suppose you are organizing a software project which has within it a requirement to process 30,000 bits of sensor data within five milliseconds. You have an algorithm which you are pretty sure will work, and if you proceed top-down to develop the program and it works, you will have to spend an estimated $40,000 in performance penalties, ending up with a loss of $50,000 on the job. The other alternatives are (1) to develop the program initially with the less efficient algorithm, accepting a loss of $10,000 on the project, or (2) to spend $10,000 to quickly develop a bottom-level prototype and test it in a way which gives a much stronger assurance, though no guarantee, that it will work in practice if it passes the tests. How do you decide what to do?

Using statistical decision theory, you would begin by quantifying such words as "pretty sure" and "stronger" into probabilistic terms. This is a very subjective step, but there are various techniques involving expert polling which can help. To begin with, let us suppose that you established a probability of 0.65 that the efficient algorithm would work. From this, we can see that the expected value of proceeding top-down with the efficient algorithm (Approach A) is:

$$0.65(\$30,000) + 0.35(-\$50,000) = \$2,500$$

clearly better than the $10,000 loss associated with proceeding top-down with the less efficient algorithm (Approach B). However, the positive expected value using Approach A is not completely reassuring, as most software performer organizations have a highly asymmetric utility function such as that shown in Figure 1. It is generally fairly linear on the profit side, but drops off steeply if the project begins to encounter losses. Thus, the expected utility of Approach A is more like:

$$0.65(0.4) + 0.35(-0.9) = -0.055$$

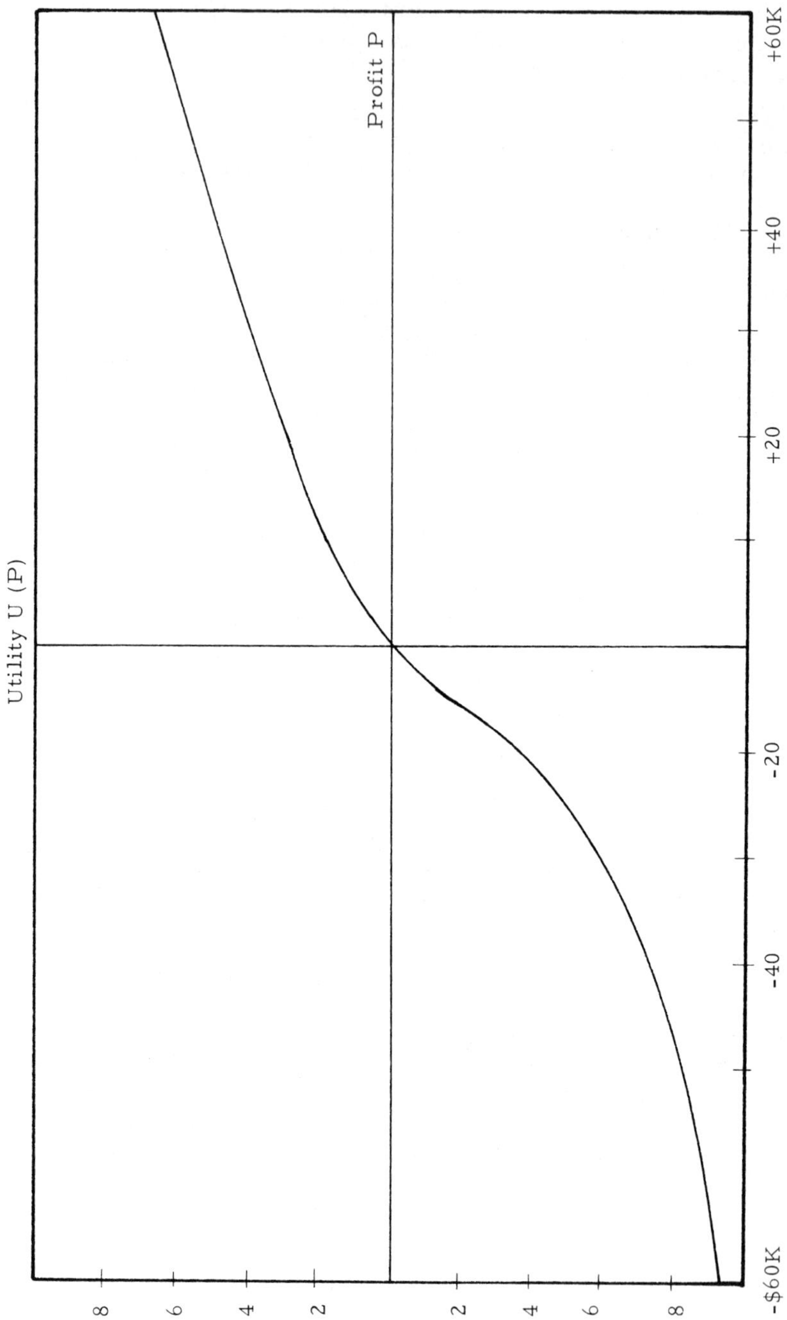

Figure 1. Utility Function for Software Project Outcome

again clearly better than the -0.4 utility resulting from Approach B, but still not very satisfactory.

In order to evaluate the expected value and utility of the bottom-level prototype approach (Approach C), we first need to estimate the effectiveness of the prototype as a predictor of the outcome of the success of the project. We do this by estimating two probabilities:

1. The probability that the prototype is successful, given that the project is tractable. Suppose we estimate this as 0.95; e.g., 5 percent of the time, the prototype would be badly done and fail, but the project would succeed if attempted.

2. The probability that the prototype is successful, but that the project would fail (due perhaps to problems of scale, or unrepresentativeness of the prototype). Suppose we estimate this as 0.15.

Then we can use Bayes' formula to calculate the probability that the project will succeed, given that the prototype succeeds:

$$P = \frac{(0.95)(0.65)}{(0.95)(0.65) + (0.15)(0.35)} \doteq \frac{0.617}{0.670} \doteq 0.92 .$$

Thus, the expected value associated with Approach C is:

$$0.670[0.92(\$30K) + 0.08(-\$50K)] + 0.330(-\$10K) - \$10K = \$2.5K,$$

where 0.670 is the probability of the prototype being successful and the decision being made to use the efficient algorithm. The expected utility is:

$$0.670[0.92U(\$20K) + 0.08U(-\$60K)] + 0.330U(-20K) = +0.009 .$$

Thus, in this situation, an expenditure of \$10K on a prototype can change the expected utility of the outcome from -0.055 to +0.009.

If we can estimate costs and probabilities with reasonable accuracy, then, the statistical decision theory approach can help us steer a proper course between top-down, bottom-up, and prototype activities. Currently, given the scanty firm knowledge we have on software cost estimation, and our lack of experience in expressing possible software outcomes in probabilistic terms, the accuracy of the estimates will not support cookbook applications of the method. However, it still has considerable value as a conceptual framework for software development decision making, and provides another reason to press for more collection and analysis of quantitative software data to support cost estimation.

4 Coding and Testing

Hopefully at the coding and testing point one has carefully done requirements analysis and design because it is at this point that the system submerges. Programmers go off and start to develop their own subroutines. The group will probably not see the entire system again until integration and testing begin. This lack of visibility is a real problem and proposals such as structured walk-throughs and chief programmer teams, (see [49, 3] in the bibliography) have been suggested as solutions to it. These are management techniques and along with them there are technical improvements which should also be considered. If we look at the coding and testing process, such improved techniques generally fall into two categories: better languages for coding and new tools for testing. In the history of computing one of the biggest innovations has come at the coding stage, namely the development of higher-level languages. Industry specialists agree that such languages are broadly applicable and result in an improved productivity of factors from 2 to 3.

Any new and "better" language has many hurdles to overcome before it will be used. First there are the people who must use it. They must be capable and more important, willing to use it. One can't stress too much the importance of human factors in all that is said here. Secondly, there is the question of how much productivity will increase if this new language is adopted. Will using ALGOL 68 or PASCAL over FORTRAN have the same effect that using FORTRAN over assembly language had? No one knows. But it is in this spirit that I discuss structured FORTRAN. Such a tool provides a cost-wise effective means for improving language facilities while minimizing the effect of the changeover. The article describes a FORTRAN super-set, discusses the development of such a tool at 6 installations and presents the pros and cons of its use. In the article by John Brown another language device, a meta or description language is presented. It was successfully used at TRW, but Brown is careful to outline the scope of its utility.

The second part of Brown's paper poses a new documentation methodology which he calls coordinated commentary programming. This device can be adopted either at the design or coding phases. The basic idea is to set up two teams who iterate over the code (or design) and check it for completeness and consistency. Though 100 percent correctness is not guaranteed the level of confidence in the code will be greatly improved.

Once the programs are written and testing begins, tools can again be helpful. Leon Stucki describes a system for instrumenting source code. The resulting programs are then run producing output such as frequency counts of statements and procedures, maximum value of variables, and results of conditional tests. Taken together the data constitutes a program profile which can be tremendously helpful. Beside aiding optimization, one can easily determine if any piece of code has been untested by the data. Though it is an elementary technique, it is surprising how little it is used today. It does aid in systematizing the testing process and in this regard it should be made available at every computing center.

GETTING BETTER SOFTWARE CHEAPER AND QUICKER

John R. Brown

I. INTRODUCTION

If one bothers to look very hard at today's world of software production, the possible (in fact, likely) result will be some degree of bewilderment. One soon begins to see that we are all, in one way or another, victims of circumstances which we have brought upon ourselves. One needn't look hard at all to begin to appreciate the number and severity of problems with which the modern-day programmer is faced; and yet, there also comes an awareness of a diverse proliferation of proposed techniques which have promised or now promise to overcome those problems once and for all.

We can credit the current state of the art of software production technology largely to a fairly widespread and very serious inability to focus on the specific issue or problem at hand. Consequently, even though we continue as we must to discover, implement and use specific tools and techniques to help with specific tasks, we almost always fall into the trap of evaluating the effectiveness and utility of such techniques in terms of general applicability, machine independence, overhead, etc. It is possible that there is some kind of overwhelming urge to solve all problems of software production technology in one fell swoop. If so, then it comes as no great surprise that individual tools and techniques, hastily put together in response to some specific and pressing problem, have so far failed miserably to measure up to that ultimate goal. It is also not surprising to hear and almost believe fantastic claims about the power and glory of such a tool or technique, because we all want so much to see the big, ugly problems disappear that we tend to close our eyes, grasp at straws, and hope for the best.

It is becoming more and more clear that faith alone will not cure the ills of software development and can lead to an even more confusing mixture of methodology and mythology than we know today. Fortunately, there are alternative approaches through which hoped for progress can be achieved. One such approach is taken in the following discussion. It involves the description of several selected techniques and associated support tools in a fashion which 1) directly supports an understanding of the relevance of each technique to one or more phases of the typical software production process, and 2) provides details essential for evaluation of current problems, limitations, and drawbacks inherent in a given technique and for evaluation of the benefits experienced or expected from the use of a technique or tool.

The techniques (i. e., methods and related tools) introduced in subsequent discussion can be best categorized in terms of the primary function of the software production process to which a given technique lends direct support. The METAFOR module-library/executive-drive-logic technique is provided as an example of a much-used program and data base construction tool. A group of tools are mentioned under the general heading of automated support to program development and maintenance; however, detailed discussion is limited to a particular combination of tools which supports data base design, development, maintenance and documentation. Extensive treatment is given to specific tools which provide various types of automated support to program testing with primary emphasis on techniques for monitoring, evaluating and increasing test thoroughness. A technique, called Coordinated Commentary Programming, is described and proposed as an approach to development of meaningful program comments which in turn directly support verification of program correctness.

II. METAFOR - An Aid to Software Construction

The term METAFOR (from META language-to-FORTRAN) is applied to both the general technique of program construction and a specific tool developed to directly support a semi-automatic construction process.

A. The Problem

A few years ago (about five), some TRW engineers were faced with a tough problem while engaged in performance of an Apollo program mission planning and analysis support function. The problem, briefly, was to find a way to build mission simulation programs which contained few (if any) errors, and to do so in less time and at less cost than previously possible.

B. The METAFOR Technique and Tool

It was determined that the problem above could be solved in large part through development and systematic use of a program construction tool which 1) supported selection and use of previously coded, tested and used modules from a module library, 2) provided a capability for complete specification of a simulation data base, 3) allowed definition of a desired sequence of events to be simulated in a natural, engineering-oriented language, and 4) automatically accomplished the appropriate chaining of modules in construction of an executable program from the engineer-supplied simulation definition. The METAFOR Program was initially developed as a tool to provide these four primary capabilities. Subsequent development added other capabilities including 1) a standard set of easily referenced utility modules for performance of general purpose arithmetic functions (e.g., trigonometric functions, random number generation, matrix operations, etc.), 2) a facility for saving, retrieving, updating and reusing previously configured programs and associated data, and 3) a means for easily adding new modules to an existing program with some support in identification of potential interface problems.

With these few, but very powerful, automated techniques, the typical user-engineer task of creating a "new" simulation program to support analysis of a "new" mission was greatly simplified. The facilities for translation from a user's specification of events to an executable program and for reusing previously developed and extensively tested software modules combine to produce significant reductions in the time and associated cost of program development. These same facilities have an equally beneficial effect in prevention of errors which can arise out of misunderstandings between engineer/user and programmer/analyst or simple coding mistakes made in the usual implementation effort.

In a typical use of METAFOR, an engineer/user will construct and operate a program as follows:

1. Identify and define top-level characteristics of the particular analysis to be accomplished.
2. Translate the top-level definition into a specification of the data upon which the analysis depends and a set of major processing functions of which the analysis is composed.

3. Search a library of previously built modules and identify those modules which alone or in combination will completely accomplish the desired processing functions.
4. Arrange for the development of new modules to support processing functions in the event that previously developed modules are not found in the module library.
5. In a high-level, FORTRAN-like, engineering-oriented language, specify:
   a. names and (where appropriate) initial values of data elements integral to the desired analysis,
   b. an explicit indication of the relationship between major processing functions and the modules selected from the module library,
   c. a sequence of special instructions to signal the desired performance of processing functions (i. e. , operation of executable modules) in the proper order, and
   d. any required intermediate operations between processing functions plus explicit identification of those data base elements, if any, required as input or produced as output as each function is performed.

The METAFOR program accepts the engineering language description of data base structure and functional processing sequence, retrieves the designated modules from the module library, and constructs a working data base and a supervisory FORTRAN program (i. e., driver or executive logic) which, when compiled and executed, will call the appropriate modules in the desired sequence and with the proper data base elements as arguments. Once the data base and program structure are built and bound in an executable process, METAFOR supports direct modification of initial values of data base elements, thus allowing a variety of engineering analyses to be performed.

C. Advantages and Disadvantages

Perhaps the best thing that can be said about the METAFOR program is that it accomplished the purpose for which it was intended; that is, it provided substantial automated assistance in the generation of mission simulation support programs and regular use led to significant savings in development time and cost, as well as a noticeable reduction in occurrence of errors when compared with previous experience.

There is, however, a serious practical limitation which derives from the very nature of the METAFOR-aided software construction methodology described here. Net effectiveness of the approach depends upon several factors. The module library must be complete and the individual modules must be reliable, easy to use, and understandable in function. In short, if one does not have and is not willing to establish a reasonably complete inventory of generally useful modules, there is little hope that a METAFOR-like software construction technique can help to create a substantially improved development process.

III. Automated Support to Program Development and Maintenance

Of all the typical phases of software production, several have received a large share of attention with regard to development and use of automated techniques. Consider, for the moment, that the term "development" actually applies to initial creation of a coded program and corresponding data base, and some debug and/or checkout effort done prior to formal testing. Then we may let "maintenance" apply to the same activities when accomplished after formal testing is initiated. With these admittedly simple definitions, it is possible to identify a seemingly endless list of automated tools which support software development or maintenance functions in one way or another. To supply such a list here would serve no purpose other than to bore or distract the reader. On the other hand, to isolate a few of the tools and to briefly describe a simple yet integrated tools-aided approach for part of the development activity may well persuade the reader to investigate and learn about automated development tools in greater detail.

A. Data Base Design, Implementation, and Documentation

Anyone who has spent much time producing large FORTRAN programs is all too aware of the tedious, time-consuming and error-prone task(s) of defining, creating, modifying, and documenting the program data base. For a reasonably complex program operating on a large data base, to either "design in" or assure consistent usage of data base elements can be and often is one of the most difficult jobs confronting the programmer. The reasons for the difficulty are many, including 1) lack of a facility for a top-level, functional definition of data base structure and content, and 2) a normal mode of operation which mixes and often confuses the creative task of data base definition (design) with the mechanical and tedious task of data base implementation (i. e., the actual coding of data specification statements such as COMMON, DIMENSION, EQUIVALENCE, type, and data value initialization). There are, fortunately, some good approaches to overcoming these difficulties. The following discussion concerns one such approach which has been developed and used extensively at TRW in recent years.

B. A Tools-aided Methodology for Data Base Construction

Over a period of approximately eight years, attempts to automate individual pieces of the data base development job have led to the creation and use of specialized tools. In most cases, the tools were seen as labor saving devices and consequently were directed primarily at the more mechanical aspects of data base construction and documentation. If FORTRAN programmers agree about anything, it is that the actual preparation (i. e., coding) of COMMON and EQUIVALENCE statements (as necessary to allow sharing of global storage by distinct program modules) is frustrating, tedious, and distasteful.

One of the earliest tools to be developed was designed to relieve the programmer of the most tedious as well as most error-prone part of the job. In the prototype version of the tool, the requirement was simply to accept a detailed specification of the complete program data base structure (provided by the programmer) and a list of the data element names referenced by each subprogram (also provided by the programmer) and, given this information, to automatically generate (e. g., punch) the proper COMMON, DIMENSION, and EQUIVALENCE statements for each subprogram. Early users of the tool soon found that it 1) required a considerable amount of effort on the part of the programmer, 2) caused a dramatic decrease in the amount of time and number of errors usually associated with major or minor data base modifications for large programs, and 3) provided a ready source of current documentation of a continually changing program data base.

In view of 2 and 3, programmers became convinced that the work required to make use of the tool was well worthwhile. It was only a short time, however, until additional tools were conceived and developed to help out with some of the programmer's remaining chores. One tool, for example, scanned the program source code, recognized global data base element names and, thereby, automatically produced part of the input for the previously mentioned tool. Another tool was developed to support generation of data base documentation in a variety of formats to permit direct incorporation in formal, deliverable program documentation. A number of tools were also developed to provide different types of cross reference information (e. g., such-and-such name referenced where, all names referenced there, etc.) to support analysis of the current data base configuration and in turn support ongoing data base maintenance.

As the tools grew in sophistication and number, it became clear that many of them could be integrated naturally and with little difficulty to form a flexible and easily used system of capabilities. It was felt that such a system could support diverse needs of data base developers in construction and documentation of large scale FORTRAN programs. Thus began the development of the COMGEN (Common Specification Statements Generator) System. In normal use, COMGEN supports data base development as illustrated in Figure 1.

C. COMGEN - Summary Remarks

The preceding discussion suggests the benefits to be derived from a COMGEN-aided data base development methodology, but not the limitations or problems inherent in the general approach. It is perhaps natural to view the strong FORTRAN orientation of COMGEN as a serious limitation. It should be remembered, however, that the very motivation for the tools was to overcome specific FORTRAN inadequacies and make possible an improved data base development process for large FORTRAN programs. Experience with many applications to date indicates that this purpose has been fully served, as COMGEN has helped to 1) ensure common vocabulary and consistent usage of data across software systems, 2) ensure centralized coordination, change evaluation, and control of common data, 3) permit more cost-effective utilization of resources, especially the time and energy of highly skilled people, 4) eliminate a significant source of programming errors through automation of mechanical aspects of the initial implementation and maintenance tasks, 5) encourage and support early documentation, and, 6) accomplish rapid and accurate data base modifications while providing for up-to-date data base documentation throughout the software development process.

IV. Automated Support to Program Testing

Computer program testing, as many of us have seen it or done it, can be a painful, thought-provoking, and unforgettable experience. One most often starts out expecting to get a heck of a lot out of testing and yet, when it's over, one can seldom make a strong and positive statement about what has been achieved. A fair indication of the magnitude of this problem can be obtained by finding and asking a few testers the simple question: "How much testing is enough?" There are other equally mind-boggling questions such as:

> How much confidence do you have in the program after testing is completed?

or perhaps best of all,

> What are your testing goals and how do you show that those goals are met?

These questions are hardly new and, in one form or another, are

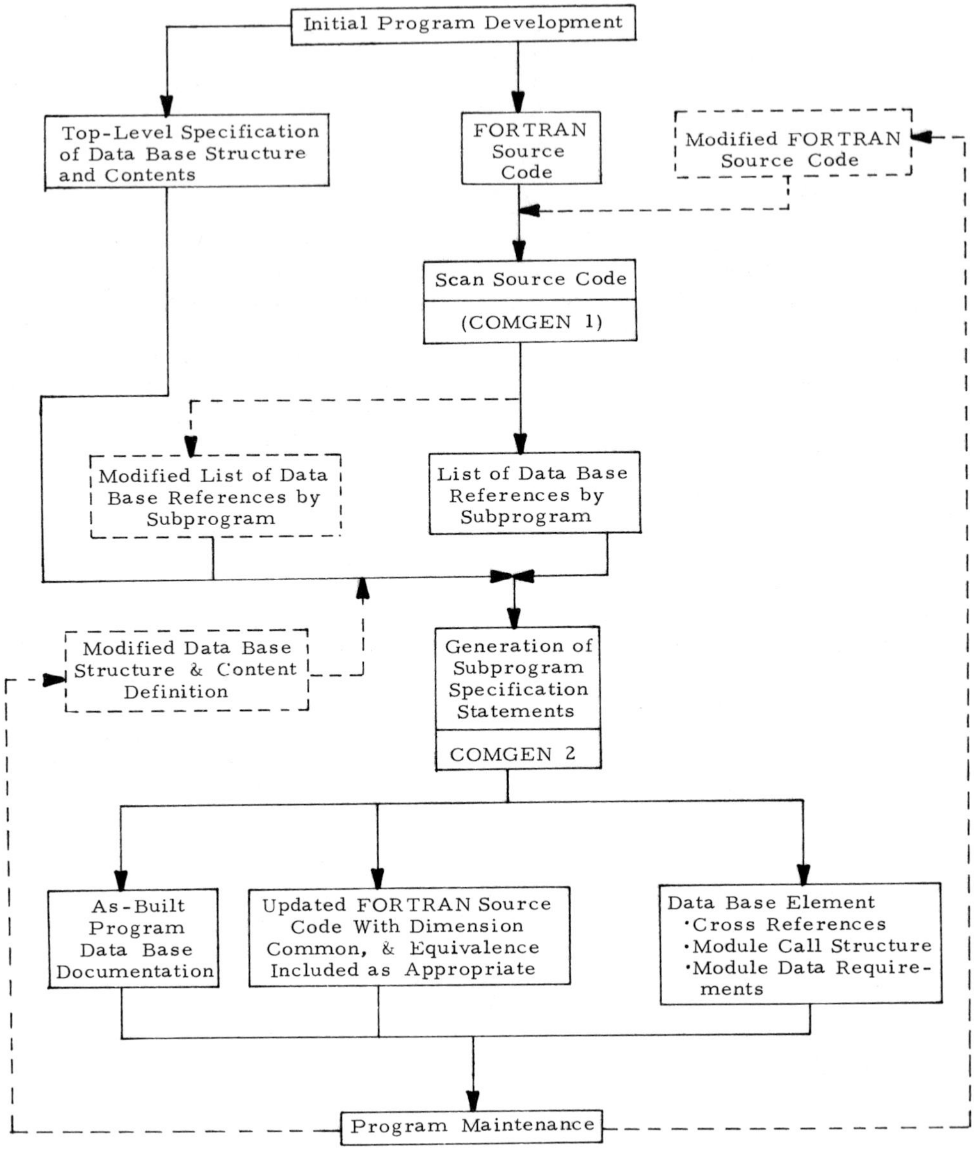
Initial Program Development
Top-Level Specification of Data Base Structure and Contents
FORTRAN Source Code
Modified FORTRAN Source Code
Scan Source Code
(COMGEN 1)
Modified List of Data Base References by Subprogram
List of Data Base References by Subprogram
Modified Data Base Structure & Content Definition
Generation of Subprogram Specification Statements
COMGEN 2
As-Built Program Data Base Documentation
Updated FORTRAN Source Code With Dimension Common, & Equivalence Included as Appropriate
Data Base Element
·Cross References
·Module Call Structure
·Module Data Requirements
Program Maintenance

Figure 1

happened upon here and there in the literature. Unfortunately, most available answers, however grand sounding, boil down to the rather unimaginative view that "testing is completed when the budget is gone and/or when the software is due to be delivered." We can get closer to the real crux of the problem through answering the questions above in the following way:

> Sufficient testing is enough.
>
> The highest possible confidence is achieved when sufficient testing is completed.
>
> To do sufficient testing is the testing goal; to demonstrate that sufficient testing has been done shows that the testing goal has been met.

Thus the three questions and their answers translate into yet another question:

> What does sufficient testing mean and how can it be measured?

In order to make any real progress toward vital and useful answers to this last question, it is worth noting Webster's definition of "sufficient"; i.e., "enough to meet the needs of a situation or a proposed end." We can conclude that "sufficient testing" has meaning only in the context of explicit, well-defined, understood, and agreed-to testing goals.

In recognition of the severe problems which can arise in the absence of carefully formulated testing goals, TRW has initiated a number of efforts to investigate, define, and promote plausible testing goals with hopes for a substantially improved software testing process. Both the feasibility and merit of establishing testing goals and measuring progress toward meeting those goals have been amply demonstrated through these efforts. But, much work remains to be done and will be done to achieve an even better understanding of what testing is, what it should be, and what can be done to make it that way.

To establish and accomplish a goal-oriented testing activity is not easy. Development of well-defined testing goals which are mutually acceptable to both contractor (i.e., the developer and tester) and the customer (i.e., the requestor and acceptor) can involve a lot of head scratching and negotiation. Measurement of progress toward achievement of the goals can require collection and analysis of a large amount of data. The latter requirement has been found to suggest a number of opportunities for automated techniques (test tools) to accomplish the collection of pertinent test information and support subsequent analysis. The remainder of this discussion is devoted to depicting the typical characteristics and usage of selected tools which directly support a goals-oriented testing process.

A. Automated Support to Program Debugging

One has to look long and hard for a computing professional who gets a big bang out of debugging. If there ever were individuals who were or aspired to be professional program debuggers, they are either very quiet about their job or have gone on to more challenging and rewarding tasks. And with good reason too, since recent years have seen the evolution of more formal and rigid testing processes and, with that formality, has come relegation of debugging to an almost mindless and highly proceduralized activity. For most of us, however, the value of and need for debugging has not been diminished. Debugging continues to be a vital and cost-effective testing activity responsible for finding and quickly fixing glaring errors which otherwise tend to be much more costly and troublesome to correct downstream in the development and testing process.

Given this general statement of purpose for a typical debugging effort, some specific tools can go a long way toward automatic accomplishment of a fairly comprehensive yet low-cost debugging job. These tools typically provide a variety of not easily distinguished capabilities. Among those capabilities, a few of the most popular involve some form of code scanning or interpretive execution of source code for the purpose of pointing out:

- violations of programming standards,
- potentially singular computations such as division by zero,
- inconsistent units, or
- coding blunders such as unreachable code, extraneous program variables (i.e., never used), and variables which are used before being set (i.e., computed or input).

A specific tool, called Code Auditor, was recently developed on TRW's Site Defense Program to support detailed audits of code for compliance with approved programming standards. In its initial implementation, Code Auditor was sought by software Product Assurance personnel charged with the task of reviewing lots of code (on the order of several hundred thousand FORTRAN source statements) in enforcement of project coding standards. Very quickly, however, programmers came to believe that they were better off finding and fixing inadvertent violations of coding standards themselves. They found, in fact, that it was desirable to do so as early as possible after code was produced in order to eliminate at least one of the possible reasons for revisiting and reworking code at a later date. Thus, the Code Auditor quickly became, and is today, a widely accepted and demonstrably beneficial adjunct to the debugging of Site Defense Software.

A desire to anticipate and protect against potential singularities has prompted the development of a specialized code scanner called the Singularity Analyzer (SINGAN). As indicated above, the primary task of SINGAN is to scan code and simply identify certain statements with some potential for attempting an ill-defined operation or singular computation. Best known examples of such operations include division by zero and attempting to compute the square root of a negative number. In actual practice, the tool need only list the statements which could conceivably cause difficulty, leaving determination of actual potential for problems to the programmer. The tool must try, however, to recognize situations where the programmer has protected against the problem (e. g. , by coding a test to jump around a given statement if necessary) in order to avoid deluging the debugging effort with irrelevant information.

Strikingly similar tools have been developed and continue to be developed to support the other types of diagnostic analysis mentioned above. A recent and very popular trend has been toward tools to automatically identify instances in which the units (i. e. , physical dimensions) of some program parameters appear to be at odds with each other. For example, the Units Consistency Analyzer (UCA) simply examines a statement such as

$$A = B + C$$

and checks to make sure that the programmer-specified units (e. g. , feet) of all parameters A, B, and C ore identical. In effect, UCA makes possible a "pretend" execution of the program through symbolic interpretation of the source code. By finding and flagging inconsistencies, UCA helps the programmer accomplish a rigorous desk check prior to first compilation and test execution.

B. Test Measurement

There are, it would seem, many ways to go about the measurement of testing. One way, however, has received more attention (in terms of development and application of support tools) than all others combined in recent years. The approach does not have a proper name so, for convenience, it will be called the "structural exercise" methodology and is so referenced in the following discussion.

The measurement technique, as implied by the term "structural exercise," is based on the simple fact that computer programs are made up of pieces or components which are strung together in some fashion to produce a program which thus has "structure." It is through execution of the components in some order prescribed by the structure that programs do the job they're supposed to do. If one thinks of a program as simply a big bunch of pieces, it is natural and not too difficult to measure program testing in terms of the pieces exercised as the program is executed.

There are a number of reasons for growth in popularity of a structural exercise test measurement methodology. For one, it can be embarrassing, if not costly, to find out that a carefully contrived set of test cases failed to exercise some piece of a program which now is giving the customer fits when he tries to use it. For another, it is often difficult to explain why a given piece of code was never executed. When an explanation is found, it is often through discovery of a logic error or some unneeded code in the program. Finding and fixing problems of this type helps the developer achieve a better understanding of internal program behavior and helps to promote a long-lasting and friendly relationship between developer and user.

In order to define a structural exercise measure of testing, one should first decide upon the basic piece or element of program structure to be used. Depending upon the level of detail at which the measurement is desired and how serious and rigorous one wants to be, some typically chosen structural elements include:

executable statement (or instruction)

transfer (or branch or arc)

segment (or node or basic block of executable statements)

path (or thread or segment string)

module (or routine or subroutine or procedure)

Regardless of which of the above elements is chosen, a measure of testing thoroughness can be defined as the ratio:

$$\frac{\text{Number of structural elements exercised by testing}}{\text{Number of structural elements comprising the program}}.$$

Seems simple enough so far and indeed it is. The hard part comes when one wants to know what got exercised and what didn't. An obvious solution to this problem lies in the development and use of a test execution monitor which can "watch" the program execute and make the needed determination automatically. There is nothing very mysterious about how such tools work or what they must do. As one might expect then, most of the large number of test measurement tools available today are pretty much the same. Since mid-1969, when TRW initiated serious efforts to formulate valid measures of structural exercise testing thoroughness and developed several prototype test measurement tools, most of the "progress" made by later entries into the test measurement arena has been in the way of new terminology to mean the same thing and new tools to do the same thing.

To a large extent, the structural program element most often chosen is the segment which is defined as a series of contiguous executable source statements for which all statements in the segment will be executed if and only if the first statement is executed. Every executable statement in a program belongs to exactly one segment and all segments taken together comprise the program. The following example is based on a recent application of one of TRW's structural exercise test measurement tools. The tool, called the Product Assurance Confidence Evaluator (PACE), is actually a system of tools which can be combined in various ways to provide automated support in test planning, test case creation and maintenance, test execution monitoring, and test evaluation. The example is primarily intended to illustrate PACE support to test monitoring and measurement, but also illustrates continued use of PACE for improvement (i. e., increased thoroughness) of testing for a specific program.

First of all, it is important to note that the example is a real one and is but one of many similar applications accomplished regularly on TRW's Site Defense Program. There is, in fact, an established requirement that Site Defense developers must construct development test cases which exercise every statement in the routines they develop and they must be able to show that they did so. Furthermore, from the preceding definition of segment, a demonstration that all segments are exercised is ample evidence that all statements are exercised as required. To complete such a demonstration without the aid of a test tool is at least a horrendous task if not an impossible one for large and/or complex programs. In order to provide the necessary support before, during, and after tests are executed, PACE is applied in a stepwise fashion as illustrated below.

The first job of the test tool is to scan the source code of a program (in this case, a FORTRAN program for the CDC 7600), identify individual fragments of code satisfying the definition of a segment, and provide the tester with a nice picture of the interrelationships among those program segments. If desired, a highly detailed description of each segment can be obtained. For each segment, a list of inputs and outputs is given, all segments which can transfer control to the segment and all segments to which the segment can transfer are identified; an index is included to permit location of the segment in the source listing, and an annotated source listing of the segmented (and appropriately indexed) program is provided.

The tester can examine the program segment structure, together with detailed information about the conditions required for executing each of the segments, and get real help in the initial formulation of test inputs which will satisfy those conditions. Now if the tester did nothing more than execute the program for each of his cases, he may think he has reason to believe that all segments will indeed be exercised. In order to confirm the belief, however, PACE adds a small amount of additional code to the program to make possible precise determination of how many times each segment is exercised as the cases are run. Actually, this addition of test monitoring code (called instrumentation) is done as part of the previously described Step 1. In view of the original requirement (i. e., exercise all segments), the mere fact that some segments were exercised zero times is a signal to the tester that more work needs to be done. PACE provides another hint to the tester by computing the previously defined measure of testing thoroughness and displaying the value as a Test Effectiveness Ratio (TER):

$$\text{TER} = \frac{\text{Number of segments exercised}}{\text{Number of segments comprising the program}} = \frac{29}{34} = .853.$$

The desired (required) TER value is, of course, 1.0, and PACE is ready to help the tester get it there. In effect, PACE explicitly identifies the as-yet-unexercised segments and, for each one, reorganizes and displays previously obtained detailed information about the specific conditions which must be met in order that the segment will be exercised.

C. Promises, Promises . . . and Pitfalls

Within the preceding discussions on debugging and test measurement, there are many suggestions as to how tools can provide automated support to program testing. In fact, the tools "promise" to lift an enormous burden from the shoulders of software developers and thereby allow development to be done in some vastly improved way. Those who might doubt the ability of tools to fulfill the promise tend to take issue with the words "enormous" and "vastly," and well they should. The born antagonist might be inclined to substitute "place" for "lift," "upon" for "from," "cause" for "allow," and "degraded" for "improved"; and there's perhaps some real benefit to be derived from doing so. The point is that one can, without much difficulty, find a case history which supports each of the extreme viewpoints. More importantly, however, the doubters and antagonists play an important (indeed essential) role in the unfolding drama of tools development. Without them, there would be no stopping the wild-eyed tools enthusiast who seems ever ready to take the plunge into never-never land. The real danger lies only partly in the plunge itself, but more so in how it may turn out. For instance, a severe, possibly fatal, blow can be dealt to an otherwise serious and productive tool development activity if one just once slips up and promises the sky but never gets off the ground. Unfortunately, there is an even greater danger. As we systematically turn over task after task to be forevermore handled by one tool or another, we tend, quite naturally, to talk ourselves into thinking that our worries are over and our problems are behind us. To the extent that we no longer have to remember how to do what we've done in the past, we are creating a situation in which we may soon lose sight of what we used to do and why we did it. If one did no more than look around at a few ongoing tool development efforts, especially those concerned with automated test data generation, it is possible to gain a greater appreciation for the potential dangers which lie ahead. Serious study, however, can help us to think of ways to continue needed development while minimizing the potentially disastrous effects of failure and eliminating the possibility that we will ultimately lose our way. This kind of thinking is essential to continued, successful tool innovation for substantial improvement of software testing.

V. Producing Probably-Correct Programs

In more or less random rambling here and there in today's software community, one can recognize the existence of certain contradictory assumptions and assertions. For example, consider the following rather ordinary remarks:

> "Program comments are meaningless. Anybody that trusts a comment to describe how a program works is asking for trouble."

> "Including frequent, descriptive comments within program source code is an essential part of producing understandable and maintainable programs."

Or the less common, but rapidly growing beliefs:

> "Proving programs to be correct is necessary if completely rigorous program verification is to be achieved."

> "Proven programs can 'correctly' solve the wrong problem" and "all of my programs are too big and complicated to permit a complete proof, anyhow."

Unfortunately, each of the statements above is all too true, and if validation of any one claim is desired, ample supporting evidence can be easily found. Nevertheless, we who have to produce software find ways to crank out a lot of code and deliver "verified" programs despite the ever-present controversy attributable to the above conflicts and numerous others.

If we take a hard look at just the two conflicts which arise from the above assertions (i. e., comment-or-not and prove-or-not), it is possible to identify a single source of difficulty which is common to both. Computer programs (especially if lengthy and complex) tend to be very hard to understand. The continuing existence of these conflicts simply implies that we have not yet come upon an approach for producing large programs which substantially helps us understand what programs really do.

The following discussion describes just such an approach in detail. The approach, called Coordinated Commentary Programming (CCP) involves the cooperative activity of two teams of programmers using specialized automated support tools in the systematic creation and use of program commentary. The discussion presents a novel use of detailed commentary to achieve succeeding levels of assurance (i. e., confidence) that a program is correct. Finally, the reader is urged to try the approach (and thus help debug it); some not-too-tough problems are discussed (and almost solved), and several additional benefits (to be accrued by the user) are thrown in for good measure.

A. Coordinated Commentary Programming: What, How, and Why

Let's assume that a large program has been written by a team of programmers called Team A. During the coding activity, a standard practice was strictly observed; that is:

> Every time a data element name is created, a textual description of the data element is added to a cumulative list of data element descriptions.

Upon completion of debug activity by Team A, the program (let's call it PROG) and the data element description list (DEDL) is given to Programmer Team B. Basically, Team B is required to achieve sufficient understanding of the program to permit the creation of textual comments which describe details of processing capability in the language of the problem domain. For example, suppose the DEDL contained:

```
        .
        .
   R  = Range of object (earth-centered) in meters
        .
        .
   RE = Radius of the earth in kilometers
        .
        .
```

And PROG contained a couple of statements like:

```
      .
      .
      .
R = SQRT (X**2 + Y**2 + Z**2)
IF  (R/1000 . . LE . RE)GO TO 936
      .
      .
      .
```

Team B should be able to construct a comment or two such as:

```
C    COMPUTE RANGE OF OBJECT FROM X, Y, Z COORDIN-
     ATES

C    HAS THE OBJECT CRASHED?
```

A very simple example was used above to illustrate the general nature of the Team B task. It is reasonable, however, to expect that Team B will face a lot of difficulty in the general case.

Some highly likely problem areas are described in succeeding paragraphs, and some basic elements of a Team B approach which serve to reduce the difficulties to an acceptable level are identified.

Frequency of Comments

There has long been (and probably will long be) a good deal of disagreement on the subject of commentary within programs. One constant dispute involves the desirable frequency or distribution of comments as they appear within a source listing. Any proposed standard (e.g., an average of one comment for every five source statements) is sure to meet up with hot, but very often sound, arguments.

Despite the anticipated arguments, however, we can see how Team B can benefit substantially if specific guidelines for commentary are established. In particular, we may adopt a policy for comments based on the previously established notion of the segment (i.e., unit) of code. Very often, the last statement of a segment is a conditional transfer of some kind. The transfer statement effectively asks a question about the current state of processing to support a decision as to how subsequent processing should proceed.

Based on a general hypothesis that a segment usually computes something and usually finishes with a question, we may establish a basic requirement for commentary. For each segment, comments should describe both the nature of the computation (e.g., COMPUTE RANGE OF OBJECT) and the nature of the transfer decision (e.g., HAS THE OBJECT CRASHED?).

It can be difficult and will probably be tedious for Team B to both identify all program segments and write one or more comments for each one. We don't know very much about automatic generation of program commentary, so it looks like Team B is definitely on the hook for that job. We do, however, know a lot about automatic identification of program segments and there are automated techniques (tools) which can accomplish that task. Use of such tools is considered to be an essential first step to be taken by Team B. The tools typically provide additional information which can help to solve some other Team B problems to be discussed later.

Understanding the Program

The "value" of the commentary produced by Team B depends largely on the ability of team members to read and understand source code written by someone else. There are certainly other potentially serious problems having to do with Team B motivation, quality of data element descriptions, time allowed to do the job, etc. We won't tackle such problems here, but will focus our attention on specific techniques and features of the approach which help Team B understand Team A-generated code.

Programs (especially large ones) have a way of becoming so complex that it is nearly impossible to develop a precise, yet concise, statement of program purpose or the meaning of the processing inherent in program purpose or the meaning of the processing inherent in program execution. Such programs often contain a large number of component parts and many decision points which imply a multitude of different ways in which the components may interact. In attempting to understand a large program, we usually are faced with a difficult dilemma. In short, in order to understand the whole, we need and seek some understanding of the component parts, but understanding a component can often require knowledge of its interactions with other components (i.e., how it "fits into" the whole).

Team B can largely overcome the dilemma through systematic use of the automatic segmentation tool mentioned earlier. First, let's see what kind of information the tool can get and keep; then, we will describe a general method of use through which Team B can draw upon the available information as needed. The tool should at least do the following:

Ingest (read in) PROG source code and DEDL

Identify all segments

For each segment:

> Identify all data element names which appear in the code and classify each as input, output or both

Identify all segments which can transfer to this segment

Identify all segments to which this segment can transfer

Accept and keep all comments and maintain correlation with appropriate segments

Support user-directed interrogation of all current information

General use of the tool is directed primarily toward the latter part of the previously stated dilemma. For example, suppose a member of Team B finds himself attempting to generate descriptive commentary for a given segment. This probably means that he has before him

a listing of the segment source code

a list of the data element names appearing in the segment, plus the classification (input, output, both) and the description (from the DEDL) for each name.

In the event that this information is insufficient, it is anticipated that some investigation of other segments will provide the necessary insight. Segments of special importance are the ones that can transfer to the given segment as well as those to which the segment can transfer. The segment of interest is designated as S_i and we define S_i^0 as the set of all segments which can transfer to or can be transferred from S_i. Similarly, the set S_i^1 contains all segments which can transfer to a member of S_i^0, plus all segments to which a member of S_i^0 can transfer. Continuing in this fashion leads to the designation of a structurally-defined, outward-expanding information base: $S_i^0, S_i^1, S_i^2, \ldots$

It is through short or extended excursions within $S_i^0, S_i^1, \ldots,$ etc., that Team B will see segment S_i in context. The tool must help Team B to conduct investigations of a very general nature as well as very detailed investigations of only selected portions of a perhaps large information base. Thus, using the tool to maximum advantage, Team B can quickly achieve a good understanding of selected segments. By the very nature of the procedure, previously commented segments provide insight into the purpose of other related segments with the end result being the completion of comments for all program segments, as required.

"Probable Correctness"

Now that we have dispelled some of the primary Team B difficulties through provision of continuous assistance with support tools, it remains to identify the principal benefits which can be derived through systematic application of the coordinated commentary programming approach.

The first, and perhaps most important benefit, involves the correctness of the program. In particular, we would like to be able to follow some procedure which would support assurance that a given program is indeed correct. The CCP approach involves Team A reviewing the comments which have been generated by Team B and comparing the independently derived statement of processing content with original Team A intentions. A good deal of assurance can be gained by simply evaluating individual segments. Much better assurance is possible, however, if Team A looks at larger pieces of the program's structure. In practice, this is accomplished by Team A using the automated segmentation support tool much the same way as Team B.

P_0-Correctness is defined to be the zero$^{\underline{th}}$ (i. e., lowest) level of assurance to be considered. This assurance can be readily obtained by Team A reviewing and accepting as valid the Team B-generated comments for each of the identified segments. The review process treats individual segments as isolated entities, thus a statement of P_0-Correct simply implies that all segments (i. e., their comments) have been looked at one at a time and each one has passed the scrutiny of Team A.

In the earlier discussion of Team B approach, the set S_i^0 was introduced. S_i^0 was defined as the set of all segments, S_j such that a) S_j can transfer to S_i or b) S_i can transfer to S_j. We may define the set, R_i, for which each element is a doublet of the form (S_j, S_i) or (S_i, S_j). Each element of R_i is interpreted as "left-most segment transfers control to right-most segment."

A statement of P_1-Correctness can be made when review and acceptance of commentary blocks (corresponding to elements of R_i for i=1 to the number of segments) has been accomplished. This is equivalent to the systematic identification of all logical transfers and, for each one, examination of the corresponding concatenation of comments from each of the segments involved in the transfer. For example, suppose PROG contains a segment 3 which can logically transfer to segment 7. Then the set R_3 would contain the doublet element (3, 7). If we assume that declarative and interrogative comments have been developed for each segment (a necessary condition for P_0-Correctness), and further consider a little more support from the automated segmentation tool, we can see that Team A will be reviewing commentary blocks something like this:

Segment 3: Input age and salary for all current employees.
More than one current employee?

Answer: Yes. (Supplied by the segmentation tool.)

Segment 7: Compute age and salary differences for two adjacent employee entries.

More differences to compute?

Note that the tool is required to not only maintain the correlation between segment number and segment comments, but to obtain (during the earlier code scan) and display assumed answers to interrogative comments. Any difficulty in doing so is strictly of the bookkeeping variety, an area in which man traditionally falls all over himself and tools come swiftly to the rescue. In this vein, the automated segmentation support tool is expressly intended to relieve Team A (and B) personnel of laborious, mechanical and mindless tasks and thereby permit concentrated attention and effort on the more thought-provoking job of achieving successively greater confidence in the correctness of a program. For example, notice that the doublet (3, 7) belongs to both R_3 and R_7. The tool "remembers" which elements have been reviewed by Team A (i.e., while marching through R_3) and can provide appropriate notification when the identical element is subsequently encountered in R_7.

If we assume that PROG is comprised of 13 segments (giving rise to $R_1, R_2, \ldots, R_{13}$) and there are a total of 20 transfers connecting these segments, then we may view the domain of interest for P_1-Correctness as the union of all R_i, that is:

$$U_1 = \bigcup_{i=1}^{13} R_i .$$

It is then a thorough investigation over U_1 which permits Team A to conclude P_1-Correctness for PROG.

The notion of P_2-Correctness follows immediately from the preceding discussion if we consider the set U_2 of elements of the form (u_i, u_j) where u_i and u_j are elements of the previously defined union set, U_1. The element formation rule for U_2 is:

$$(u_i, u_j) \in U_2 \rightarrow u_i = (S_k, S_l) \in U_1 \text{ and } u_j = (S_m, S_n) \in U_\ell \text{ and } \ell = m$$

where an element of U_2 is simply a segment triplet.

Similarly, P_3-Correctness is defined over the set U_3 of segment quadruplets which are formed by combining elements of U_1 and U_2. P_4-Correctness corresponds to the set U_4 of segment quintuplets from combinations of elements of U_2 (or alternatively from U_1 and U_3), and so on for succeeding P_i.

In general, P_i-Correctness is defined over the set U_i containing elements which are i+1-tuplets of segments. The formation of elements of U_i can be accomplished through appropriate concatenation of elements of U_1 and U_{i-1}.

B. CCP - An Evaluation

The primary objectives of the preceding discussion dealing with probable correctness were to:

1. describe an innovative approach which can lead to succeeding levels of assurance that a given program will probably perform in the intended manner, and
2. provide enough detailed information to support implementation of the approach by the interested reader.

The reader is urged to play with the approach. Experimentation should result in identification of some of the following inherent problems as well as additional benefits (and/or characteristics) which were not explicitly treated above.

Problems

Although a fairly long segment-to-segment transfer sequence looks simple enough on paper, (e.g., (1, 3, 5, 6, 9, 10, 11, 13)), the corresponding commentary block can be cumbersome. In general, one quickly becomes very irritated when forced to re-examine large commentary blocks which have been previously evaluated. One possible solution to this problem requires the reviewer to substitute a more palatable comment which summarizes the processing content of the segment sequence. This solution, however, introduces some problems (e.g., the loss of pertinent information), which require further study.

A more easily solved problem is one which is due to the existence of paths (i.e., segment sequences) which are in fact impossible to execute. It is, fortunately, a simple matter to delete the impossible sequence when recognized by Team A and, by the very nature of the process for composing subsequent U_i, the impossible path problem can be overcome without too much difficulty.

Another problem arises when either Team A or Team B detects an error in the program. In general, some effective techniques for controlling, documenting, and coordinating program changes are essential to the CCP methodology. Accommodating program changes will most likely require a cooperative and iterative mode of interaction in performance of the Team A and Team B functions.

Benefits

The realizable benefits of adopting and strictly adhering to the two-team, coordinated commentary programming methodology are thought to be numerous. Some of the more important benefits (in fact, a few receiving most of the study to date) are either listed below or are assumed to be easily derived from the summary characterization of the CCP methodology.

1. Although originally conceived as a very practical and essentially informal (i.e., not mathematically rigorous) way to evaluate and express confidence in program correctness, the unbiased activity of Team B plus the continuous support of automated tools lend a more formal, complete and rigorous flavor to the approach than planned.

2. The data element description list (DEDL) and segment sequence commentary blocks provide significant, direct support to detailed program documentation. The approach supports achievement of several long sought, but seldom attained, goals:

   to treat documentation as an integral element of the software development/verification process, and

   make effective use of automated support facilities in final document preparation.

3. The Team A programmer who habitually writes overly "sophisticated" programs to solve simple problems will soon learn that he has created unnecessary headaches for himself and others. Those who insist upon developing "monolithic monsters" will inevitably have to cope with assuring correctness through evaluation of a large number of long, ugly, and perhaps only marginally meaningful commentary blocks. In short, the approach provides positive incentives for writing straightforward, common sense, structured (at least, well-structured), and functionally modular programs as well as corresponding negative incentives which are hard to ignore.

4. Finally, and perhaps most important of all, the coordinated commentary programming methodology can be effectively employed within the framework of proven organizational structures and existing software production processes. In fact, an even stronger statement is possible. Experiments to date have shown that the methodology as a whole fits very nicely into the present "scheme of things" and ultimately serves as a natural and important adjunct to current development practices. In particular, the CCP methodology is considered to be

   compatible with known organizational (i.e., people) structures for software design, implementation, testing and documentation, complementary to current program testing methodology, consistent with efforts to prove programs correct, and

a practical set of techniques upon which innovative organizational structures and improved software production methodology can be based.

And yet, CCP does not promise to right all wrongs of the software development process, and this shortcoming is perhaps its greatest virtue. Although somewhat harsh, it is possible to view CCP as little more than a super-rigorous desk check requiring a lot more effort from programmers than one can ever expect to get. But, in this regard, CCP is certainly not alone. It is sad, but true, that real progress toward improved software production depends largely on "a lot more effort from programmers than one can ever expect to get." If that required effort can be successfully defined in terms of activities essential to software production (e.g., design, coding, verification, etc.), then we are at least headed in the right direction. Furthermore, if we carefully proceed to automate the drudgery, but avoid supplanting human judgment, then the chances of actually getting that extra effort will be significantly improved. Real improvement of software construction and verification technology can only come from an in-depth understanding of the functions we perform and a conscientious and constructive effort to do each one of them in a better way.

FORTRAN—CAN IT BE STRUCTURED AND SHOULD IT BE?

Ellis Horowitz

There is no doubt about it, structured programming (s. p.) is making waves. Wherever one goes within the computing community people are asking what it is and how they can use it. And they are receiving answers, but sometimes very different answers. This inability to pin down a precise definition has caused s. p.'s original conception to be widely distorted. For example, a recent advertisement described s. p. as follows "a means of improving the quality of the code, improving project control, reducing the debugging phase of the project, forcing good software documentation as an integral part of the system design, and making programs less sensitive to turnover of project personnel." [1] Thus portrayed as a panacea for the entire programming process, it is not surprising that in a recent week-long seminar given by Dr. Dijkstra, he refused to use the term at all.

To put s. p. in perspective let us consider the entire software development process as it is usually thought of, divided into four phases: requirements, design, coding, and testing. Let us look at these four stages to see what maxims s. p. preaches.

A literal analysis of Dijkstra's Notes on Structured Programming [2] would lead us to the coding stage. One message here is that the programming language we write in should provide constructs which allow us to easily express what it is we want to accomplish. The expressive limitations of our language can limit our ability to describe complex processes. Though no ideal s. p. language exists today, one can point to several desirable features which are clearly absent in the popular COBOL and FORTRAN languages. Another message of s. p. for the coding phase is that the static text should mirror as closely as possible the dynamic execution of the program. Another way to say this is that the flow of control during execution should be forward except, obviously, for loops. This and the previous maxim have as a corollary that only careful use of the GO TO statement should be made. Unfortunately the GO TO controversy temporarily overshadowed the broader implications of s.p. and is still mistakenly associated by some as its major message. But this emphasis seems to be waning. To quote from Knuth, "What we really want is to conceive of our program in such a way that we rarely even think about GO TO statements, because the need hardly every arises." [3]

Another maxim of s.p. at the coding stage is proper indentation of code. The goal here is to exploit the two-dimensional possibilities of the paper we write on rather than forcing us to concentrate our understanding on a linearly written text. If I had to sum up these three maxims into one word, readability would be it; accomplished through the use of good language features, program organization and program cosmetics.

But a literal analysis of Dr. Dijkstra's notes does not really do them justice. Dijkstra himself says that he would prefer to speak of large systems, but he is constrained to use small examples. Many of his rules exhibited for a small program hold equally well for doing top level design of a large system. As applied to the design phase, s.p. emphasizes the notions of top-down construction via levels of abstraction or refinement. His strategy begins with a well-defined task, and calls for breaking it into manageable pieces. At each breakpoint one must carefully consider the alternatives and, to whatever extent possible, the implications of one design choice over another. In any case only a single design decision should be made at each stage. By following this process one creates a tree structure where the nodes represent further refinements of the design of the program.

By way of a brief example consider Dijkstra's development of the primes program. The root node of his tree is simply the statement of the problem:

"print the first 1000 prime numbers"

and his first refinement is to create for the root 2 sons, one which is

"compute the first 1000 primes"

and the other

"print the first 1000 primes."

As trivial as they may seem the decision to hold all 1000 primes before printing is not necessarily the best answer in all contexts. Such a decision might have been unwise if, say, the machine is very fast but short on memory. But right or wrong, the virtue of a single, well-defined decision at each node makes it easier to go back and modify the program. The careful delineation of module interfaces and the notion of reducing module interconnectivity is not new, but is accepted as a valid design principle.

S.p. has another goal which it hopes to achieve via these levels of abstraction and that is provability. Where it is possible to prove that a program is correct the absence of errors are guaranteed. But program proving is an art, perhaps more difficult than program writing and testing. By introducing these levels of refinement one breaks the program proving process down into smaller pieces. Thus at each node of the tree one need only prove the newly refined code while the code which comes from a higher level remains intact and is still valid. By the way, a proof does not necessarily have to be done by formal techniques of axioms and rules of inference. Informal methods may be just as valid and far easier for generating a proof.

In conclusion, s.p. emphasizes three criteria for the design and coding phase in addition to the two commonly accepted criteria of correctness and efficiency. These are that the program should also be 3) readable, 4) modifiable and 5) provable. The aggressive pursuit of these goals will have positive impact on the design, coding, and testing phases of any software project. But the ultimate effectiveness of s.p. will depend upon the ability of people to apply its rules.

Other methodologies and tools have recently been suggested for improving programmer productivity. One such technique is the concept of the chief programmer team as described by Baker and Mills [13]. Another tool is the structured HIPO which stands for hierarchical, input, process, output. This is basically a set of forms within which one can describe the top-down refinement of a process plus specify precisely the different modules. Figure 1 shows a typical HIPO package of forms. The top diagram numbers the different modules and reveals through the tree structure their interrelationships. The PROCESS form allows for the specification of input and output variables plus a description of the actions to be performed on them.

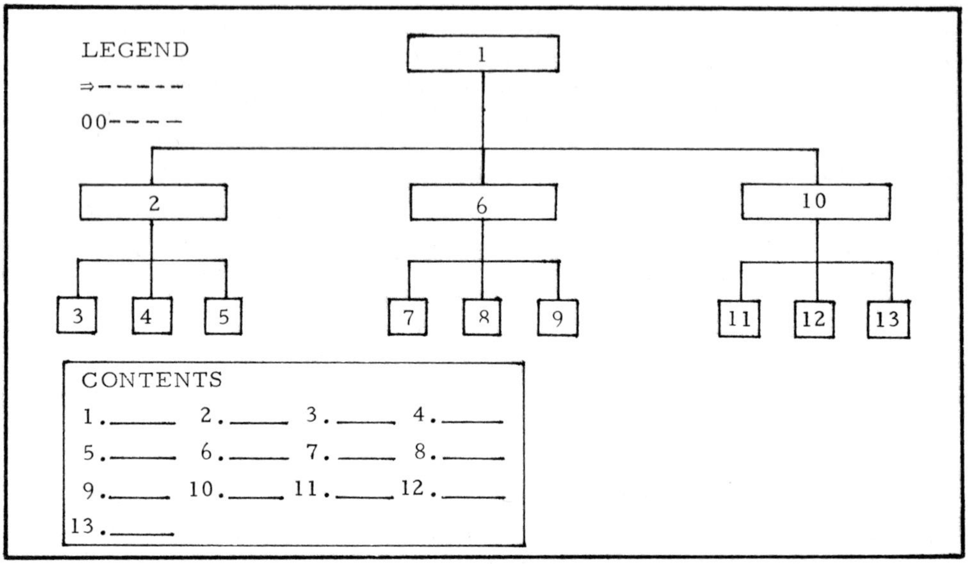

TABLE OF CONTENTS

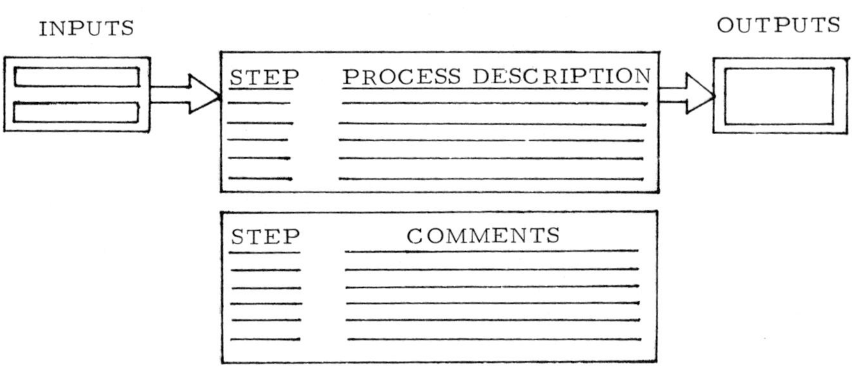

PROCESS FORM

Figure 1. A HIPO Package

Another technique is the idea of the structured walk-through [14]. This is primarily a management tool which calls for periodic project reviews that concentrate on specific parts or persons within the project. A group convenes with the purpose of critically analyzing the work product of the reviewee. This work product may be expressed using the previously described HIPO documentation or it may already be in coded form. The objective of the walk-through is to check that all specifications have been included within the design and further on that particular subsystems have no internal or external inconsistencies. A side effect of the walk-through is to create greater visibility of the entire project among its members.

Structured HIPOs and walk-throughs represent two reasonably well defined practices for improving the quality control of software development. Unfortunately there is no quantitative data on the effectiveness of these procedures. Moreover, any existing data is always subject to the variations in attitude and ability of the people who used them. This proviso has also been a factor in judging the effectiveness of s.p.

Nevertheless all of these ideas have proved useful and it is with this spirit that I come to the main subject of this paper, structured FORTRAN or s. F. As I am writing this I cannot help but be somewhat fearful of the rancor I will receive from my academic colleagues by even mentioning such an idea. To perpetuate FORTRAN with some cosmetic surgery will doubtlessly seem like a cardinal sin, designed to impede even further its eventual demise. Personally I find such an attitude parochial in the sense that it lacks an understanding of the factors which influence the commercial (as opposed to the academic) computing marketplace. Though some of these factors are deleterious, others reflect real strengths of the language. One factor which helps FORTRAN (and COBOL) to maintain their preeminence is the lack of a truly outstanding better successor. Other factors such as the cost effective facility of independent compilation, existing subroutine libraries, a standardized subset and the existence of good compilers almost everywhere represent great strengths. Any tool for beefing up FORTRAN should not destroy these advantages.

What exactly is s. F.? It is an attempt to add new syntactical constructs which allow for greater clarity of expression and consequently improved readability. At the same time the intent is to stay very close to FORTRAN so as to make adoption by programmers easy and, perhaps, conversion of programs easier than normal. The mechanism for implementing this idea is via the notion of a preprocessor. Such a program accepts statements in s.F. and produces statements which accomplish the same task, but in conventional FORTRAN, (see Figure 2).

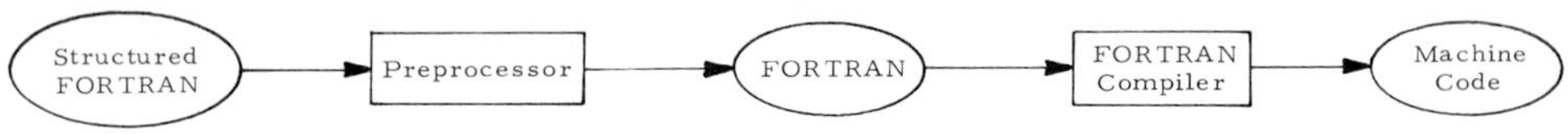

Figure 2. Structured FORTRAN to Machine Code

Basic Features

S.F. is not exactly a new idea, it has already been tried by many groups and used successfully. This author is now aware of six such preprocessors and this section is a compendium of their efforts. None of the systems have adopted all of the features I will describe but several are quite close. Though one or two of the efforts have not caught on, the others seem to be thriving. To describe the statements let S, T, $S_1, \ldots, S_N$ represent arbitrary size groups of FORTRAN statements having no restrictions. Also let BEXPR stand for any legal Boolean expression and AEXPR any arithmetic expression. Each statement is described below by giving its syntax and its translation into conventional FORTRAN. Figure 3 represents an IFTHENELSE statement

```
syntax                         translation
IF(BEXPR)                    IF(.NOT.(BEXPR))GO TO 100
   THEN                          S
      S                          GO TO 101
   ELSE                   100    T
      T
ENDIF                     101
```

Figure 3. IF Statement

The ELSE part is optional and either S, T or both may contain other s.F. statments. Note how separate lines are used for the IF, THEN, ELSE and ENDIF. These are not necessary though they are convenient for the preprocessor. Looking at the translation we see that two new labels had to be generated. Most of the systems start internally generated labels at 99999 and work down, presumably minimizing the chance of any conflict. In practice the label 100 above can be attached to the first statement of T if that statement is unlabeled. Otherwise we can use that label except for one or two circumstances; e.g., T begins with a FORMAT statement.

Figures 4 and 5 describe two common forms of iteration statements, the WHILE and UNTIL loops. Both statements have been used extensively by Dr. Dijkstra. In fact, Bohm and Jacopini have shown that all proper programs can be rewritten using only the IFTHENELSE, and the WHILE or UNTIL statements to alter the normal flow of control. But this does not mean we should constrict ourselves to use only these forms. On the contrary the most powerful and descriptive devices we can think of should be employed where it is appropriate.

syntax		translation
WHILE(BEXPR)	101	IF(.NOT.(BEXPR)) GO TO 100
S		S
ENDWHILE		GO TO 101
	100	

Figure 4. WHILE Statement

syntax		translation
DO	100	S
S		IF(.NOT.(BEXPR)) GO TO 100
UNTIL(BEXPR)		

Figure 5. UNTIL Statement

We now come to a generalized form of the FORTRAN DO statement, see Figure 6 below. The notation <vble> stands for any legal FORTRAN identifier, while AEXP1, AEXP2, AEXP3 are arithmetic expressions. Semantically AEXP1 is the starting value for <vble> and AEXP2 is the terminating value. AEXP3 is the difference by which <vble> is changed each time execution returns to the beginning of the loop. Note how this permits increasing and decreasing values for <vble>. All of the variables making up these three expressions can be altered within S with subsequent effects on the difference added and the terminating condition. Though this corrects many of the major deficiencies of FORTRAN's DO loop it has its own pitfalls of which the programmer should be aware.

```
        syntax                          translation

FOR <vble> = AEXP1,             <vble> = AEXP1
          AEXP2,AEXP3           GO TO 100
        S                   101 <vble> = <vble> + AEXP3
ENDFOR                      100 IF((<vble> - AEXP2)*AEXP3.GT.0)
                                                   GO TO 102
                                      S
                                      GO TO 101
                            102
```

Figure 6. FOR Statement

For example if (<vble>- AEXP2)*AEXP3 is a floating point zero, how will that compare with the fixed point zero in the translated IF statement? Another difficulty may occur as seen in this descending loop:

```
N = 10
FOR I = N, 0, -I/2
    S
ENDFOR
```

which causes I to take on the values 10, 5, 3, 2, 1 while -I/2 or AEXP3 will be -5, -2, -1, -1, -0. Is there any distinction made between zero, minus zero, fixed or floating point zeros. The only consolation is that if these problems of mixed mode arithmetic and different representations of zero are understood within the FORTRAN context, then the same rules apply to s.F.

Another useful statement is called the LOOP WITH EXIT as defined in Figure 7.

syntax		translation
LOOP	100	S
S		IF (BEXPR) GO TO 101
IF (BEXPR) EXIT		T
T		GO TO 100
ENDLOOP	101	CONTINUE

Figure 7. LOOP with EXIT

The LOOP-ENDLOOP is an infinite loop and so there must be a way of exiting. One way this is done is by the EXIT statement which is a transfer to the statement immediately following ENDLOOP. The EXIT statement can also be used unconditionally as it is shown above. The LOOP statement is often useful since the WHILE/UNTIL statements can cause clumsy things to be done because their test is at either the beginning or the end of the iteration. A good example of this difficulty is revealed by the code of Figure 7 which is not easy to express using only the WHILE or UNTIL loops. The use of the EXIT is not restricted to a LOOP statement, but it can be used to exit from any innermost iteration.

The final statement is the CASE, first proposed by C.A.R. Hoare Its form is a conceptually clear way of describing a multiway branch.

The statement as described below is considerably more general than with what one can achieve if the translation uses a computed GO TO. Though more expensive, the rewards seem worth the cost. For example, if AEXP evaluates to an integer in the range 1 to N, then AEXPi should be i. But if we would like AEXP1 to work in the range 1 through 5 and 7, then we can introduce some more syntax and write

(AEXP1) as (1.TO. 5, 7).

Other generalizations are easily imagined.

```
syntax                          translation

CASE(AEXP)                      IF(AEXP1.NE.AEXP)GO TO 101
  (AEXP1)                          S1
          S1                       GO TO 100
  (AEXP2)          101          IF (AEXP2.NE.AEXP) GO TO 102
          S2                       S2
         ...                       GO TO 100
  (AEXPn)                          .
                                   .
          Sn                       .
  ELSE             100+n-1      IF(AEXPn.NE.AEXP) GO TO 100+n
        Sn+1                       Sn
ENDCASE                            GO TO 100
                   100+n        CONTINUE
                                   Sn+1
                   100          CONTINUE
```

Figure 8. CASE Statement

An Example

Armed with these new constructs we are now ready to tackle an example. Suppose we have an ordered array of integers stored in ITEM(1), . . . , ITEM(N) and we wish to determine if NUMBER is present in this list. N is small enough so we can do an in-core binary search of this array, returning either zero or the index into the array where NUMBER is found. In s. F. the program becomes

```
      INTEGER FUNCTION BINSRH (NUMBER, ITEM, N)
C     NUMBER IS AN INTEGER
C     ITEM IS AN ORDERED ARRAY OF INTEGERS FROM 1 TO N
C     IN INCREASING ORDER
C     BINSRH APPLIES THE METHOD OF BINARY SEARCH TO
C     DETERMINE IF NUMBER IS PRESENT. IF SO ITS PLACE
C     IN THE ARRAY IS RETURNED ELSE ZERO.
      INTEGER BOT, TOP
      BINSRH = 0
      BOT = 0
```

```
      TOP = N+1
      WHILE (BOT+1.LT.TOP)  $ITEM(BOT)< NUMBER<
                                 ITEM(TOP)$
        MID = (BOT+TOP)/2
        IF(ITEM(MID).LT.NUMBER)
          THEN
            BOT = MID
          ELSE
            IF(ITEM(MID).GT.NUMBER)
                THEN
                  TOP = MID
                ELSE
                  GO TO 10
            ENDIF
        ENDIF
      ENDWHILE
C     NUMBER NOT PRESENT, BOT+1.GE.TOP
      RETURN
C     NUMBER IS FOUND
10    BINSRH = MID
      RETURN
      END
```

The above program is written in s. F. and makes use of the WHILE and two nested IF statements. The GO TO seems preferable here since we wish to exit but not immediately outside the WHILE clause. Below is the resulting FORTRAN which would be produced by the preprocessor.

```
      INTEGER FUNCTION BINSRH(NUMBER, ITEM, N)
C     NUMBER IS AN INTEGER
C     ITEM IS AN ORDERED ARRAY OF INTEGERS FROM
C     1 TO N IN INCREASING ORDER
C     BINSRH APPLIES THE METHOD OF BINARY SEARCH TO
C     DETERMINE IF NUMBER IS PRESENT. IF SO ITS PLACE
C     IN THE ARRAY IS RETURNED ELSE ZERO
      INTEGER BOT, TOP
      BINSRH = 0
      BOT = 0
      TOP = N+1
C     ITEM(BOT)< NUMBER< ITEM(TOP)
 101  IF(.NOT.(BOT+1.LT.TOP))GO TO 100
        MID = (BOT+TOP)/2
        IF(.NOT.(ITEM(MID).LT.NUMBER)GO TO 102
          BOT = MID
          GO TO 102
 102      IF(.NOT.(ITEM(MID).GT.NUMBER)GO TO 104
```

```
                TOP = MID
                GO TO 105
   104          GO TO 100
   105          CONTINUE
   103          GO TO 101
C NUMBER NOT PRESENT,BOT+1.GE.TOP
   100   RETURN
   NUMBER IS FOUND
   10    BINSRCH = MID
         RETURN
         END
```

I believe that if one looks at these two programs the virtue of the structured version will be evident. A binary search program written by hand would not be much better, but at least the .NOT.'s would be removed. Notice the double GO TO which starts at statement 102 through 104 and out of the WHILE loop to 100. Such code could be greatly refined with a two pass processor but it causes only slight overhead in the resulting machine code.

Other Features

As with all languages there are often auxiliary frills which make them more attractive. Such is the case for s.F. One feature was shown in the previous example where a comment was added to the right of a WHILE statement. Some of the systems allow for commenting on all statements using a special character as a delimiter. These comments are then reformatted by the preprocessor to agree with the FORTRAN comments convention. Another feature is the automatic indentation of both the s.F. source and the resulting object FORTRAN. This can relieve the keypuncher of a lot of tedium.

A third facility is the ability to define macros within a subroutine. There is considerable variation here among the systems that were studied, but the most general facility allows both for parameters and the nesting of macro calls. Such a feature can be usefully employed with the notion of levels of refinement as advocated within the s.p. philosophy.

Another feature allows one to write a FORTRAN DO loop without supplying a label, which is automatically generated by the preprocessor.

Finally a most important requirement for the preprocessor is the ability to do error detection. Missing END statements is a common occurrence. Some of the early trials with s.F. have done poorly because of strange, unintelligible diagnostics emanating from the preprocessor. If evangelism followed by conversion is to take place the path to salvation must be made clear and smooth.

Figure 9 gives a capsule summary of the six systems on which I have statistics. It summarizes their features at the point of time when they either wrote their documentation or spoke to me on the phone. However many of these efforts are evolving and may have improved or changed their facilities by the time this is read.

Other features, not directly connected with s.p. suggest themselves. A nice way of handling character strings would be very useful. Simplified facilities for doing fancy output such as report generation would be nice. Given almost any application area, new attributes for the preprocessor could be conceived. In fact an entire conference on FORTRAN preprocessors for numerical software was held recently [15].

Pros and Cons

Finally we come to the balance sheet for s.F. Let us begin with its positive aspects. First and foremost it corrects the paucity of language constructs which now exist in FORTRAN. These new elements, it is argued by our most prestigious computer scientists, lead to improved thinking on the part of the programmer and to more transparent programs. Such claims were supported in one test made by J. Flynn at J.P.L. [11]. He reports a 10 : 1 ratio of time saved on a project that used his SFTRAN. If other experiments observe even more modest improvements, then this tool will be worth its while.

Another positive aspect is that these preprocessors are simple to implement and inexpensive to run. All of the systems studied had sizes of around 8k words. Though compilation speeds were not generally available, the IFTRAN system at TSC, which double buffers it I/O, processes about 100 cards per second on a CDC 6400. Therefore such a system can be easily built in-house, is efficient to run, and can be maintained internally with little trouble.

Finally a third virtue is its closeness to FORTRAN. All of the advantages of writing in FORTRAN are preserved; e.g., relative portability and the ability to use previously developed programs. The other aspect of this closeness to FORTRAN is the psychological impact of transferring to a new language. This impact is considerably lessened with s.F. and will not pose the same kind of threat for the programmer than other conversions do. The evolution to newer (and hopefully better) languages will be a slow process.

EFFORTS / FACILITIES:	IF	WHILE	UNTIL	CASE	FOR	LOOP	EXIT	MACROS	INDENTS
1) IFTRANX	√	√		√			√	√	√
2) SFTRAN	√	√	√	√		√	√	*	√
3) SPIFFY	√	√	√	√	√		√	* ↑	√
4) IFTRAN	√	√						√ ↑	√
5) DEFT	√			√		√	√	√ ↑	√
6) SPFORT	√	√	√	√				* ↑	√

* means available without parameters

↑ means no nesting of macros allowed

FIGURE 9: Summary of Capabilities for 6 Structured FORTRANs

Now for the negative factors. An important issue is the question of what to do if the software product is a deliverable. Does one supply the s. F. source with the preprocessor or the resulting object FORTRAN? The former might be a nice solution, but a customer might soon find he has as many different s. F. preprocessors as he has contract software. The alternative solution is more practical, but would probably require a pass, either manual or automatic, to clean up the code. This will include removing extraneous CONTINUE's, eliminating double jumps, and getting rid of some .NOT.'s. Much of this could be accomplished by the preprocessor at the expense, however of increased compilation time. For in-house development though, a local s. F. would not have to overcome this consideration.

Another factor is that the object FORTRAN may be 10-15 percent longer than if handwritten. This overhead may be intolerable for small machine configurations.

A rather interesting difficulty arose at TRW where they have an on-line debugging system [12]. They decided to try and use it on s. F., but the system is designed to break at labels. Since s. F. discourages the use of GO TO's, it also discourages labels and the people at TRW found that they could not make easy use of their debugging tool. This is now corrected.

CONCLUSION

In the end s. F. is just a tool like so many others. Writing in it does not necessarily mean that one is doing s. p., since we have seen that using the special language features is only one part of the concept. But it is a step forward. Finally one must ask the question: why should we not just go to an entirely different (and better) language where the "structure" has been built in in a more natural way. Hopefully the answer to this question will be clear.

REFERENCES

1. Computerworld, June 26, 1974, p. 3.
2. Dijkstra, E., "Notes on structured programming," Structured Programming, Academic Press, New York, 1972, pp. 1-75.
3. Knuth, D., "Structured programming with GO TO statements," Computing Surveys, vol. 6, no. 4, January 1975, pp. 261-302.

4. Steele, G. and A. E. Sedgwick, "DEFT: a disciplined extension of FORTRAN," Technical Report No. 62, Department of Computer Science, University of Toronto, 1974.

5. Cohen, M., "IFTRAN, a structured extension to FORTRAN," Technical Report, Technology Service Corp., 225 Santa Monica Boulevard, Santa Monica, California, March 7, 1974.

6. Press, B., three sheets describing structured FORTRAN at TRW called SPFORT, TRW, 1 Space Park, Redondo Beach, California 90278.

7. Miller, Edward F., IFTRANX, FORTRAN Preprocessor for Structured Programming, Program Validation Project, General Research Corporation, 5383 Hollister Avenue, P.O. Box 3587, Santa Barbara, California 93105.

8. Flynn, J.A., "SFTRAN User Guide," Jet Propulsion Laboratory, 4800 Oak Grove Drive, Pasadena, Calif. 91103, July 31, 1973.

9. Carpenter, Loren, "Spiffy," Boeing Company, Seattle, Washington, (206) 237-8090.

10. Cook, J., "MORTRAN," SLAC, computation group at Stanford University, Stanford, California.

11 Flynn, J., personal communication.

12. Press, B., personal communication.

13. Baker, F. T. and H. D. Mills, "Chief programmer teams," Datamation, December 1973, pp. 58-61.

14. "Structured walk-through: a project management tool," IBM Data Processing Division, August 1973, 14 pages.

15. Workshop on FORTRAN Preprocessors for Numerical Software, sponsored by JPL and ACM-SIGNUM, JPL, Pasadena, California, November 7-8, 1974.

AUTOMATED TOOLS AND TECHNIQUES ASSISTING IN SOFTWARE DEVELOPMENT

Leon G. Stucki

THE NATURE OF THE PROBLEM

Programming has been described by Dijkstra as the most complex mental activity ever undertaken by mankind [1]. Advances in computer hardware capabilities have brought previously unsolvable problems into the scope of solvability. Rapidly increasing reliance upon the correct behavior of complex software systems is being experienced by both government and private industry alike. As new systems realizing more complex hardware and software functions continue to evolve, accurate and efficient implementation of these systems is of critical concern.

The analogy comparing software to a "black box" tends to illustrate the mysticism attached by many to a software system whose internal behavior is not clearly understood. Any given software module contains many decision points, each branch of which may be exercised with varying frequency. The problem of measuring the actual behavior of complex software affects the validation of that software and represents a new phase in the measurement of computer systems.

Various monitoring and measuring processes have been applied to ensure hardware performance and quality. For these systems criteria have been established against which reference measurements can be clearly defined. Early attempts to apply measurement techniques to computer systems centered on efforts to monitor hardware utilization. In the attempt to further improve hardware utilization and performance, many aids ranging from optimized compilers to execution monitors have been developed. Performance has been the primary consideration in these attempts.

The problem of software validation calls for a deeper understanding of software behavior. Questions of performance and speed, though important, become secondary to the question of whether or not the software produces valid answers meeting problem requirements. New techniques are needed to develop specific tools that will validate and verify evolving software systems.

THE PROGRAM EVALUATOR AND TESTER SYSTEM

The Program Evaluator and Tester (PET) is a prototype program test evaluation tool which automatically generates self-metric (self-measuring) software from existing software. FORTRAN implementation of this technique demonstrates its value for other higher-level languages such as COBOL and JOVIAL. Further, the design and implementation of PET suggest a pattern applicable to the development of more powerful software testing systems. The PET system employs a technique for measuring computer systems through probes selectively applied to the software. The self-metric instrumentation approach to the measurement of dynamic program behavior is a technique to build self-measurement capabilities into source language programs by preprocessing the original program or by augmenting the compiler to perform the necessary instrumentation. After the program is made self-metric, it is then executed; and a subsequent post-processing step generates a report on actual program behavior.

SOURCE PROGRAM INSTRUMENTATION

Figure 1 shows a sample FORTRAN program segment and its related flow diagram. Optional instrumentation points are identified for three sets of sensors applicable to this particular program segment. The execution-count sensors are shown at all points on the flow diagram where the internodal traversal frequency is not obvious.

These execution-count sensors can be realized most efficiently by associating a unique counting cell with such sensor and by inserting these sensors at only those points where logical program breaks occur. The min/max/first/last sensors for assignment statements appear following nontrivial assignment statements. A trivial assignment statement, or one in which a constant or literal is assigned to a variable, generates no instrumentation. The min/max/first/last sensors for DO-loop control variables are inserted after the label or statement number, if present, and before the invocation of the loop if variable parameters are used in any of the three loop-controlling fields.

```
      .
      .
      .
      N = 100
   5  DO 15 I = J, N, K
      IF(I-K) 10, 10, 15
  10  C = A(I)* B(I) + C
  15  B(I) = 1
      N = 10
      .
      .
      .
```

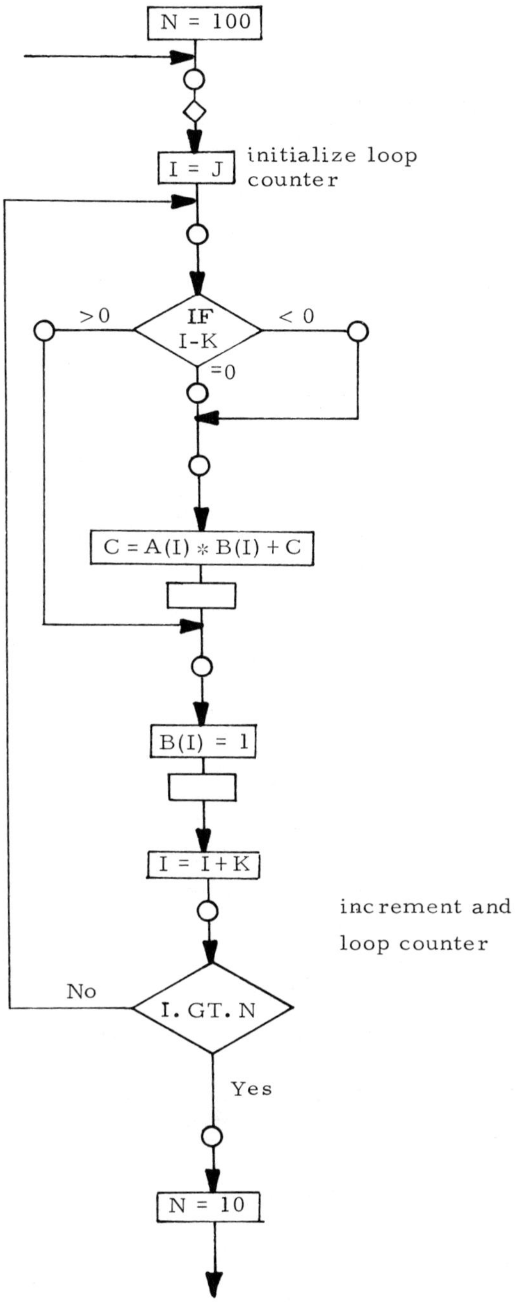

Legend of Optional Instrumentation

- ○ Execution-count sensors
- ▭ MIN/MAX/FIRST/LAST Sensors for nontrivial assignment statements
- ◇ MIN/MAX/FIRST/LAST sensors for DO-LOOP control variables

Figure 1. FORTRAN Program Segment Showing Optional Instrumentation

Two techniques have been used experimentally to implement these and several other types of software sensors: (1) direct code insertion, and (2) invocation of run-time routines. The direct code insertion of placement of all counters directly into the source program appears to be faster in most cases; but invoked by instrumented CALL statements are more flexible, for measurements can be more easily altered at execution time.

The profile produced by running the instrumented application program contains part or all of the following measurements:

1. The number and percentage of all potential executable source statements which were executed one or more times.
2. The number and percentage of those program branches taken.
3. The number and percentage of those subroutine calls which were executed.
4. The number of times each subroutine was called, together with a list of those subroutines that were never entered.
5. Relative timing on the subroutine level.
6. Specific data associated with each executable source statement.
   a. Detailed execution counts.
   b. Detailed branch counts on all IF and GOTO statements.
   c. Optional data range values (min/max/first/last) on assignment statements.
   d. Optional min/max ranges on DO-loop control variables.

These summaries and detailed reports can be employed to quantify the degree of testing to which the program has been subjected.

The measurements performed allow examination of the internal structure of a software system rather than mere treatment of it as a "black box." While the testing process does not technically prove the correctness of the algorithms used, it does allow observation of the behavior of the algorithms with actual test data. From these observations, the effectiveness of the software validation process can be greatly improved.

DEVELOPMENT OF THE PROGRAM EVALUATOR AND TESTER

The Program Evaluator and Tester consists of two major components: (1) a highly structured preprocessor which instruments the source program to make it self-metric, and (2) a postprocessor which generates reports from the execution measurement data produced by the instrumented self-metric software. Both of these test system components are written in a high-level language to create a more easily maintained system. Development of the preprocessor was accomplished through the use of the McDonnell Douglas Metatranslator.

This powerful software development system provides a concise well-structured language for the specification and automatic generation of language processing systems. The Metatranslator written in its own Metalanguage has been used to generate the current FORTRAN versions of the Program Evaluator and Tester, a Metaassembler for NASA's SUMC computer family, and the Metatranslator itself.

The language processors generated by the Metatranslator are easily extensible. The structured Metalanguage of the Metatranslator is transformed into a machine-independent, high-level language (currently ASA standard FORTRAN IV); thus, the language processors generated by the Metatranslator are machine independent and will run on any machine supporting an ASA Standard FORTRAN IV Compiler.

The postprocessor component of the Program Evaluator and Tester will generally be written in the same high-level source language for which the test system was designed. For the current FORTRAN Program Evaluator and Tester systems, a FORTRAN postprocessor was built. For a proposed COBOL system, a COBOL postprocessor is specified.

SAMPLE TEST RESULTS

Some sample parameters currently being produced by the Program Evaluator and Tester appear in Figs. 2 through 5. Figure 2 shows various detailed program behavioral measures: (1) the frequency with which each potentially executable statement is executed; (2) the number of times each potential branch within a program is executed; (3) the data range information associated with each nontrivial assignment statement. The program segment shown in Fig. 2 is from an actual eigenvalue and eigenvector routine which had been in a production status for a period of time. (Note the logically impossible program flow path which was found when executed by the Program Evaluator and Tester.)

Original Source Code	Count	Branch Counts, Truth Values MIN/MAX/FIRST/LAST Values			
360 E(I) = NORM	1066	MIN = 3.897 E-04	MAX = 4.213 E-10		
380 CONTINUE	3790				
TEMP = C*E(NUM1)*S*D(NU)	117	MIN = -1.56 E-03	MAX = 3.143 E-03		
D(NU) = S*E(NUM1)*C*D(NU)	117	MIN = -1.20 E-01	MAX = 3.238 E-01		
E(NUM1) = TEMP	117	MIN = -1.36 E-03	MAX = 3.143 E-03		
GO TO 210	117	BRANCH1 117			
500 PP = ABS(P)	3790	MIN = 1.285 E-03	MAX = 9.425 E-01		
QQ = ABS(Q)	3790	MIN = 1.340 E-13	MAX = 4.213 E-01		
IF (QQ.GT.PP) GO TO 510	3790	TRUE 1071	FALSE 2719		
NORM = PP*SQRT(1.0+(QQ/P)**2)	2719	MIN = 4.584 E-04	MAX = 9,423 E-01		
GO TO 520	2719	BRANCH 1 2719			
510 IF (QQ.EQ.0) GO TO 530 (NEVER TRUE)	1071	TRUE 0	FALSE 0171		
NORM = QQ*SQRT(1.0+(PP/QQ)**2)	1071	MIN = 1.684 E-03	MAX = 4.213 E-01		
520 C = P/NORM	3790	MIN = 1.00 E+00	MAX = 1.000 E+00		
S = C/NORM	3790	MIN = -9.89 E-01	MAX = 9.999 E-01		
GO TO RETURN, (31-, 340, 340)	3790	BRANCH1 117	BRANCH2 2607	BRANCH3 1066	
530 C = 1.0	0				
S = 0.0 Impossible to reach	0				
NORM = 0.0	0				

Figure 2. Sample PET Program Output

Syntactic Profile

Total Number of Source Statements		1246
Type of Statement	Number	Percent of Total
Executable Source	792	63.6
Nonexecutable Source	168	13.5
Comment	266	23.0
Nonstandard	10	0.8
Branch	274	N/A
Call	24	N/A
Unformatted I/O	0	N/A
Formatted I/O	61	N/A

Operational Profile

Total Execution Count		1889544
Type of Statement	No. Executed	Percent Executed
Executable Source	288	36.4
Branch	77	28.1
Call	14	58.3
Unformatted I/O	0	100.0
Formatted I/O	3	4.9

Figure 3. Program Evaluation and Tester Report for Program AB33A

Program Evaluator and Tester Report Subroutine Timing Survey

Total Execution Time for this Case	157,814 sec.
Total Time in Monitored Routines	08,010 sec.
Total Time in Other Routines	49,804 sec.

Detailed Subroutine Time Monitoring

Subroutine Name	Time Relative to Maximum Subroutine Execution Time (* = Two Percent)	Actual Time in Seconds	Percent of Total Monitored Time
AB33		0,011	0,01
AB33A		0,071	0,07
ATTERR	****	3,207	4,82
ATTRES	**************	21,170	19,60
CHG	***	73,960	68,48
CROSS	***	3,716	3,44
CRPROU	***	3,847	3,56
ERCOND		0,003	0,00
ERNOTE		0,019	0,02
EULER		0,006	0,01

Total Time in Postprocessor 7,243 sec.

Figure 4. Sample Module Timing Summary

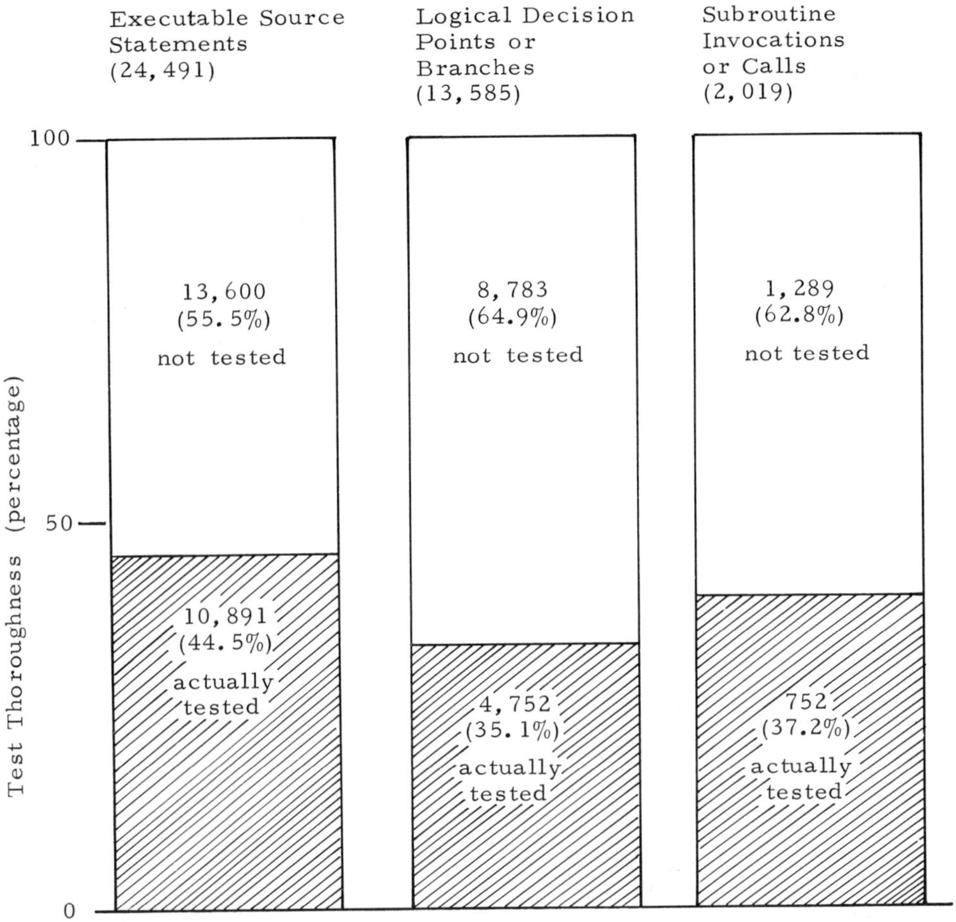

Figure 5. Test Effectiveness Statistics
(Sample size 40,869 source statements)

Figure 3 shows a summary report for a subroutine under test. This report presents, in a concise fashion, several interesting statistics, including the number of times the module was accessed, the complexity of the module (in terms of statements and branches contained in that module), and the internal documentation present in a module (as denoted by the number of inserted comments within the program source code). Figure 4 presents a timing summary.

Figure 5 and Table 1 summarize the results of some of the early programs run on the Program Evaluator and Tester System. They point out several interesting results, including the fact that only 44.5 percent of the possible executable source statements was actually tested and only 35.1 percent of the possible branches was tested. Both of these numbers are rather surprising; yet they may well be more typical than one would think.

TABLE 1

PET SOURCE STATEMENT STATISTICS

SOURCE STATEMENT PROFILE:		
Total Number of Source Statements in the Sample	40,869	
Number of Comment Statements	12,193	(29.8%)
Number of Other Nonexecutable Statements (e.g., declaratives, type statements, etc.)	4,185	(10.2%)
Number of Executable Statements	24,491	(59.9%)
OTHER SOURCE STATEMENT MEASUREMENTS:		
Number of Source Statements Containing Coding Standards Violations	519	(1.3%)
Number of Branches Contained in the Source Code	13,535	
Number of Subroutine Invocation Points (CALL Statements in FORTRAN	2,019	

ARTIFACTS

Both space and time artifacts are introduced when using selfmetric instrumentation. The time artifact ranges between approximately a 1.25 to 2.5 factor for the execution time of a self-metric program depending on the measurement options specified.

The space artifact also varies widely depending on the types of measurements being performed. Space artifacts are introduced in the following areas:

1. Additional memory is allocated for counters, timing cells, and data range storage cells.

2. Additional code is added to make the program self-metric.

AN AUTOMATED APPROACH TO SOFTWARE VALIDATION

An Automated Program Support System (APSS) is currently being designed to incorporate present tools and techniques within a comprehensive collection of automated aids for software development and certification. This extensible system contains five major components. The organization of a general Automated Program Support System (APSS) is shown schematically in Fig. 6. The intent of the diagram is to show that each component tool of the APSS may be applied to a given program separately, as well as in a rational sequence. This variability of application is motivated by the pragmatic desire to be able to apply the functions of the system to both the development and the maintenance of future software. Execution of the APSS tools will be performed on the support computer.

The general APSS configuration contained in Fig. 6 comprises in the following components:

1. A Program Development Subsystem Interface for guiding the development of well structured programs in a top-down fashion;

2. A Test Statistics Subsystem for both gathering static measurements and monitoring the dynamic behavior of software;

3. A Documentation Subsystem for assisting in the generation and maintenance of detailed software documentation.

4. A Simulation Subsystem for monitoring the behavior of assembly language software and scaling real-time data used for validation testing; and

5. A Test Data Generation Subsystem for synthesizing and assessing tests of critical software components.

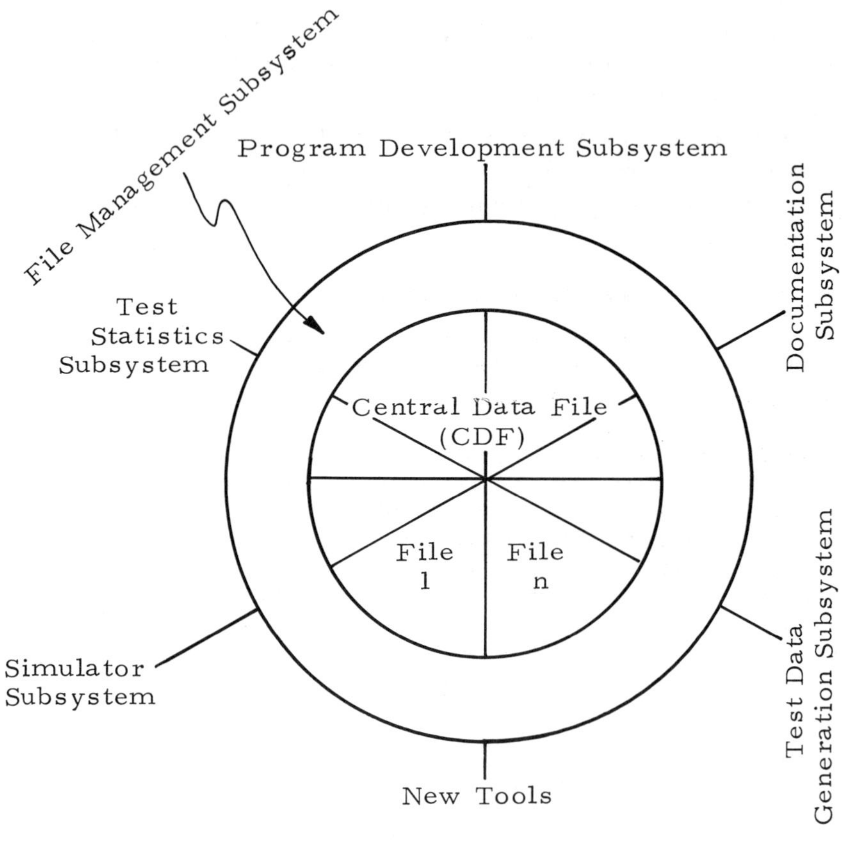

Figure 6. Automated Programming Support System

The general APSS provides substantial assistance in a number of verification tests. APSS

1. Aids in the preparation of a comprehensive set of test cases for exercising every executable statement, branch, or segment in a program.
2. Assists in preparing test data to exercise any specific portion (logical block, class of paths, or procedure of a program.
3. Assesses the impact of a prospective change in a block upon the unchanged blocks.
4. Identifies singularities and critical values of the input domain and of computed variables.
5. Assures that no combination of input data will result in reaching a block before the required block input is available.
6. Traces the flow of program control for given test data to find where the program computation first departed from expected results.
7. Flags assertion violations whenever a new or previously acceptable test data set no longer produces correct results because of program enhancements or modifications.
8. Identifies blocks of code that are impossible to reach by any combination of input data.

The following strategy for optimum application of the APSS suggests its inclusion in a well defined top-down structured approach to software development.

1. Provide the end user with a structured design capability for expressing his requirements in near-English using a minimal set of basic functional control structures.
2. Facilitate the continued expansion of the basic user requirements by the programmer with an automatically maintained design/audit trail.
3. Generate functional simulations of critical system segments in order to evaluate proposed implementation techniques.
4. Allow for the incorporation of critical assertion or verification conditions within the evolving code.

5. Apply analysis tools to the source program, inserting instrumentation and various user-selected options as desired.
6. Determine, through the application of selected test tools, a comprehensive set of requirements for complete testing, taking advantage of all structural data compiled via analysis.
7. Define simulation requirements for various test phases.
8. Compile the instrumented program and execute it using the test data derived as above.
9. Run one or more data reduction tools to display and summarize the data collected.
10. Maintain historical data for refinement of statistical software reliability models.

INCREMENTAL IMPLEMENTATION OF AN AUTOMATED PROGRAM SUPPORT SYSTEM

The characteristics of a general APSS show how it provided automated aids to assist in many areas of software testing and retesting. These highly desirable aids promise reduced manual efforts, higher visibility of program behavior, assurance of adequate testing and more reliable system software. Not all of these aids have been implemented, even in prototype form. Those test aids which have been developed for other software systems and have proven utility will form a basis for the further development of additional capabilities. An effort will be made to analyze the existing tools and techniques and to identify their current costs and benefits.

A large gap exists between exhaustive testing of all potential program paths and the statement that all program branches or segments have been exercised at least once. Advance research efforts are being conducted in several areas to help bridge this gap. Two of these research areas will be mentioned here. The first area involves the incorporation of an assertion capability into existing languages. The second area explores the automated selection and construction of meaningful test cases.

ASSERTION CAPABILITIES FOR EXISTING LANGUAGES

A number of new languages are currently being investigated by researchers for possible use in proving the correctness of programs. Although the various proof techniques differ to some extent, one common requirement is the development of logical assertions describing the nature of the algorithm. Enabling the user to establish his own logical assertions at key points within his algorithms in the languages he is now using is a practical step toward more reliable software design and implementation [5].

The proposed assertion capability will provide for two levels of assertions. Global assertions will be located with the declaratives and have control over the length of their enclosing module or block. Local assertions will be position dependent and will consist of any legal logical expression of the host language. While it is acknowledged that global assertions could be replaced by numerous local assertions, human factors motivate the inclusion of these additional global assertions.

The assertions are transparent to the normal language compilers and must be preprocessed in order for dynamic execution checking to take place. The preprocessor will instrument the assertions by augmenting the original source program with self-metric (self-measuring) instrumentations [4].

The use of the assertion capabilities will be emphasized throughout all phases of program development. Designers will be encouraged to include as assertions all critical requirements to be placed upon the key program algorithms. Interface requirements between system modules can be documented and validated through the use of appropriate assertions. Quality control and configuration management can be analyzed and enhanced by means of assertions. Listed below you will find illustrations of the proposed assertion language.

Local assertions as previously mentioned, may appear as comments at any point within the executable program code. They serve to enhance the documentation of critical algorithms during regular program development while later on providing meaningful check points for the validation and maintenance of complex systems. Local assertions appear as special comment directives of the form:

ASSERT <logical-expression>.

Global assertions are designed to extend our capacity to inspect and monitor the behavior of larger program modules or blocks. Two basic types of global assertions are provided. The first type checks on the enforcement of a specific set of logical requirements while the second type consists of a monitoring or data-gathering process on actual program behavior. Global assertions appear as special comment directives of the form:

```
ASSERT    RANGE (list of variable-names) (min, max)
ASSERT    VALUES (list of variable-names)
                 (list of legal values)

MONITOR [RANGE] [,] [{ FIRST/LAST }]
                    [{    F/L     }]

                    [{ (list of variable-names) }]
                    [{           all            }]
```

```
FORTRAN  { C      ASSERT   N.GT.5.AND.A.LT.100
         { C      ASSERT   1.NE.0

PL/1     { /*     ASSERT   N> 5 & A> 100          */
         { /*     ASSERT   1 ¬ = 0                */

JOVIAL   {    "   ASSERT   N GR 5 AND A LS 100    "
         {    "   ASSERT   1 NQ 0                 "
```

Figure 7. Examples of Local Assertions

EXAMPLES OF GLOBAL ASSERTIONS (FORTRAN)

```
C   ASSERT     RANGE (N) (-10,100)
C   ASSERT     VALUES (SEX) ('F','M')
C   ASSERT     VALUES (J) (-1,1,10,20)
C   MONITOR    RANGE (X,SUM,ITOTAL,Y,I)
C   MONITOR    FIRST/LAST (ABC,FG)
C   MONITOR    RANGE, FIRST/LAST (IVAR)
C   MONITOR    RANGE ALL
```

The incorporation of an assertion capability in existing language support systems appears to offer a sophisticated yet practical approach to the validation task on today's programs while at the same time as a powerful capability for future system designers.

AUTOMATIC SELECTION AND CONSTRUCTION OF TEST CASES [6]

A second area of current research addresses the problem of providing automated assistance in the selection and construction of meaningful test cases. A key issue in this area involves the identification of a significant set of criteria for grouping together a number of "similar" program paths. We are faced with the problem of forcing ourselves to find a means of cutting down the number of paths through a program. Structured programming can assist us in the better organization of our programs; yet we still will find that exhaustive testing of even structured programs is not always feasible.

Investigation in the area of automatic selection and construction of test cases has lead to the design of a general methodology addressing this problem. The goals of this research work are to design a test case generation methodology and to reach a better understanding of the basic program testing problems. The methodology is general and can be applied to programs in different languages although it was designed with FORTRAN programs in mind.

The methodology breaks a program down into a finite number of standard sets of program paths. It then attempts to generate test cases which cause one path from each class to be tested. A complete set of test cases contains one test case for each standard set of paths. The methodology attempts to generate a large subset of the complete set of test cases.

GENERAL APPROACH

The methodology contains five phases. Phase one analyzes a program and constructs descriptions of the standard sets of inner-program paths. These sets are characterized by the input data which causes a path element of each set to be followed. This characterization is described in terms of the assignments, loops, function calls, and branch predicates affecting the traversal of each set of inner-program paths [3].

The second phase of the methodology constructs descriptions of the input data causing each set of paths to be followed. The descriptions generated by the second phase are in intermediate format described as "implicit descriptions." They do not explicitly describe a set of data in terms of simplified predicates and relations. They contain assignments and loops and other program-like constructs.

Phase three of the methodology attempts to transform the "implicit descriptions" into equivalent but greatly simplified explicit descriptions. An explicit description consists entirely of predicates and relations with all other program-like constructs removed. In general, it is not possible to transform all arbitrary implicit descriptions into an explicit description.

The fourth phase is therefore designed to construct explicit descriptions from subsets of the input data sets where phase three was unable to construct the desired explicit descriptions.

Phase five of the methodology solves the equations from phase four by generating input values which satisfy the explicit descriptions. Explicit descriptions of numeric input data consist of systems of equalities and inequalities. Values which satisfy numeric explicit descriptions can be obtained by the application of inequality solution techniques.

CONCLUSIONS

The automatic generation of self-metric software has been shown to be a powerful approach to the measurement of program behavior. The power of the self-metric instrumentation approach lies in the fact that software need no longer be treated as a "black box." The internal structure of the program can be examined and automatically rebuilt into a self-metric form. Many new measures beyond simple performance figures can provide new insight into the actual behavior of a program during execution and can facilitate the establishment of new yardsticks and new procedures for validating large-scale software systems.

HOW DO WE ATTAIN MORE RELIABLE SOFTWARE?

The author feels that a two-pronged approach is necessary for attaining increased software reliability:

1. We must design with verification and validation constantly in mind, using basic yet well structured techniques whereever possible.
2. We must continue to develop an integrated set of automated support tools and a management discipline requiring their use and refinement.

REFERENCES

1. Dijkstra, E. W., "The Humble Programmer," 1972 Turing Award Lecture, Comm. of ACM, October 1972.
2. Dijkstra, E. W., "Notes on Structured Programming," Report 70-WSK-03, Technological University Eindhoven, The Netherlands, Department of Mathematics, April 1970.
3. Stucki, L.G., "A prototype automatic program testing tool," AFIPS 1972 Fall Joint Computer Conference, Anaheim, California, December 1972.
4. Stucki, L.G., "Automatic generation of self-metric software," Proc. IEEE Symposium on Software Reliability, N. Y. March-April 1973.

5. Stucki, L.G. and N.P. Svegel, "Software Automated Verification System Study," McDonnell Douglas Document No. MDC G5103, January 1974.

6. Howden, W. and L.G. Stucki, "Final Report Methodology for Effective Test Case Selection," McDonnell Douglas Document No. MDC G5301, January 1974.

5

Management

MANAGEMENT

A story I first heard from Jules Schwartz tells of a seminar at M. I. T. One of the directors of SAGE was discussing why the programming had gotten out of hand. He was then asked, "If you had it to do all over again, what would you do differently?" His answer was to find the ten best people and write the entire thing themselves. I'm sure that similar thoughts have occurred to many other managers. With a small group the communication problems are greatly simplified and so too is the management task. Of course, the other side of the coin is that each person becomes very critical to the effort. Given a choice, the small group is a most effective means for producing software.

However, the complexity of today's operating systems or management information systems makes it unfeasible to build them with a small group. Therefore, the proper management of people enters as a significant aspect of the programming process.

This book does not do this subject justice, for it is beyond the book's scope. The article by Schwartz in the introduction is addressed to managers; and he emphasizes their leadership role.

Countering this personal approach of Schwartz is the article by Harvey Bratman. His basic thesis asks to what extent the managing process can be automated. With the growing use of technical methodologies such as top-down design plus the use of personnel arrangements such as the chief programmer team, an automated system becomes more feasible and desirable. But a balance must be struck between eliminating the tedium of existing procedures on the one hand and creating an additional level of useless work.

Bratman outlines his proposal for such a system. It integrates both the structured programming and the chief programmer team methodologies. It is, however, a proposal; and, hence, it is too early to speak of its usefulness or effects. Because many groups are presently considering such proposals, we hope that exposing it will spawn some future ideas.

AUTOMATED TECHNIQUES FOR PROJECT MANAGEMENT AND CONTROL

Harvey Bratman

INTRODUCTION

1.1 Problems in the Management of Software Development Projects

The process of producing a large software system is the successive refinement of a system solution to greater levels of detail through a series of phases, from the system specification into a more and more detailed representation of a system solution until the final solution is reached: the checked-out program representation. The lack of an organized approach or methodology to advance a system solution from phases to phase, and the lack of a unified representation of the system solution as it advances from the initial to the final phase, are partly responsible for systems that are overly complex, difficult to manage and control, difficult to check out, and difficult to modify and maintain. The repeated restatement of the system at each development phase poses serious problems for all levels of project management. Managers have difficulty in tracking the progression of the system from phase to phase; and, as a result, they have problems in planning and controlling the developing system. The discontinuous representation of the system solutions makes it very difficult to validate the system's performance with respect to the original requirements.

The software project manager has the very real problem of maintaining the visibility of his project not only to higher management and his customer, but sometimes to himself. This is especially true if the software system is only part of a larger system that involves a hardware system and the "system platform"--the facilities and vehicles in which the software and hardware systems are installed. The high visibility of physical facilities, computing machinery, and display and sensor equipment, overshadows the insubstantial software product. Physical interfaces are more readily perceived than logical interfaces. Software, because it is more flexible and easily adapted than hardware, must often bear the brunt of absorbing system changes and buffering hardware incompatibilities. Software, since it embodies much of the procedural, decisional, and control aspects of the system, tends to be more interrelated than hardware. Software, since it determines many of the behavioral characteristics encountered in using and operating the system, is more sensitive to customer dissatisfaction. Software, since it deals with all the minute details and operational interactions of the applications, tends to be more complex than hardware components. Thus, software is harder to define, more subject to change, and less visible to management and the customer than hardware is. This lack of visibility, great complexity, and propensity to change make project progress difficult to measure, hard to evaluate, and resistant to control.

1.2 Automating Project Management

Known techniques and new concepts such as structured programming, top-down program development and program production libraries that can help these problems are either not used at all or, when they are used, are not used in an integrated manner but are put together ad hoc each time a large system programming project is begun. If it were not necessary to retool a software development facility for each new system, considerable benefits would accrue in getting projects underway quickly and in improving program design, code production methodology, and project management.

An automated approach to these problems must attempt to integrate the project management process into the structured programming and project team approach to software development. Visibility is improved by keeping up-to-date status records on all system elements and by providing a variety of reports on system configuration and project progress. Complexity is reduced and understanding of the system is improved by recording the system structure and its interrelationships, and by orienting schedules and budgets and other managerial information toward this structure. Greater control over change is achieved by tracing and evaluating the impacts of changes on both system requirements and project plans. Better measures of progress make evaluations easier and more precise. Finer planning is encouraged to improve project guidance, to aid in the early detection of deviations from plans, and to enhance control. "What if" modeling with project plans is used to evaluate the possible consequences of various actions and emergent events. Automating this process will reduce the manual labor that project managers must do when preparing reports, evaluating progress and changes, and completing other administrative tasks.

The process of developing a large software system results in two coordinated projects being undertaken. One is the project that designs, programs, tests and validates the software system. The second is the project that manages the project that designs, programs, tests, and validates the software system. Some managers mistakenly act as if these two projects were really one; but they have different personnel, use different data, and require different tools. The principal objective of this discussion is to outline the data and tools required for each project, but emphasizing the management project, and to indicate how the activities of both projects can be coordinated.

1.3 Elements of an Automated Project Management Facility

An integrated software development facility is unified through a Project Development Data Base established for each project using the facility. The data base consists of two parts: a Software Development Data Base and a Project Control Data Base. The Software Development Data Base contains the development of program modules from their first functional definition, through the definition of their interface with other modules and system data, and finally as developing source- and object-language programs. System and program descriptions and supporting management data are maintained in the Project Control Data Base from early in the design phase. The management data is oriented toward the software system structure and the activities performed to develop the software system. This use of a Project Development Data Base furthers the automation of program development, management visibility, configuration control, and documentation.

The objective of this system is to present a standardized program production methodology for developing and recording program data throughout the implementation phase, that will provide management visibility and control. This methodology will not require any change in or addition to existing techniques for program generation, compilation, and verification.

In small programming projects, programmers may simply keep programs in a deck of punched cards. However, when more than a few hundred cards are involved, the chances for error in maintaining a program on cards invite disaster. Cards can be dropped, or assembled out of sequence, or even misplaced. For this reason, a large programming project will usually use the computer to store the programs in a programming library, thereby reducing the chance of error in program handling, as well as minimizing the effort required to maintain the library.

Programmers can perform library operations along with their other work. However, a programmer is not necessarily a good librarian and should spend the bulk of his time doing programming. More important, a library system that is organized poorly, or not kept accurate and up-to-date, can necessitate extra debugging and rewriting of programs.

The Software Development Data Base will be organized around a Program Production Library concept designed to reduce error and to increase programmer productivity, by providing a well organized, accurate, and up-to-date information base for programmers to work from.

The Program Production tools that enable programmers to use the Program Production Library will consist of operating systems utility routines or, if they are not suitable, specially written utility routines. In either case they record in the Software Development Data Base useful management data, such as program size, the number and type of operation (edit, compilation, execution) performed on each program module, and the test cases used.

The Automated Project Managers' Information System (which will be called APMIS) is a software tool that assists the manager of a software project in doing his job. It helps him plan, monitor, and control the work, define and control the software configuration, and ensure the observance of quality assurance measures. It assists him in the preparation of management reports, in the evaluation of project progress, and in spotting potential difficulties and developmental trends.

APMIS also strongly supports the Software Development process. It furthers the concepts of structured programming and module design by fostering the creation and integration of a hierarchical structure of program modules. It supports the members of the project management team from the project manager to the chief programmer charged with producing a program module. It helps the system architect by recording the system structure and module interrelationships and by tracing chains of interrelationships through the system for functions, data, equipment, and modules. APMIS helps the system architect evaluate the impacts of change, select routines for integration and testing, and determine the completeness of designs, programs, and tests.

2. Program Production

The discussion in this section will highlight those aspects that relate to Project Management. Emphasis will be placed on the use of the Software Development Data Base throughout the software development cycle and its relationship to the Automated Project Managers' Information System. The techniques that will be presented have been influenced by the concepts of Structured Programming, Top-Down Program Development, Chief Programmer Team and the Program Production Library. The concept of the Program Production Library as originally proposed by H. Mills of IBM has been augmented by configuration control and automatic record-keeping techniques. Although the techniques presented are supportive of these concepts, they do not depend on their use.

2.1 Chief Programmer Team

The Chief Programmer Team is a concept developed and tried out successfully by IBM. It represents a management structure that parallels the modular design of program structure. It is characterized by

Restructuring the programming effort into specialized jobs;

Defining relationships between specialists; and

Developing tools to permit specialists to interface effectively.

The motive behind restructuring the programming effort into specialized jobs is to distribute the scarce capabilities for program design thinking deeper into the coding process by technical and organizational means. The use in the Chief Programmer Team of Top-Down program development and structured programming ensures that the implementation of a system parallels its design. The Chief Programmer Team organization also results in increased productivity and reliability. The structure of the Chief Programmer Team defines the relation between its members: the Chief Programmer, the Backup Programmer, and the Program Secretary.

The Chief Programmer is a technical manager to whom all other members of the Chief Programmer Team report directly. His principal job, however, is to design and code programs. The Chief Programmer codes central, critical segments of a program himself and defines program stubs for other team members to complete, using structured programming techniques. The entire work of the team is reviewed and incorporated into one unit by the Chief Programmer. The Chief Programmer's managerial duties are simplified by the degree of structure in the team and the continuous team interaction in a project. He must be a manager to maintain the team's organizational discipline and bear project responsibility for the team's performance.

The Backup Programmer, a peer of the Chief Programmer in program design skills, assists in developing the design in order to help ensure that global system considerations are discussed and defended, thus providing a check on the correctness of the developing design. It is prudent that a second person be totally familiar with the design decisions that have been made. The Backup Programmer can serve also as a research assistant for the Chief Programmer in areas of programming strategy and tactics, freeing the Chief Programmer to concentrate on the central problems of system development. He can also provide independent test planning for the system.

The Program Secretary maintains the records of a project, the project notebook and the Program Production Library (PPL), in both an internal (machine-readable) and an external (human-readable) form. The Program Secretary is a full-fledged team member, not simply a pooled assistant to the programmers. The job of maintaining the PPL is an integral part of the Chief Programmer Team; it is to preserve and maintain a project asset--program and test data--for highest possible productivity and manageability of programming operations. Therefore, the Program Secretary, while reporting to a Chief Programmer, has overriding professional accountabilities as well, just as a comptroller has financial record-keeping accountabilities that override any specific reporting relationship.

Programmers also call on the Secretary for all assembling, compiling, linkage-editing, and test runs required in the project. The results of these runs are filed by the Secretary as part of the PPL. The main function of a Program Secretary, however, is not to save the programmers clerical work, but to maintain the status of program and test data in a form that serves as the primary source of communication between programmers on the current definition of program modules so that they can work more effectively and with fewer errors.

Other programmers and analysts perform duties precisely defined by the Chief Programmer to meet project requirements, as needed, in designing and coding modules that are originally specified, and finally accepted, by the Chief Programmer.

In large projects, many Chief Programmer Teams can be organized into a traditional management structure, each team handling a subsystem in a system hierarchy. The classical way of incorporating programmers into a management structure has been to put them at the bottom of the management pyramid. Technical personnel with design talent may be sprinkled through the hierarchy, as staff members, but they usually have no actual coding responsibilities. It is in such organizations, where all coding is done at the lowest organizational level, that the program structure gets lost in a mass of coding.

The Chief Programmer Team differs from this classical organization only in the placement of the programmers. Chief Programmer Teams, as self-contained program design and coding units, incorporate the entire programming hierarchy. In this form, there are design and coding teams at all levels, each reporting to higher-level teams, with the highest reporting to the project manager. This ability to distribute programming teams throughout a management hierarchy results from the fact that Top-Down program development and the management structures naturally coincide. The code used to handle high-level functions can be identified with, and maintained by, Chief Programmer Teams at the appropriate levels. In this way, the integrity of program structure can be preserved during the detailed coding process.

2.2 Top-Down Program Development

The highest level of a program describes the flow of control among the major functional segments of a module. Names are given to these segments; and the names are replaced with code later, either through a procedure call or by a coded segment. First, however, the functional specifications of these segments are stated, explaining their input and output and identifying the functions they are supposed to perform. The code for these segments describes the flow of control among still lower-level program segments. The process stops when no undefined names remain.

The Top-Down development of a structured program is thus an iteration of the following sequence given the functional specification of a structured program segment:

1. Design the program to accomplish the specification.
    a. Define the functional requirements of the next-level segments.
    b. Devise the test cases.
2. Implement the program using structured program techniques --a combination of program steps and calls to dummy lower level segments. The dummy segments, called program stubs, contain enough code to establish linkage with the higher-level segment.
3. Test the program and the calls to the dummy program segments with the test cases. An informal proof of correctness can show that the code of the segment matches its spe-

cification. The proof should not be too difficult because the use of the restrictive set of control constructs makes the segment small and logically straightforward. The proof will be based on axioms stating that lower-level segments match their specifications.

4. Verify that the dummy program has been coded successfully by repeating the testing procedure.

The result is testing of the system successively downward from the top levels of abstraction to the bottom levels, continuously exercising the actual interfaces. The bottom level may be standard packaged routines--data access methods, sort routines, etc.--or interfaces with other systems. The Top-Down approach is the reverse of the usual approach of checking the bottom-level modules first and working up, finally integrating and testing the entire system. In the Top-Down approach, the integration of modules is a continuous process.

2.3 The Software Development Data Base

The Software Development Data Base will record the development of program modules from their first functional definition, through the definition of their interface with other modules and system data, and finally as developing source-and object-language programs.

Components of a problem system exist in many forms (source language, object code modules, executable load modules, link, edit commands) and are stored in various sections of the data base. The data base also contains program stubs, stub simulator representations, module linking records, and test cases. Operations on the various components will be performed using existing processors and utilities wherever possible.

The Software Development Data Base is a hierarchically structured data base comprised of at least the following sections: SOURCE, OBJECT, LOAD, LEL, STATUS, TEST, and OPLOG.

- SOURCE - The members are source programs - BAL, COBOL, FORTRAN, ECC.
- OBJECT - Object modules from language processors are stored as members of this section.
- LEL - Link-edit language directs the formation of load modules from object modules and other load modules.
- LOAD - The members of this section are load modules; i.e., modules of executable code produced by the link-editor.

STATUS - Status keeps information about each source member.

TEST - Test cases are stored here.

OPLOG - Operations Log records the operations performed on various members.

Each section is a partitioned data set comprised of members. Members of the SOURCE section will be the source programs of the problem system. The SOURCE section consists of all known modules of the system. In the design phase a module may be represented by just its name and description; later, by a program stub; and finally, by the complete module. The source programs will be operated on by the various language processors to produce object programs that will be stored as members of the OBJECT section. Object programs will be processed to form load modules that are stored as members of the LOAD section. Member A of the SOURCE section will give rise to member A of the OBJECT section, which in turn will give rise to member A of the LOAD section.

An alternate means of forming load modules is via the LEL section. Members of this section contain link-edit commands that direct the information of load modules from combinations of object modules and/or other load modules. Member X of the LEL section will cause the creation of member X of the LOAD section. Members of the LEL section control the combining of program modules for testing and for building sub-systems.

The TEST section will contain test cases to be read during the execution of load modules of the problem system.

Information about each member of the various sections will be kept in the member STATUS section. This section will provide a basis for checks to enforce naming conventions and initiate module currency warnings. The initial contents of this section will be established as member definitions are entered into the data base. Subsequent operations on the various members will be reflected in the status description of the members.

A record of all operations performed is maintained in the OPLOG section. This record will be periodically processed by the Automated Project Managers' Information System. The OPLOG will indicate the operation performed, the degree of success, the time at which it was performed, the responsible user, and certain other items of information judged useful.

Each PPL will be associated with a particular project of the factory. As such, a project name will be assigned. Since more than one version of a project system can exist, the PPL name is assigned a minor qualifier according to its version name. A PPL will be uniquely identified, then, by both its project name and its version name.

3. Automated Project Management Information System (APMIS)

3.1 Concepts and Principles

The Structured Programming concepts that will be supported by APMIS are the "stepwise refinement of the system solution" and Top-Down program development. In the stepwise refinement case, a program module, defined in terms of what its function is, may be redefined in terms of lower-level program modules that define how the function is accomplished. Or a program module may be defined as owning a data set or piece of equipment. For Top-Down program development, a program module may "call" the next-lower-level program modules. In all instances the relationship among modules, data, equipment, etc., has to be input to APMIS and must be stored in the Project Control Data Base.

All items that come under configuration control must be definable. These include programs, documents, equipment, requirement and design changes, and other project activities and products. The definitions are stored in the Project Control Data Base. This will allow for baselining, accounting and design change control later on.

All projects activities will be input to APMIS. The links among requirements, design documents, program modules, equipment, tasks, etc., will also be input and are stored in the Project Control Data Base. Also the activities, modules, documents, milestone events, and other items pertinent to the project at each phase of development--definition, design, implementation, test and integration, installation, and maintenance--will be entered. The links connecting these items from phase to phase will be entered so that the project manager can track their development; e.g., from requirement to baseline design to project module to the operation of a piece of equipment. The project manager must be permitted to structure these inputs in a form most natural to him and to his situation.

3.2 Requirements

The overall requirement for APMIS is to assist project managers at all levels in the planning, monitoring, controlling, and modeling of a project. The preparation of input for a tool like APMIS enforces upon the project manager a necessary discipline that is valuable even if the tool is never used. The manager must know and define the entities of the project and the relationships between them, such as

requirements and deliverable items,
requirements and program functions,
program functions and program modules,
high-level program modules and lower-level program modules,
program modules and equipment,
deliverable items and the activities that produce them, and
activities and the resources necessary to support them.

Once these entities and relationships are entered into the data base, APMIS can be used to optimize scheduler and resource allocation using the techniques of PERT, CPM and Graphic Network Analysis. Progress and resource expenditure are recorded and attached to specific activities and thus to the deliverable items they produce. Usually, plans will be modified and refined as the project develops.

The project manager can obtain reports on progress and resource expenditures based on activities producing the items supporting a requirement, a function, a piece of equipment, a generic activity (design, code, test or implement) or a program module.

A change can be attached to a requirement, function, equipment, etc.; and its effects on schedule and resource allocation can be evaluated. Implementing the change can be tracked. Finally the project as well as the system can be modeled. The effects of different resource allocations, different sequences of activities, and different schedules for deliverable items can be input; and their effects on the overall schedule can be evaluated.

3.3 Operational Functions

The functions needed to implement the basic activities of APMIS are Information Storage and Maintenance, Planning and Control, Information Retrieval and Report Generation.

3.3.1 Information Storage and Maintenance

The information entered is error-checked and stored in the data base. Implicit and explicit links between data are automatically maintained. Data entered periodically in the data base, such as activity start and stop dates, execution-run history and resource expenditures, can also be entered or accumulated.

With the passage of time, resource expenditures must be accumulated and schedules updated. With the occurrence of unscheduled and unexpected events, slippages, and early completions, resources may have to be shifted to meet changing demands, and obsolete information purged from the active files. To meet this need, the project manager may request the UPDATE function to update the data base to reflect the passage of time, incorporate a cost report, or replace existing schedule and resource information with newly planned data.

Management data will be extracted from other project files located in the Software Development Data Base and formulated for insertion into the Project Control Data Base. Typical information includes computer time expended on compilations or tests, number of recorded errors, verification data for system-wide set used, number of compilations per module, number of tests executed, cross-references or module environments, and module sizes and running times.

3.3.2 Project Planning and Control

Developing and improving plans, evaluating project performance, and assessing the impacts of project and product changes will be supported by three major functional modules. These modules are the SCHEDULER, which derives and optimizes critical path schedules and resource allocations; the THREADER, which assesses the effects of modifications and interprets the hierarchical structure of the software system and the organization of project work; and the TRENDER, which evaluates project performance and data stores. These three tools represent an integrated set of capabilities that help the project manager create and work with plans. Together they also constitute a powerful project-modeling capability that can increase significantly the project manager's efficiency and effectiveness.

Scheduling and resource allocations essentially include four elements.

Determine what is to be produced; i.e., modules.

Determine the activities necessary to produce the product or attain the objective; i.e., tasks.

Determine constraints on plans, such as externally imposed delivery and due dates, limitations on resource (men, machine, facilities, time) and interdependencies of modules, tasks and resources.

Allocate the resources to attain objectives within constraints in an optimum fashion.

Information on modules, tasks, resources, and the constraints upon them are generated and stored in the Data Base. Both modules and tasks can be hierarchically structured. These structural relationships are recorded so they can be used by the SCHEDULER, THREADER, TRENDER, and the report-generation routines in selecting groupings of items for schedules and resource computation and reports and for summing over module and task hierarchies in making summary reports.

3.3.3 Information Retrieval

The THREADER is a valuable adjunct to the information-retrieval and report-generation functions. First, designers are required to state explicitly what a module is to do, what functional requirements it is to satisfy, and what tests are to verify its proper performance. If the system architect desires to ascertain how completely a functional requirement is being satisfied, or if a project manager wants to check on the developmental status of such a functional requirement, they may request the THREADER to "pull a thread"; i.e., to trace the various elements associated with the requirement through the system. The "linking" nature of the data base permits such threading to be done at several levels. For example, the pulled thread may represent only gross, high-level program modules and data elements, or, by descending through the levels of abstraction, a detailed, step-by-step trace of the element through the smallest modules. The thread that is pulled now forms an information-retrieval template. With the template, the architect can pull and compare statements from the data base of requirements, designs, data, validations requirements, test procedures, and schedules related to the items in the template. A complete set of functional threads through a complex system represents a great deal of information which the THREADER may access via functional requirements, design specifications, test plans, and such system elements as modules, data, and equipment.

3.3.4 Reports Generation

In addition to the trends and anomalies reports for which the TRENDER derives data, the REPORTER will output standing reports in standard formats. Via an internal call to the THREADER, reports may be requested for any subset of modules or other elements that the THREADER can find and for nested elements such as modules, tasks, and equipment configurations.

Examples of some of the standard reports that can be requested are the following: (1) Management Summary Report, containing schedule and resource progress information; (2) Resource Allocation Report, giving schedule and budget information; (3) Configuration Index and Status Report, describing deliverable program modules and pertinent milestone data; (4) Configuration Summary Report, indicating program modules, specification references, and accumulated changes; (5) Modification Index Report, describing proposed and approved design changes and scheduled milestones and authentications; (6) Modification Summary Report, summarizing modification status; and (7) Module

Run Summary, covering the compilation and test run history for a module or set of modules.

3.4 The Project Control Data Base

To support the three major capabilities of the Automated Project Managers' Information System--Project Planning and Control, Data Base Maintenance and Reports Generation--a Project Control Data Base with unique structure will be considered. It will record the planning and control aspects of program development and will contain the following:

> Such project planning and progress data as schedules and activity status, resource allocations and expenditures, personnel responsibilities and accomplishments, and project documentation references;
>
> Such configuration planning and control data as performance requirements, configuration structure and content, quality assurance criteria and evaluation, and authentications of configuration baselining and configuration control events.

4. Development of Software System

4.1 System Definition Phase

Most of the activities of the system definition phase are associated with planning: planning the project, general product planning, and general quality assurance procedures planning. Although these plans are broad in scope, a great deal of information is generated. This information is stored in the Project Control Data Base to assist the planner in defining the project and the software product and to guide the project to a successful completion.

The Software Development Data Base and the Project Control Data Base are initiated with the top-most program modules as they become defined. As modules and tasks are identified and entered in the Project Control Data Base, the SCHEDULER can assist the planner in estimating resource requirements and in making schedule computations. As planning iterations are made, APMIS can help the planner allocate and reallocate his resources.

For project management, comprehensive schedules, budgets, organization and accounting information are submitted. For configuration management, initially identified modules, module interrelationships, externally required milestones and cross-references to the software performance specifications are created; and descriptive information on all of these diverse elements is entered as Development Item Descriptions. For quality assurance, the initial product review milestones and testing schedule are recorded; and validation criteria are entered for each identified module. If there is a separate interface specification document that will later guide integration testing, specification cross-references for the interface document as well as the performance specifications are also generated.

In addition to the valuable assistance given in generating schedules and resource allocations, APMIS can assist the system architect by crosschecking functional designs against performance requirements to assess their completeness and accuracy. APMIS will generate initial Configuration Index Reports and assist the system architect in monitoring the design of the system and officially reporting the evolving configuration. Initial cost accounting and progress reports will also be generated.

4.2 System Design Phase

In addition to replanning, progress monitoring, and progress reporting, the major activity of the system design phase is the identification of the program modules and the system structure. Consequently, the Program Control and Software Development Data Bases increase greatly in size during this phase. Configuration indexing and status reporting are now relatively comprehensive and result in large reports.

The generation of the preliminary or system-design specification results in document descriptions and their attendant cross-reference files. As the logical and physical structure of the system is laid out, many additional key-word descriptions and changes to them may be expected, resulting in many data-base changes.

For quality assurance during the system design phase, validation criteria continues to be recorded; and specification descriptions and cross references for test plans and more detailed interface specifications are generated. At the end of this period, the system or preliminary design-review meeting should be held, which may result in many specification changes and in the first external certification of the passing of a milestone event (unless a previous performance specification was produced and certified). The system design is now baselined.

The use of APMIS to check on the completeness and accuracy of designs and tests increases during the system-design phase. Crosschecks of various specifications should continue. Configuration and progress reports are generated regularly; and trend reports are made for the purpose of discovering anomalies in the Project Control and Software Development Data Bases and detecting potential difficulties and deviations in progress.

4.3 Component Design Phase

Replanning, monitoring, and reporting of project progress continue during the component design phase. In addition, since the system design has now been baselined, design-change procedures become operational; and the first modification descriptions, milestones, and cross references enter the Data Base and are included on configuration status reports. Module identification may continue. Specification cross reference and document subsection descriptions for the detailed design specifications, the test procedure specifications, and the data base specifications (if separately produced) are created. At the end of this phase, the detailed design specifications are reviewed (the Critical Design Review), revised, and certified.

During this phase, the THREADER is used to evaluate the impacts of design changes on software design, to trace strings for assembly test builds, and to track the increasingly complex hierarchical structure of the system. The SCHEDULER may be used more frequently to evaluate slippages and schedule breakthroughs; and the TRENDER is used to detect present and potential difficulties in project progress. Modification Index and Status Reports are added to other configuration-accounting reports during the component-design phase.

4.4 Implementation Phase

The implementation phase is one in which computer programs are coded and debugged and the system data base generated if it is part of the project. The Automated Program Production Library begins to record compilation and test-run statistics, module-size and execution-time statistics, and expenditures of machine time. APMIS extracts this data and incorporates it in the Project Control Data Base. Replanning, monitoring, and reporting continue. System-wide set-used cross-reference information, as reflected in programmed modules, may be checked against the set/used-as-designed information previously generated. Run statistics may be helpful in replanning and directing the programming effort.

The system design should be frozen at this time; and additional models and versions of the system may be identified to accommodate system changes and adaptions. Much time and effort are usually spent in processing design changes. If the system is large and changes are packaged into a sequence of models to be developed in parallel, it might be advantageous to initiate new projects for each model.

The evaluation of changes in the design plans is a continuing activity. Module validation criteria are used in the debugging and parameter-testing process as input for the automatic program validation processor.

4.5 Integration and Test Phase

Proposed modifications are accounted for; and a discrepancy reporting and processing procedure is instituted during the integration and test phase. Since processing a discrepancy report is analogous to processing a design-change proposal, the Modification Milestones and Descriptions are used for both. During this phase, model and version accounting is important for the scheduling of design changes and discrepancy corrections, and for the adaptations of the system configuration to reconcile differences in locations and applications. In addition, the normal replanning, monitoring, and reporting functions continue.

Test-run statistics and certification that a module has passed a test are very useful to project planners who are scheduling runs for string testing and assessing the current status of programs being tested and integrated. If programs are to be certified provisionally, lists of pending modifications and corrections provide the bases for discussions of their known limitations. In addition, to test a function or construct optimum testing sequences, the THREADER is invaluable in selecting strings of modules and tests.

Specification cross references to documentation for using, operating, and maintaining instructions may also be inserted in the data base and cross-comparisons run to ensure the comprehensiveness and accuracy of coverage.

Careful certification of program quality is important if warranties are to be issued covering program performance and correctness. APMIS keeps the records for program certification and helps the project manager ensure that his warranties may be given with a low probability of future program faults.

4.6 Installation and Maintenance Phase

During the installation and maintenance phase, APMIS is usually engaged in tracking proposed and approved design changes and error corrections and in helping plan the activities associated with the implementation of these changes. If there are enough modifications, additional models and versions of the system may be scheduled. If each model or version is large enough to be managed as a separate project, managing through APMIS proceeds as indicated in the above phases, except that the large amount of information about existing modules may be extracted from the old Project Control Data Base and transferred to the new Project Control Data Base.

The emphasis is then upon rewriting or converting the transferred records and merging in the activities associated with implementing the approved change package. Tracking many detailed changes and discrepancy corrections is an onerous task for integration contractors. Updates of interface specifications and benchmark tests to reflect changes are often almost as expensive as producing new specifications and modules. For large systems, voluminous modification status reports covering requested design changes and reported errors may be produced.

Evaluating the impact of change through the THREADER and using it to track the completeness and accuracy of change packages and establish test threads are valuable applications of APMIS. Status reports also help monitor a complex set of change implementations and discrepancy corrections. Precise records may be kept of integrated system "tape" and adaption "tape" contents. In brief, APMIS is an excellent vehicle for the configuration control of a system during operational and maintenance stages.

5. Summary

In brief, APMIS is a set of program tools that supports software project managers. APMIS is based on the concepts of structured programming and chief programmer teams and incorporates hierarchically structured program modules as the basic unit of production. The hierarchical and interdependent structures of software system and programming tasks are recorded and used to evaluate project and program changes and to assist the system architect in building the system and ensuring the completeness and accuracy of his designs and tests. APMIS is intended to serve as an initial planning tool and as an integrated subsystem that supports software configuration management from the inception of a project through the post-delivery maintenance of a system. The major innovations in APMIS are the ways in which activities are scheduled, resources are allocated, and the impacts of design changes and project developments are traced through the system. Equally important are the comprehensiveness of the Project Control Data Base and the manner in which it is structured, as well as the tools used for creating, maintaining and utilizing the data structures and links.

ACKNOWLEDGEMENT

The work discussed in this paper has been performed as part of the Software Engineering Project in the Software Development Department of the System Development Corporation, Research and Development Division. Many of the concepts and much of the material described herein under the names of the Automated Project Managers' Information System and the Automated Program Production Library were contributed by Paul F. Cudney, Bruce G. Johnson, and N. E. Willmorth.

6

Annotated Bibliography

There seems to be common agreement that an annotated bibliography adds to the value of a book. So much has been written on these subjects that a complete bibliography would swamp the reader and serve no purpose. Therefore, this bibliography has been constructed with some rather stringent criteria. First of all, only references which are readily available are included. Therefore, many in-house reports were immediately rejected. A second criterion was continued relevance: anything older than five years was carefully screened as to its continued relevance today. Finally, emphasis was placed on general treatments of these many subjects. Already published bibliographies are included in references 16, 21, 23, and 52.

Many new people are entering the field of software construction. I hope that this bibliography, by presenting an abbreviated list of references, makes their task easier: people may at least come close to reviewing the relevant literature in this field. Those already working in this area may be curious to see how their own lists compare with mine.

[1] Ashcroft, E. and Z. Manna, "The translation of GO TO programs to WHILE programs," Proc. IFIP 71, North Holland, 1972, pp. 250-255.

A theoretical paper giving two algorithms for transforming programs so they have no GO TOs. Extra Boolean variables are added to keep track of previous states. A proof is given that, in general, extra variables are always needed.

[2] Baker, F. T., "Chief programmer team management of production programming," IBM Systems Journal, vol. 11, no. 1, 1972.

A description of how the methodology of chief programmer teams (functional organization, program production library, top-down programming, and structured programming) was actually applied in implementing the New York Times information bank system.

[3] Baker, F. T. and H. D. Mills, "Chief programmer teams," Datamation, December 1973, pp. 58-61.

This entire issue is devoted to structured programming. This particular article defines the chief programmer team concept and how it interfaces with the technical aspects of a project. The New York Times project is discussed as an example of these ideas.

[4] Bohem, B. W., "Software and its impact: A quantitative assessment," Datamation, May 1973, pp. 48-59.

This article discusses the first stage in collecting data, showing that software is the major source of difficult problems and operational performance penalties. Also discussed are means for reducing software development delays, the distribution of effort among analysis/design, checkout/test and coding/auditing, and the importance of software development criteria and improved validation techniques. The survey includes a discussion of where software errors are made and other technical problems encountered in software design and development.

[5] Bohm, C. and G. Jacopini, "Flow diagrams, Turing machines and languages with only two formation rules," CACM, May 1966, pp. 366-371.

By now, a classic article. These authors were the first to show that most flowcharts could be redone using only IFTHENELSE and DO WHILE statements. Later algorithms by Ashcroft and Manna do more to preserve the original "topology" of the program. Theoretical, but nevertheless an important milestone.

[6] Brown J.R., et al, "Automated software quality assurance," Program Test Methods, Prentice Hall, Englewood Cliffs, N.J., 1974, Chapter 15.

This paper describes three example-testing modules which have been implemented or are in the process of implementation. The authors believe automatic testing and analysis of computer software will generate significant rewards during the 1970s. The three case studies presented here demonstrate some of the recent achievements.

The system studies are composed of a Data Base module, which includes both data and program inputs; a Program module, which includes all machine instructions; and a Results module which includes all forms of output, irrespective of the storage medium.

[7] Buxton, J.N. and B. Randell, Software Engineering Techniques, Brussels, NATO Scientific Affairs Division, 1970.

The proceedings of a conference held in October 1969. Articles are by such luminaries as Dijkstra, Falkoff, Needham, Schwartz, Aron, and Brown. There are chapters on software specification, quality and portability.

[8] Chapin, N., "Flowcharting with the ANSI standard: A tutorial," Computing Surveys, vol. 2, no. 2, June 1970, pp. 119-146.

Discussed in detail are the system chart and the flow diagram as important tools for the analyst and the programmer in preparing and documenting work for implementation on computers. Carefully prepared, flowcharts can enhance the rigor with which analysts and programmers think through the systems, programs, and associated procedures. This greater rigor should in turn reduce the cost of debugging. However, the main contribution of the system chart and flow diagrams is to communicate essential aspects of information processing work from one human to another. The quality of this communication is enhanced by a consistent use of the standard which is described in detail in this paper.

[9] Cougar, J.D., "Evaluation of business system analysis techniques," ACM Computing Surveys, September 1973, pp. 167-198.

The trend towards automating business procedures is explained full blast in this survey article. Such mechanisms as SOP (study organization plan), automated ADS (accurately defined system), TAG (time automated grid), PSL (problem statement language), Hoskyns system, and the ISDOS project at Michigan are all covered.

[10] Davis, R.M., "Quality software can change the computer industry," Program Test Methods, Prentice-Hall, Englewood Cliffs, N.J., 1973, Chapter 23.

The chapter is a discussion of software management, customer and industry needs. It presents the varying aspects of software as it is viewed from different stand points: those of the recipient of computer services, the software producers and the suppliers of software services. The writing emphasizes the role of the National Bureau of Standards, which requires the Bureau to simultaneously associate with both sides of the marketplace in order to equitably promote the use of technology.

[11] Dijkstra, E.W., "The humble programmer," CACM, October 1972,

This article is a transcript of the author's 1972 ACM Turing Award Lecture. In it, Dijkstra describes the major developments in his programming career and in the software field: he gives his opinions on the current situation in programming and on its future development. Extremely provocative and thought-provoking.

[12] Dijkstra, E.W., "GO TO statement considered harmful," CACM, vol. 11, no. 3, March 1968, pp. 147-148.

Quality of programmers is a decreasing function of the density of GO TO statements in the programs they produce. GO TO statements should be abolished. Programmer is not involved in his program's behavior (and whether or not it satisfies the desired spec). People are geared to master static relations rather than dynamic, time-evolving processes. Values of indices are outside the programmer's control. GO TOs are an invitation to make a mess of one's program.

[13] Dijkstra, E. W., "Notes on structured programming," Structured Programming, O. J. Dahl, E. W. Dijkstra, C.A.R. Hoare, Academic Press, London, 1972.

This is an expansion of Dijkstra's privately distributed article with the same title. In it are discussed the reasons behind structured programming and stepwise program construction. Examples are given illustrating Dijkstra's methods.

[14] Elmendorf, W. R., "Controlling the functional testing of an operating system," IEEE Trans. on System Science and Cybernetics, vol. SCC-5, no. 4, October 1969, pp. 284-290.

The paper defines test plan, control of test effort and quantitative measure of test coverage. Explained in detail, within the test control process, are survey, ID, appraisal, review and monitor. Specification testing versus program testing is discussed. With regards to the extent of testing, a coverage matrix is defined. The functional variations eligible for testing are identified. Detailed are the criteria for appraising; i.e., relative significance, yield and cost of variations, leading to test resources allocation to the higher payoff variations.

The article contains very good generalities and fairly good details.

[15] Graham, R. M., G. L. Clancy, and D. B. DeVaney, "A software design and evaluation system," CACM, February 1973, pp. 110-116.

This paper describes a methodology for evaluating the performance of a software system. This is done by combining performance evaluation with design and implementation using a high-level language to describe the system at all phases of its development.

[16] Hetzel, W. C., Program Test Methods, Prentice-Hall, Englewood Cliffs, N. J., 1972.

A collection of articles delivered at the symposium on Computer Program Test Methods held at Chapel Hill.

Several of the articles are individually listed here. It gives a nice overview of what to do during the testing phase. It also contains an extensive bibliography.

[17] Hoare, C.A.R., "An axiomatic approach to computer programming," CACM, vol. 12, October 1969, pp. 576-580, 583.

This is the first of several papers by Hoare which axiomatize a programming language. The basic idea is to give a rigorous set of axioms and rules of inference so that rigorous proofs of programs can be accomplished. A simple example is carried through.

[18] Holland, J.R., "Acceptance testing for applications programs," Program Test Methods, Prentice-Hall, Englewood Cliffs, N.J., 1973, Chapter 20.

Applications program acceptance testing affects anyone who designs, develops, monitors or uses functional systems; but it is a subject which has received little serious consideration, either procedural or theoretical.

In this chapter, pertinent literature is reviewed; the acceptance tester and the developer in a common environment are compared; and the acceptance tester is discussed. Some considerations toward development of a theoretical model which treats an acceptance test as an empirical rather than an analytical process are suggested.

[19] Kernighan, B.W. and P.S. Plauger, The Elements of Programming Style, McGraw-Hill Book Company, N.Y. 1974.

A unique approach to teaching programming style. The authors have collected many program exercises from introductory books and explain why they are poorly written. Keyed to FORTRAN and PL/I it contains many useful rules for improving readability.

[20] Knuth, D.E., "An empirical study of FORTRAN Programs," Software Practice and Experience, vol. 1, 1971, pp. 105-133.

The study shows quantitatively "what programmers really do." Statistical result are given, based on actual programs executed. Examples of statement quantized are IF, GO TO, DO, WRITE, CONTINUE. Also discussed are statistics on static and dynamic use of statements; the importance of a program "profile," namely, a table of frequency counts of statements executed; and implications for future work in compiler design.

[21] Knuth, D., "Structured programming with GO TO statements," Computing Surveys, vol. 6, no. 4, January 1975, pp. 261-302.

In this important article, Knuth discusses the problem of creating efficient, reliable, and well-structured programs. He discusses possible syntaxes for repetition and error exits. He proposes that what is needed to aid in the creation of "good" programs is a program manipulation system which can be interactively used to convert algorithms into programs. The final sections discuss the nature of structured programming and possibilities for the future.

[22] Kosy, D. W., "Annotated bibliography of debugging, testing and validation techniques for computer programs," RAND Corp., WN-7271-PR, January 1971.

Some of the many topics treated in this paper are program development checkout, activities and management, debugging concepts and tools, testing reliability versus least testing cost, test effort management, selective testing, real-time system test, quality control, and management control in program testing.

[23] Lecht, C. P., The Management of Computer Programming Projects, American Management Association, N. Y., 1967.

Replete with charts for management reporting, this book is aimed at the manager of a programming project. Though it missed the boat on top-down and structured design, it still has value. The fundamentals of project management are explained. Everything from sizing and costing to debugging is covered from the viewpoint of management.

[24] London, R. L., "Bibliography on proving the correctness of programs," Machine Intelligence, 5, Edinburgh, 1970, pp. 569-580

A superb bibliography, it is now getting out of date but nevertheless contains most of the fundamental papers in the area of program proving.

[25] McCracken, D. D. and G. M. Weinberg, "How to write a readable FORTRAN program," Datamation, October 1972, pp. 73-77.

It is imperative that programs be adequately documented, so that someone studying them can determine what they were intended to do. A complete package of documentation contains a number of factors: a precise statement of what the program is supposed to do, a complete set of flowcharts, a complete set of sample input and output including test cases, a set of operating instructions for the computer operator. Other factors affecting software quality are examined.

[26] Miller, E. F. and G. E. Lindamood, "Structured programming: top-down approach," Datamation, December 1973, pp. 55-57.

An overview of what is meant by the terms structured programming and top-down design. An example of structured FORTRAN is also discussed.

[27] Mills, H. D., "Mathematical foundations for structured programming," IBM Report, FSC72-6012, February 1972.

The report is an excellent source document which discusses a multitude of topics: structured programming, technical standard, error-proneness, structure theorem, GO TO free program segments, free structure, top-down corollary (programming), correctness theorem, expansion theorem, programming analysis versus synthesis.

[28] Mills, H., "Top-down programming in large systems," Debugging Techniques in Large Systems, R. Rustin (ed.), Prentice-Hall, Englewood Cliffs, N. J., pp. 43-55.

A clear statement which proposes structured programming as a methodology for developing large systems. Modules should be constructed top-down with interfaces forming a tree structure. The size and complexity of modules should be limited and top-down testing procedures used.

[29] Myers, G. J., "Composite design: The design of modular programs," TR 00.2046, IBM Poughkeepsie Laboratory, January 29, 1973.

The document elaborates on the ideas of Constantine as regards program design. Emphasis is on minimizing module connectivity.

[30] Paige, M.R. and E.F. Miller, Jr., Program Validation Bibliography, General Research Corp., November 1972.

Thirty-two pages of papers and books on the subject of program verification.

[31] Parnas, D.L., "A technique for S/W module specification with examples," CACM, vol. 15, no. 5, May 1972, pp. 330-336.

This paper presents an approach to writing specifications for parts of software systems. The main goal is to provide specifications sufficiently precise and complete so that other pieces of software can be written to interact with the piece specified without additional information. The secondary goal is to include in the specification no more information than necessary to meet the first goal. The technique is illustrated by a variety of examples from a tutorial system.

[32] Parnas, D.L., "More on simulation languages and design methodology for computer systems," Proc. Spring Joint Computer Conference, 1969, pp. 739-743.

Continuing to expand on his language for design, SODA, Parnas extends its capabilities to handle multilevel modeling as defined by Randall and Zurcher. This new system, SOCS, is compared to SIMULA. Strong arguments are given for certain features which will aid in designing such complex software as operating systems.

[33] Phelan, P.F., "Writing and debugging computer programs," Chemical Engineering, vol. 80, no. 13, June 1973, pp. 98-106.

Program checkout, or "debugging," usually demands a greater effort than writing the program itself. The novice programmer can make his programs more efficient by adopting techniques professionals use in debugging their programs. Some of these techniques are discussed in this paper: the value of output statements, i.e., how they can aid in pinpointing errors; pre-keypunching check (or desk-checking of computer programs) as an aid to eliminating errors prior to program execution; and the elimination of syntax errors, i.e., statements that are incorrectly formatted.

[34] Rice, J.R., "GO TO statement reconsidered," CACM, vol. 11, no. 3, August 1968, p. 538.

This paper is a rebuttal to E. Dijkstra's article. The claims made there are discredited in this reference. What should be done to keep track of which GO TOs are encountered and where they transfer control.

[35] Rubey, R.J. and R.D. Hartwick, "Quantitative measurement of program quality," Proc. 23rd Nat'l Conf. ACM, 1968, pp. 671-677.

Many software attributes and their metrics are defined and discussed. There is a total of fifty-seven attributes distributed among seven categories. They are related to mathematical calculations, program logic, computation time and memory usage, program modifiability, etc. The metrics are realized as formulas and are explained in detail.

[36] Rustin, R., Debugging Techniques in Large Systems, Courant Computer Science Symposium 1, Prentice-Hall, 1971.

A collection of papers by people such as H. Mills, J. Schwartz, J. King and R. Gaines. Includes a variety of techniques which have been proved useful for debugging different kinds of software.

[37] Sadowski, W.L. and D.W. Lozier, A Unified Standards Approach to Algorithm Testing, Program Test Methods, W.C. Hetzel, (ed.), Prentice-Hall, Englewood Cliffs, N.J., 1973, pp. 277-290.

The book shows how portability of fundamental algorithms in terms of desired level of accuracy is achieved by using primary, transfer and working standards to "calibrate" the subject software.

[38] Sharpe, W.F., The Economics of Computers, Columbia University Press, New York, 1969.

A superb in-depth study done while the author was at RAND. The basic subject is the microeconomic theory of computer usage. Though it is getting out of date, there is no successor in sight. It also includes a valuable overview of the computer industry and its interactions with other segments of society.

[39] Stevens, W. P., G. J. Meyers, and L. L. Constantine, "Structured design," IBM Systems Journal, no. 2, 1974, pp. 115-139.

Considerations and techniques are proposed for reducing the complexity of programs by dividing them into functional modules. The relationships between these concepts and the idea of HIPO is discussed. This is a practical article on forming small modules and making larger, yet reliable computer structures from them.

[40] Stucki, L. G., "Automatic generation of self-metric software," Proc. IEEE Symposium on Software Reliability, New York, March 1973.

This paper describes in greater detail the PET system, which Stucki discusses in the appendix of his paper in this volume.

[41] Stucki, L. G., "A prototype automatic program testing tool," AFIPS 1972 Fall Joint Computer Conference, Anaheim, December 1972. TK 7885 A1J6 P2, pp. 829-836.

This article describes a "Program Testing Translation" which measures the number of executions of each statement of a FORTRAN routine, and gives an example of how the translator was used to optimize and find a bug in an eigenvalue-eigenvector subroutine.

[42] Taliaferro, W. M., "Modularity: the key to system growth potential," Software Practice and Experience, July 1971, pp. 245-258.

This correspondence between hardware and software development is made with emphasis on modularity. Various proposals are given including independent testing of modules as they are being prepared.

[43] Teichrow, D. and H. Sayori, "Automation of system building," Datamation, August 1971, pp. 25-30.

This article summarizes the steps necessary to build a computer-based information system and concludes that, because of the number and complexity of these systems, manual methods are inadequate. Thus automated methods are needed; and one of them currently being developed, ISDOS (Information System Design and Optimization System), is described.

[44] Weinberg, G. F., The Psychology of Computer Programming, Van Nostrand Reinhold, 1971.

An entertaining book on a subject for which very little has been written. The term "egoless coding" was started in this book. Weinberg expands on the social aspects of programming with the ultimate goal of getting the job done.

[45] Weinwurm, G. G., (ed.), On the Management of Computer Programming, Auerbach, Inc., New York, 1970.

Though 5 years old now, it remains a fine overview from the management perspective. A collection of twelve articles by people such as D. Brandon, H. Sackman, A. Peitrasanta and others. It also has a annotated bibliography. I view this book as the logical predecessor of the one you are now reading.

[46] Wirth, N., "Program development by stepwise refinement," CACM, vol. 14, April 1971, pp. 221-227.

A strong proponent of structured programming, Wirth discusses how to refine a program so that correctness is highly probable. He tackles the well-known 8 Queens problem. A model of how to choose identifier names.

[47] Wolverton, R. W., "The cost of developing large scale software," IEEE Trans. on Computers, vol. C-23, no. 6, June 1974, pp. 615-636.

This is the expanded version of the paper in this volume. It is filled with detailed charts of costing data, categories for the costing algorithm plus more depth on the conclusions which one can obtain. A must for those actively involved in this part of the business.

[48] Wulf, W. A., "Programming without the GO TO," Information Processing 71, Proc, IFIP-71, booklet no. 3, pp. 84-88.